Conservatives Betrayed

10   09   08   07   06   1   2   3   4   5

Library of Congress Cataloging-in-Publication Data

Viguerie, Richard A.
  Conservatives betrayed: how George W. Bush and other big government republicans hijacked the Conservative cause / Richard A. Viguerie.
      p. cm.
  Includes bibliographical references and index.
  ISBN-13: 978-1-56625-285-0 (hardcover : alk. paper)
  1. Conservatism--United States. 2. Republican Party (U.S. : 1854-) 3. United States--Politics and government--2001- I. Title.

  JC573.2.U6V533 2006
  320.520973--dc22

                                              2006016993

Bonus Books
9255 Sunset Blvd., #711
Los Angeles, CA 90069
www.bonusbooks.com

Conservatives Betrayed

How George W. Bush and Other
Big Government Republicans
Hijacked the Conservative Cause

Richard A. Viguerie

Bonus Books
Los Angeles

DEDICATION

This book is dedicated to my five lovely and much-loved grandchildren: Virginia, Kathleen, and Matthew Coffman and Megan and Shannon Kelley.

It's their generation that will bear the burden of the irresponsible actions and lack of leadership by the governing class—Democrats, Republicans, Big Business, Big Labor, the legal community, the educational establishment, and others.

This burden includes a country on a rapid road to socialism and financial bankruptcy, as well as a world that is a far more dangerous place to live and raise a family than we faced even during the Cold War.

But, because man does not live by bread alone and is a spiritual being with an eternal soul, the collapse of moral values is perhaps the foremost threat facing my grandchildren's generation. The amorality and greed of the entertainment industry, combined with the silence of most religious leaders, is threatening the very foundation of the free world.

Virginia, Kathleen, Matthew, Megan, and Shannon, my generation has done some good things, but we've also made too many things far worse. You've got a big challenge, but with reliance on God and faithfulness to the values you've been taught by your parents, you can be victorious.

THEN, AND LATER

"Although I held public office for a total of sixteen years, I also thought of myself as a citizen-politician, not a career one. Every now and then when I was in government, I would remind my associates that, when we start thinking of government as 'us' instead of 'them,' we've been here too long."

— Ronald Reagan, in an address to the
Los Angeles Junior Chamber of Commerce, 1991

Tom Delay, the House Republican Leader, held a fundraiser for his political action committee at a well-known Washington restaurant. The restaurant leased space in a building owned by a federal agency, so smoking was prohibited. The prohibition was posted on numerous signs inside and outside the restaurant. After the main course, DeLay pressured the restaurant manager to let him smoke. The manager said, "I'm sorry, sir, but this is a federal building, and it's against the law of the federal government."

DeLay replied: "I *am* the federal government."

— adapted from a *Washington Post* story
by Lloyd Grove, May 15, 2003

TABLE OF CONTENTS

Introduction

When conservatives are unhappy, bad things happen to the Republican Party.

In 1948, conservatives were unhappy with Tom Dewey's liberal Republican "me-too" campaign of mimicking the Democrats, and the result was Dewey's unexpected loss to Harry Truman.

In 1960, conservatives were unhappy with Richard Nixon's divide-the-spoils negotiations with Nelson Rockefeller, and the result was Nixon's razor-thin loss to John F. Kennedy.

In 1974, conservatives were unhappy with the corruption and Big Government policies of Nixon's White House and with President Gerald Ford's selection of Nelson Rockefeller as his vice president, and this led to major Republican losses in the congressional races that year.

By 1976, conservatives were fed up with Ford's adoption of Rockefeller's agenda. The result was Ford's narrow defeat by a peanut farmer from Georgia.

In 1992, conservatives were so unhappy with President George H. W. Bush's open disdain for them and their beliefs that they staged an open rebellion with the candidacies of Pat Buchanan in the primaries and Ross Perot in the general election. The result was an incumbent president who got a paltry 38 percent of the vote, and Bill Clinton's election with only 43 percent of the vote.

And in 1998, conservatives were unhappy because Republican leaders in Congress had abandoned conservative principles to go on a wild spending spree and failed to put forward a conservative issue agenda. The result was a failure to make the major gains suggested historically in the sixth year of a president's administration. Instead, Republicans lost House seats, and Newt Gingrich resigned as Speaker of the House.

Warning to the Republican Party: Conservatives Are Unhappy Again

Conservatives are unhappy right now because Big Government Republicans have hijacked our cause. We are questioning why we should continue to vote Republican if the GOP acts like the

Democrats on spending, corruption, and lack of progress on social issues. And if we desert the GOP, or just stay at home on Election Day, the Republicans will lose again, just as they did in 1948, 1960, 1974, 1976, 1992, and 1998. How many times does the GOP have to be hit on the head before it learns not to take conservatives for granted?

Why in the world are conservatives unhappy?

At first glance it might seem counterintuitive to say that conservatives are unhappy today. After all, a supposedly "conservative" Republican Party controls the presidency and both houses of Congress for the first time in a lifetime. And with the appointments of John Roberts and Samuel Alito to the Supreme Court, the mainstream, constitutional faction on the Court appears to be one seat away from a majority.

That's great news for the Republican Party as a power-seeking organization. But it's deeply disappointing news for true conservatives who still believe in the principles of limited, constitutional government that motivated us over the years. Just take a look at the facts.

Conservatives have always stood for limited government, and our goal upon achieving power has always been to downsize the federal government and restore power to the states and the people as mandated in the Constitution. Yet the GOP in control of the White House and Congress has gone on a spending binge such as we haven't seen since the days of Lyndon Johnson. Before there always was an excuse—a Republican Congress could complain that the Democrats controlled the White House, or a Republican president could complain that Democrats controlled one or both houses of Congress. Today there's no excuse—the Republicans control everything. So they must take the blame and the responsibility for this awful state of affairs.

I'll prove that case against the Bush GOP in this book.

And it's not just the overall spending that has been exploding since the year 2000. The scope of the government has been exploding too. Conservatives and Republicans used to fight the intrusion of the federal government into entire areas where it has no business. In recent presidential election years, Republican platforms have called for elimination of the cabinet departments of Education and Energy, and the return of those powers to the people (in education) and the market (in energy). Instead, the Bush GOP has turned federal education dictates into one of its priorities, making Washington, D.C., the schoolteacher-nanny to the nation. And in energy, it is playing the subsidy (read: pork) game as deftly as the Democrats ever did. Moreover, these are just two conspicuous examples of the GOP flip-flop. Pork barrel spending is pervasive everywhere in this Republican administration, and is far worse than what the Democrats had done.

Taxpayer-funded subsidies to Big Business have never been higher. Taxpayer-funded subsidies to left-wing organizations and interest groups have never been higher.

I'll prove thos]e charges against the Bush GOP in this book.

As for the Supreme Court, we'll give President Bush guarded credit, with our fingers crossed. His first nominee to the Supreme Court, Judge John Roberts, is not a liberal but he is a Washington establishment insider, not visibly a "movement" conservative. We are painfully aware that of the 17 Supreme Court justices appointed by Republican presidents in the past half—century, only three (not counting recent appointees Roberts and Alito) have built solidly conservative records. We won't prejudge Roberts, but he will have to prove himself to us.

President Bush's next Supreme Court nomination, that of Harriet Miers, was an inexcusable act of cronyism that precipitated a conservative outcry forcing her to withdraw her nomination. Samuel Alito appears at this writing to have been a wise and conservative substitute choice. Still, it is telling that, of Bush's three nominations for the Court, not one had a significant paper trail as a conservative legal scholar. Young conservatives have gotten the message: If you want to be on the Supreme Court some day, you must not take the conservative position in the great public debates of the day. You must keep your mouth shut and take care not to write anything down that might be incriminating from the standpoint of a Ted Kennedy or Chuck Schumer, who are the Senate voices for Ralph Neas, Nan Aron, and the radical Left interest groups.

On immigration, the Bush GOP has failed utterly to protect our borders with a firm but compassionate immigration policy. Instead, the Bush administration has allied itself with the shortsighted interests of

Big Business, with disastrous consequences now and down the road for our system of government, our economy, and our society. The president has even neglected his most important cause — protecting America from terrorism — by allowing an open door to illegal immigration.

It's time for conservatives to stand up to a Republican Party that uses their votes to get elected, then refuses to stand up for conservative principles.

Conservatism for the Future

Today, I see a void in American politics. We have no concise explanation in clear English of what conservatism stands for in an era of bloated government fed by both major parties, a society in denial of some of the first principles of civilization, and post-Soviet threats from abroad in the form of terrorism. Somebody's got to do it, and since nobody else had, I am making my own modest stab at it.

My main goal in this book is to explain what conservatism stands for in the 21st century. In 1960 Barry Goldwater defined the essence of conservatism with his history-changing book, *The Conscience of a Conservative*. In the 1960s through the 1980s, Ronald Reagan did the same with his stirring speeches. Well, the world has changed a great deal since their days, and the conservative cause has to be redefined with the times. I hope this book will begin a debate about what conservatism means in today's rapidly changing world.

Let me be clear: The present leaders of the Republican Party are not conservative. Rather, knowing that the great majority of the American people are conservative and reject liberalism, these Big Government Republicans have hijacked the term "conservative" and they have hijacked the conservative movement itself.

Conservatives and the Republican Party

It's obvious that conservatives have a GOP problem.

On the one hand, we have to work within the two-party framework of American democracy in order to be effective and not be marginalized. When you look at third-party efforts on the Right, whether of the Libertarian Party or Constitution Party variety, you can perhaps agree with their platforms and principles more than with those of the Republican Party—but as minority parties they have next to zero influence on national policy.

On the other hand, putting all of our marbles on the Republican side hasn't worked either, as we've seen since 2000. Oh, a few hundred or a few thousand conservatives get some of the spoils from being in power in Washington, but the conservative *movement* fails to achieve its objectives, to the nation's detriment. Republican lawmakers *talk* conservative but *vote* for bigger and more intrusive government. They've been getting away with this—so far—because they think conservatives have nowhere else to go.

Instead of creating a new party, we conservatives need to think of ourselves as a Third Force—an independent outside force that holds *both* parties accountable for their actions. In this book I will explore some of the ways we can do this. This is not a pipedream—we've done it before. In the 1970s the "New Right" was becoming so successful precisely because its leaders thought of *themselves*—not the Republican Party—as the alternative to the Left and the Democrats. And during the second half of the 1970s and the early 1980s, this alternative New Right leadership planned strategy every Wednesday at my McLean, Virginia, home. For six or seven years, the New Right independent operatives would meet for breakfast sessions. For a couple of years, those sessions were followed by evening gatherings where we would be joined by six or seven key Republican congressmen, with Newt Gingrich as their leader. The organizational leaders thought of themselves as the "outside" leadership group, with the congressmen as the movement's "inside" leadership.

For another example, some of the greatest conservative successes over the years have come with independent single-issue groups that have managed to take liberal issues off the table—perhaps the ultimate in political success. Phyllis Schlafly's Stop ERA took the proposed Equal Rights Amendment issue *off the table* in the 1980s, and more recently the National Rifle Association took the "gun control" issue off the table. The critical strategic point is that they battled for bipartisan support of their aims, and held politicians of both parties responsible for their votes. The fact that few Democrats but most Republicans saw the light on these issues explains a lot about why Republicans have been winning elections and Democrats losing them.

The fact that the conservative *cause* triumphed on these issues is my interest, and I say it's time to let 1,000 new conservative single-issue organizations bloom.

Finally, this book can serve as a primer for conservatives who want to do more than gripe, and who are willing to help lead grass-roots conservatives to victory. And nowhere is our lack of leadership more obvious than in the presidential sweepstakes. In this book you'll find the issues, and the stands on those issues that could make some individual the winner in the presidential lottery.

Barry Goldwater became the leader of the fledgling conservative movement precisely because he held his own party and president accountable—not just the Democrats. There were other solid conservatives in Congress in the 1950s and 1960s, but only Goldwater had the guts to stand up on the floor of the U.S. Senate and call President Eisenhower's policies a "dime store New Deal." That forthrightness and honesty endeared him to us conservatives, and we made him our leader. Unfortunately, Goldwater never really wanted to be the movement's leader, and it showed. But someone else, in California, did want to be our leader, understood and believed in our principles and positions, and rode our movement to the White House in 1980.

After January 20, 2009, George W. Bush will not be president of the United States. The position is available to someone who understands that the vast majority of the American people are conservative, and who is willing to speak out as forthrightly as Goldwater and Reagan did in their day. If a politician assumes that mantle, he or she will be the conservatives' candidate, and therefore the GOP's nominee for president, in 2008.

In his 1947 classic *The Mainspring of Human Progress*, Henry Grady Weaver examined a mystery.

He noted that, "down through the ages, most human beings have gone hungry, and many have always starved. . . . The Roman Empire collapsed in famine. The French were dying of hunger when Thomas Jefferson was president of the United States. As late as the 1840s, the Irish were starving to death; and no one was particularly surprised because famines in the Old World were the rule rather than the exception. . . . Hunger has always been normal.

"Then suddenly, in one spot on this planet, people eat so abundantly that the pangs of hunger are forgotten. Why did men die of starvation for 6,000 years? Why is it that we in America have never had a famine?"

From the beginning of the conservative movement, conservative thinkers have pondered the revolutionary impact of America in the world. What was the secret of our success in throwing off the shackles of political oppression and rising above bare economic sustenance? The answer invariably comes to an amalgam of three factors:

1. Our Judeo-Christian heritage
2. Economic liberty
3. Political liberty (limited, decentralized government)

Our Judeo-Christian heritage: All pagan cultures, including the Greeks and the Romans, endowed the political state with sacred religious authority. "Since it was secular and religious authority rolled into one," explained conservative author M. Stanton Evans, "there was no alternative source of loyalty, no challenge to its power, and no higher truth accessible to the average citizen by which its power could be judged."[1] The other side of the coin was that the individual citizen had no particular value, and even outright slavery was the norm. The greatest of the pagan philosophers, Aristotle, reflected the universali-

---

[1] See the excellent discussion of our philosophical roots in M. Stanton Evans, *Clear and Present Dangers: A Conservative View of America's Government* (Harcourt Brace Jovanovich, 1975).

ty of this viewpoint when he said: "Do not suppose that any of the citizens belong to themselves; for they all belong to the state."

Judaism, then Christianity, changed all that, Evans wrote, due to "the Biblical conception of a transcendent Deity who lifts up the individual and scales down the assertions of the state. This view confers on us our Western notions of personal freedom, equal individual worth, privacy of conscience . . ." In short, "the distinctly libertarian (and thus distinctively Western) aspects of our politics are Biblical in origin."

Judaism and Christianity gave men the notion that they had intrinsic worth that took precedence over the claims of government. Still it took centuries of struggle to give the world a workable formula for curtailing the power of government and providing economic abundance. The pivotal year for both these revolutions was 1776.

Economic liberty: In 1776, Adam Smith published *The Wealth of Nations*, which established him as the father of economics as a science. His key insight, wrote Nobel Prize-winning economist Milton Friedman, is that, in a truly voluntary economic exchange, both sides must "believe that they will benefit from it. Most economic fallacies derive from the neglect of this simple insight, from the tendency to assume that there is a fixed pie, that one party can gain only at the expense of another."[2]

"The price system," Friedman explained, "is the mechanism that performs this task without central direction, without requiring people to speak to one another or to like one another. When you buy your pencil or your daily bread, you don't know whether the pencil was made or the wheat was grown by a white man or a black man, by a Chinese or an Indian. As a result, the price system enables people to cooperate peacefully in one phase of their life while each one goes about his own business in respect of everything else."

Adam Smith's insights gave birth to the notions of free trade and a free market — free, that is, of the government controls that had characterized economic affairs for centuries. And what better place for

---

[2] Milton Friedman and Rose Friedman, *Free to Choose* (Harcourt, Inc., 1980), p. 13.

these ideas to blossom than in America, where equivalent notions of *political* freedom were becoming dominant. This economic freedom, coupled with political freedom, is the reason America has never had a famine and why we have enjoyed growth and prosperity unprecedented in world history.

Political liberty: That same year, 1776, brought the birth of political freedom in America, as proclaimed in the Declaration of Independence. The patriots who signed it put their lives on the line to affirm:

> We hold these truths to be self-evident, that all men are created equal, that they are endowed by their Creator with certain unalienable Rights, that among these are Life, Liberty, and the pursuit of Happiness. That to secure these rights, Governments are instituted among Men, deriving their just powers from the consent of the governed, That whenever any Form of Government becomes destructive of these ends, it is the Right of the People to alter or to abolish it, and to institute new Government . . .

First that independence had to be secured by winning a long and bloody war. That was followed with the equally daunting task of *maintaining* our newly won independence by crafting, in Evans' words, "a political system that had sufficient authority to perform [its] basic tasks, but would be so constrained and limited in the reach of its power that it would not become a hazard to the freedoms it was instituted to protect."

More than two centuries of survival as a constitutional republic testify to the value of the system created by the Founders. The critical features of that system include strict limitations on what government could do.

First, the Constitution strictly limited the powers of the federal government to those specifically listed. The Tenth Amendment, part of the Bill of Rights, declared that "the powers not delegated to the United States by the Constitution, nor prohibited by it to the states, are reserved to the states respectively, or to the people." The first eight articles in the Bill of Rights listed specific rights possessed by the people, and the Ninth Amendment made clear that the people possessed other rights[3] as well.

Second, the powers of this strictly limited federal government were further divided between three branches – the legislative, the executive, and the judicial. This three-way division was crafted as a system of "checks and balances" to prevent any individual politician or group of politicians from amassing too much power.

This system of limited power, spread out among different branches of government, is something that conservatives fight to protect.

Liberalism is easy: See something that you think is a problem, declare that "there oughta be a law" against it, then pass a law and use the power of the government to bend people to your will. Conservatism is hard, because conservatives demand that all laws fit into the framework of the Constitution, and we attempt to think through all the possible repercussions before using the power of government.

When conservatives insist, for example, that the federal government has no right to be involved in education, our belief is grounded firmly in the Constitution, the supreme law of the land. Federal involvement in education is clearly unconstitutional because the Constitution does not enumerate public education as one of the tasks of the federal government. (Remember that, under the Tenth Amendment, the federal government has only those powers that are specifically listed.)

And, as a general principle, conservatives believe that decisions should be made at the level closest to the people – at the state level, at the city or county level, at the neighborhood level, at the family level, or at the individual level. With education, which intimately shapes children's perspectives on life, that means decisions should be

---

[3] Because the term is often misused, it is important to note the definition of a "right." A "right" is (a) a restriction placed on government, or (b) the designation of an activity in which the government cannot intervene. So, for example, "the right to a job" refers to the idea that a person can take any job he pleases, for whatever compensation he can obtain, without interference from the government. It does *not* mean that the government provides employment, any more than "freedom of the press" means that the government buys you a printing press.

made by the parents themselves, with whatever assistance they need from local authorities (such as local school boards) and, as a last resort, the state government.

In addition to our belief in upholding the law and in keeping power at the grassroots level, there is another reason we oppose the federal government's involvement in education. We believe that it is too important to be placed in the hands of federal politicians and bureaucrats. The framers were wise to omit education from Washington's enumerated powers because the power to educate is the power to indoctrinate, and indoctrination is the goal of many in the government school system. (See, for example, the magazines *Green Teacher* and *Radical Teacher.*)

This line of reasoning on all issues is what differentiates conservatives from liberals. Liberals believe in turning to the government first, preferably at the highest level, regardless of constitutionality, and regardless of the fact that this empowers bureaucrats and politicians, while it weakens the power of the people. Conservatives believe that the Constitution has proved its worth, and we believe in keeping power as close to the people as possible. Such an approach is prudent from the standpoint of preserving our liberties, and efficient in terms of solving problems.

Now, conservatism as a way of thought is as old as this country. But the conservative movement—conservatism as an organized political force—is something that has arisen in my lifetime.

Birth of the Conservative Movement

By the middle of the 20th century, it was clear that American liberties were in great danger. In the late 1920s and the 1930s, Herbert Hoover Republicans and Franklin Roosevelt Democrats had ushered in an era of unlimited and centralized government. The result was the Great Depression and the beginning of Big Government in the United States. When the New Deal Democrats were finally turned out in 1952, the self-styled "modern" Republicans under Eisenhower ratified the New Deal with just a few minor adjustments.

By the 1950s, the Constitution was seen as an interesting but no longer particularly relevant document of history. It was seen as "impractical" in an age when a strong central government was deemed necessary to correct problems caused (allegedly) by private enterprise. Americans were being reprogrammed to believe that they were no longer able to secure their own future, and that they needed the help of federal bureaucrats with every task. At the same time that the government was meddling in a wide range of tasks for which it had no constitutional authority, it was failing at the primary task assigned to it by the Constitution: national defense. The Soviet Union was on a march to world domination; it was interfering in U.S. internal affairs with networks of espionage cells, Communist Party members and "fellow travelers," and the nation's leading pseudo-intellectuals were describing Soviet-style centralized planning as efficient and as the wave of the future. Our individual liberties and our nation's survival were at risk.

Many Americans were alarmed by this state of affairs, but it wasn't until the appearance of *National Review* magazine in 1955 that these dissidents from liberal orthodoxy began to think of themselves as an opposition movement. The journal's editor, witty and erudite William F. Buckley Jr., became the intellectual spokesman of the new movement, just as Arizona Senator Barry Goldwater became its political spokesman when he dared to criticize his own party, the Eisenhower administration, of being a "dime store New Deal."[4]

Since its formation, the conservative movement has gone through three distinct periods.

The Goldwater era: The fledgling movement mobilized enough grassroots support to wrest control of the Republican Party from the Rockefeller wing—supporters of New York Governor Nelson Rockefeller—and to nominate Goldwater as the GOP candidate for president in 1964. Liberals had near-total control of the national media, however, and succeeded in persuading many Americans that Goldwater was a dangerous radical who would, for example, start a nuclear war. The result of the anti-Goldwater smear campaign was a decisive Republican defeat in November.

Conservatives were discouraged, but determined to fight on. We

---

[4] For the story of this exciting era, see Chapter 5, "The Birth of a Movement," in *America's Right Turn: How Conservatives Used New and Alternative Media to Take Power* (Bonus Books, 2004).

realized that we'd never get a fair shake from the liberal Establishment media, so we started creating our own alternative media. The first alternative medium was direct mail, which I used to help build conservatism as a political movement. By connecting conservative organizations and causes directly to the conservative grassroots, through their mailboxes, we were able to bypass the liberal media that either ignored or defamed us.

A new political star had been born in the closing days of the 1964 campaign, when actor Ronald Reagan made a passionate TV plea for Goldwater. Soon, Reagan was governor of California.

The Reagan era: During the '70s, the conservative movement adopted a more aggressive stance. Led by the so-called New Right, we were no longer content to wait for direction from conservatives in Congress; we created new leadership and seized the agenda. Grassroots organizations mobilized the troops, while new foundations and think-tanks spread the conservative message.

The growing movement used direct mail and grassroots mobilization to secure the presidential nomination for Ronald Reagan in 1980. Reagan served two terms as president, pursuing a military and diplomatic policy of strength that resulted in conservatism's greatest triumph , the peaceful destruction of the Soviet Union. On the domestic front, Reagan was able to slow down, but not reverse, the growth of government. Nevertheless, conservatives' efforts to restrict governmental power kicked off an era of dramatic economic growth and technological advancement. Despite the many successes of Reagan and the conservatives in national security and domestic policy, liberals were still entrenched in Congress and in Washington power circles when Reagan left office.

The Bush era: George H. W. Bush was never a conservative, but he was able to use his role as Reagan's vice president to secure the GOP nomination and be elected president in 1988. His one term of office was an affront to Reagan conservatives, as he broke his promises to us and the American public, most famously his "read my lips" pledge never to raise taxes. Many conservatives responded in 1992 by staying home or supporting third party candidates, and as a result, Arkansas Governor Bill Clinton brought the White House back under the Democrats' control.

This was a setback to the Establishment liberals in the GOP, but it was a boon to conservatives, who channeled a rebellion against Bill and Hillary Clinton's Big Government initiatives to win conservative GOP control of the House of Representatives in 1994, ending 40 years of Democratic rule. In the media, conservatives expanded beyond direct mail and used the new and alternative media of talk radio, cable TV, and the Internet to spread the conservative message.

In 2000, Texas Governor George W. Bush learned from his father's mistake in alienating conservatives. The younger Bush worked hard to convince conservatives that he was one of us, and he succeeded well enough to eke out a 271-266 Electoral College victory in November. Some of us were disturbed by his use of the term "compassionate conservatism," which seemed to imply that regular conservatism was *not* compassionate. We remembered how our first political leader, Barry Goldwater, scorned the liberals' use in his day of the term "progressive conservatism." "This is a strange label indeed," he wrote in *The Conscience of a Conservative.* "It implies that 'ordinary' conservatism is opposed to progress. Have we forgotten that America made its greatest progress when conservative principles were honored and preserved?"

Well, we soon learned what "compassionate conservatism" meant. It meant an orgy of federal spending that made the Clinton Administration look like a bunch of penny-pinchers. It meant Big Brother and Big Nanny government that expanded Washington's power in new directions, intruding ever more into our daily lives. And it meant expanded old and new "entitlements" that threaten to bankrupt our nation in just a few years.

And those are just Bush's *domestic* sins against conservative principles. In foreign policy, he initially responded magnificently and appropriately against the terrorists who attacked the United States on September 11, 2001, and against the Taliban regime in Afghanistan that sheltered them. But then he inexplicably turned from finishing the job of eradicating Al Qaeda to regime change in Iraq. The post-war occupation has been a direct violation of Bush's promises as a presidential candidate not to engage in the liberal practice of "nation-building."

The result of "nation-building" in Iraq is that the U.S. is stuck in a

Middle Eastern quagmire that shows no promise of ending, at a human cost of more than 20,000 Americans dead or disabled, not to mention a monetary cost of nearly $1 trillion and rising. Reagan won the Cold War peacefully by bankrupting the Soviet Union; Bush threatens to lose the peace by bankrupting the U.S. The result has been a drop in his public support from more than 80% after 9/11 to the low-30s as this is written.

Big Government "Conservatism"

As he pursued these policies, President Bush's strongest support came from Big Government Republicans and from so-called "Big Government conservatives" who, of course, are not conservatives at all.[5]

Now, these "Big Government conservatives" – sometimes confusingly called "neoconservatives" – have not been shy about their intentions to hijack (or, from their point of view, "lead") the conservative movement. Irving Kristol, often called "the grandfather of neoconservatism," wrote in *The Weekly Standard* (August 25, 2003) of "the historical task and political purpose of neoconservatism": "to convert the Republican Party, and American conservatism in general, against their respective wills, into a new kind of conservative politics suitable to governing a modern democracy."

---

[5] As I note above, "Big Government conservatives" are sometimes referred to as "neoconservatives." Sometimes they call themselves by that name. This use of the word "neoconservatives" has led to a great deal of confusion, because the term originally referred to a very specific group of people – academics and intellectuals who were former liberals and socialists but joined the conservative movement in order to fight the excesses of liberalism. Those liberal excesses included government social engineering (such as tearing down neighborhoods as part of "urban renewal") and, most especially, liberals' failure to stand up to Communism. Prominent neoconservatives, in the original sense of the term, included two anti-Communist U.S. ambassadors to the UN, Jeane Kirkpatrick and Daniel Patrick Moynihan (later a Democratic senator from New York).

It is true that some "Big Government conservatives" are neoconservatives in the original sense of the term. But some, such as Fred Barnes of the *The Weekly Standard*, are religious conservatives. Others, such as Vice President Cheney and Defense Secretary Rumsfeld, have roots in the Big Government wing of the Republican Party.

This new kind of conservative politics, Kristol wrote, feels no "alarm or anxiety about the growth of the state in the past century, seeing it as natural, indeed inevitable." Seeming to overlook the popularity of Ronald Reagan's brand of conservatism, Kristol proclaimed that "neoconservatism [Big Government conservatism] is the first variant of American conservatism in the past century that is in the 'American grain,'" and that these positions "have helped make the very idea of political conservatism more acceptable to a majority of American voters."

When the flagship of American liberalism, *The New York Times*, needed to replace the retiring columnist William Safire on its editorial page, it picked someone with views similar to Kristol's, David Brooks. In his advice to the GOP just before the 2004 election, Brooks declared that "reducing the size of government cannot be the governing philosophy for the next generation of conservatives."[6]

Here are the facts.

Ronald Reagan won his first election as president with 51% of the popular vote, a ten-point margin over the incumbent. He carried 44 states. When he ran for reelection, he won 59% of the vote and carried 49 states.

Big Government "conservative" George W. Bush won his first election by five Electoral College votes and actually finished second in the popular vote, with 48%. Running for reelection, he won 50.76% of the vote against some of the most pitiful opposition in recent political history.

As a political force, I'll take conservatism over "Big Government conservatism" any day of the week.

Conservatism at a Crossroads

Conservatism, as a political movement, was founded in the middle of the 20th century as a response to the failures of liberalism.

Liberalism had gained power and consolidated its power during the first half of the century. That was long enough to demonstrate that, as a way of solving society's problems and advancing freedom, liber-

---

[6] "How to Reinvent the GOP," *The New York Times Magazine*, August 29, 2004.

alism just didn't work. It took conservatives roughly another half century to become the dominant philosophy in America and to elect, to Congress and the White House, people who at least *claimed* to be conservatives.

A half century gaining power, a half century losing power – that was the trajectory of liberalism in the 20th century.

But what about conservatism? Will conservatives fare any better than liberals? We spent a half century gaining power. Are we now fated to spend the next half century in decline?

Twentieth century liberalism failed because it turned its back on the core principles and values of Western civilization. It rejected our Judeo-Christian heritage and the principles of economic and political freedom and limited government. It replaced these ideas with moral relativism and ever-bigger government. Moral relativism only breeds moral chaos, and ever-bigger government simply doesn't work. Big Government doesn't solve problems, it magnifies them.

Today, in the 21st century, the Republican Party and much of the machinery of the conservative movement has been hijacked by people who do not believe in the core principles of conservatism. Unless conservatives reclaim our heritage, conservatism will be discredited, and it will go the way of liberalism. Republican Big Government doesn't work any better than Democratic Big Government.

I haven't spent a half century fighting Big Government run by liberals and Democrats, only to succumb to Big Government run by pork-barrel Republicans and pseudo-conservatives.

I say we fight.

A Conservative Manifesto for the 21st Century

CATEGORY 5: THE DISASTER COMING TO AMERICA, AND HOW REPUBLICANS MADE IT WORSE

When Hurricane Katrina hit New Orleans, the city as we knew it was destroyed.

We will never forget those television images of desperate survivors on the rooftops of their flooded houses, or the thousands of abandoned refugees begging for food and water, while the buses that could have been used to evacuate residents were left sitting in the parking lot.

Politicians explained that they didn't foresee such a disaster as Katrina. They made that claim despite the fact that a catastrophic hurricane hitting New Orleans had been the recent subject of a government-sponsored disaster simulation. They made that claim despite the fact that, time after time over the millennia, catastrophic storms had changed the course of the Mississippi in the area. And despite the fact that, as anyone who understood Louisiana politics was aware, most of the money that was supposed to be used to prevent such a disaster had ended up someplace else. And despite the fact that the average 10-year-old could look at a scale model of New Orleans and realize that, in all probability, the city would one day be swallowed up.

It's like those claims that it was unforeseeable that someone would use a plane in an attempt to destroy the Capitol or other populated landmark. Tom Clancy foresaw it and wrote about it, counterterrorism experts foresaw it and warned about it, and a friend of mine who worked on Capitol Hill in the early 1980s used to talk about it with his friends when they walked outside to go to lunch and saw planes flying nearby.

When the coming political and economic disaster hits America, I guarantee you, the politicians will say it was unforeseeable.

They will say: **Nobody could have foreseen** the consequences, once the Baby Boomers retire from the workforce, of failing to reform Social Security, Medicare, and seniors' part of Medicaid.

They will say: **Nobody could have foreseen** the consequences of the government guaranteeing private pensions that were underfunded. (This policy allows Big Business corporations to promise their employees more than they can possibly deliver, as a way of negotiating for lower wages and salaries. Then, when these pension programs fail, the corporations can dump their obligations onto the backs of the taxpayers.)

They will say: **Nobody could have foreseen** what would happen when the number, size, and scope of federal programs became too large for any group of 535 in Congress, or any group of about 5,000 presidential appointees, to oversee.

They will say: **Nobody could have foreseen** what would happen after the government simply stopped enforcing the immigration laws against criminal aliens.

They will say: **Nobody could have foreseen** what would happen after the government made it impossible to fully develop our energy sources, including oil from the Alaskan wasteland and nuclear power.

As it approached New Orleans, Katrina was rated a Category 5 hurricane, a near-perfect storm with winds above 155 miles per hour. It was a monstrous force of Mother Nature. America now faces a man-made disaster, the consequence of decades of misjudgment, procrastination, and cowardice by generations of politicians. And the most frustrating aspect of this is that the politicians who are responsible for this mess will get away with it. Most of them are long gone, like Richard Nixon and Lyndon Johnson, or invulnerable, like Teddy Kennedy. They and hundreds of others like them benefited from promising the supposed benefits of such policies; the costs will be borne by future generations.

I'm not exaggerating. Consider just one measure of the mess we're in, the government's unfunded liability. That's the difference between

(a) the money the government is expected to spend in the years to come, and (b) the amount of tax revenue the government is expected to collect. This liability amounts to (depending on the calculation) between $600,000 and $1,000,000 per family.

One way or another, the typical American family will pay that amount – between $600,000 and $1,000,000 – in loss of promised benefits, in higher taxes, or in higher prices for everything that family buys (the result of bureaucratic regulations and of inflation from deficit spending). That's if the government never adds another program! What's the chance of that?

You may be thinking that there's no way people can afford to pay so much, and you're right. Which means that, at some point, the irresistible force of government spending will meet an immovable object, the limited wealth of the average American.

That's when we get the perfect storm.

David M. Walker, Comptroller General of the United States and head of the Government Accountability Office, refers to just one aspect of the problem—the federal deficit—"a fiscal challenge unprecedented in American history." (He might think I've underestimated the danger, though. He called the coming disaster a "Category 6.")

Because Congress and the president have been spending far more of our money than they've managed to raise as revenue, even with today's ultra-high tax rates, the federal government runs a deficit each year and the debt grows. Those deficits now total more than $7 trillion, which is more than two-thirds the size of the U.S. economy.

Add in all the government's other future obligations beyond what it can pay for under current tax levels, chiefly Social Security and Medicare benefits, and America's total debt is nearly $46 trillion. Other estimates are higher. Even the lower figure is –

- Four times the size of the U.S. economy
- More than $150,000 for each man, woman, and child in America, or at least $600,000 for a family of four
- Five times as much per capita as the annual disposable personal income per person, $29,475
- $350,000 for every fulltime worker in the nation
- And almost enough to buy two homes for each worker in

America (the median existing home price was $188,900 in December 2004)

Moreover, this debt is growing like a Southern California fire fueled by Santa Ana winds.

Walker says that "every American would have to give up around 90% of his or her net worth just to cover the government's current liabilities and unfunded promises for future spending."

This is insane. No private business could survive with this kind of debt load and debt growth. Americans personally have a dismal record of saving money—individuals now spend more than they take in, for the first time since the Great Depression. But a non-mortgage *debt* per worker of $350,000 or more, with the interest on that debt added on, is beyond the imagination.

Hold on, though. It's going to get worse.

We've been growing this debt in "good times" – a growing economy, no recession in sight, a healthy stock market. You may not think we're in good times if you are out of a job, of course, but for the nation as a whole we've been chugging along much better than most of the rest of the world.

In 2005, TV talk show host John McLaughlin asked Walker if the U.S. growth in debt is due "to circumstances beyond our control." Walker's reply: "Absolutely not. Most of them were within our control. If we were in a recession, if we had slow economic growth, if the deficit was explained by the war or incremental homeland security costs, it would be understandable. But the fact of the matter: It is not."

If we won't put our financial house in order during "good times," what happens if we *do* have a recession or stock market crash? What happens if rising interest rates pop the housing bubble?

Actually, we don't have to envision bad news like that for the future. *Even with a continuation of our "good times,"* we are headed for what Walker calls "a demographic tsunami" which "threatens to swamp the ship of state if we fail to act." And "unlike most natural tsunamis, evacuation isn't an option with our demographic challenge."

America Gets Older

The cause of this economic tsunami is the aging of America, combined with the entitlements we've built into the federal budget.

The population of the U.S. as a whole has been getting older for decades, thanks to lower birth rates and longer life spans. By 2030, the nation will have a higher percentage of senior citizens than Florida has now. Our current life expectancy of 77 years – 74 for men, 80 for women – is projected to rise to 86 by 2075.

Rapidly rising life expectancy presents a major problem, but another problem is more immediate: the retirement of the Baby Boomer generation, people born between 1946 and 1964. Starting in 2008, some of these Baby Boomers will take early retirement. And beginning in 2011, members of this huge generation start to retire at age 65 with full Social Security and Medicare benefits.

By their very nature, these programs serve as budget-busters. That's because entitlement law mandates the payment of benefits to any person meeting the eligibility requirements. Money is no object.

Any attempt even to limit the growth of such programs is falsely depicted by the news media and by liberals in general as "benefit cuts." Any politician who tries to control spending on these programs is depicted as Scrooge or worse; Newt Gingrich was caricatured by the media as "The Gingrich Who Stole Christmas."

The largest entitlement programs are Social Security, Medicare, and Medicaid, but this category of the budget also includes retirement benefits for military and civilian government employees. In addition, payment of interest on the public debt is not an "entitlement" but is mandatory.

The Baby Boomer Effect

Here's a dramatic example of the effects of an aging population. The GAO's Walker said that in 1950, "more than 16 workers were paying into the [Social Security] system for every retiree drawing benefits. Today, that ratio is a little more than three to one. By 2040, it'll be about two to one."

We can expect the number of people getting Social Security benefits to grow from 47 million today to 68 million in 2020, 83 million in 2030, and 91 million in 2040.

Over the next 25 years, Social Security spending will grow much faster than our economy. We can expect Social Security outlays to rise 147% (after adjusting for inflation). That's more than twice the 72% expected growth in the economy, as measured by figures for the Gross Domestic Product.

Social Security, as you may have heard, is currently projected by the federal government to go broke in a decade.

Claims that the system is sound until mid-century are based on the belief in mythical "Social Security Trust Funds." Those funds consist of IOUs the government writes to itself. As the *Wall Street Journal's* David Wessel once noted, that's like a father who saves $3 a day for his daughter's college education, then, at the end of each day, takes $3 out of the jar and puts in an IOU for $3. The so-called trust funds are money the government owes itself, represented by certificates in a filing cabinent in Parkersburg, West Virginia, as President Bush himself has pointed out. So, by the middle of the next decade, when Social Security starts to take in less money than it pays out, there will be no real "trust funds" on which to draw. Social Security will be broke, and it will continue to operate only through some combination of benefit cuts, tax increases, and much more deficit spending.

But Social Security is only part of the scenario. "Social Security's problem is a fraction of Medicare's," Walker said, noting that Medicare is "seven to eight times worse" off than Social Security.

In 1970, Medicare expenditures were $7.5 billion (about $35 billion in 2002 dollars). By 1999, Medicare expenditures had grown to $213 billion. The number of enrollees nearly doubled in that time period, but the inflation-adjusted expenditures per enrollee *tripled*. So we have to worry not only about ever greater numbers of people going on Medicare, but also about the much greater increase in their health care costs.

More recent history: Medicare's spending and unfunded obligations increased 43% in just two years, between 2000 and 2002. In the next two years, 2002 to 2004, they more than doubled (an increase of 112%).

This sky-high jump was thanks to the Medicare prescription drug benefit enacted in 2003 by our Republican Congress and Republican President. And the prescription drug program provides a built-in incentive for politicians to promise more and more benefits, especially as prescription costs rise.

Prescription costs rise because, with advances in technology, more and more diseases can be treated by drugs rather than by surgery and other methods. It costs more than $800 million to develop a new drug, on average, and the profits from one discovery are used to finance the next discovery. Of course, it would be possible to put price controls on prescription drugs, if we didn't care about the new drugs that would never be created and about the people who would suffer and die as a result. It *would* be possible to reduce the price of medicine by restricting excessive lawsuits.

As I mentioned, the economy is projected to grow 72% between 2005 and 2030 and Social Security is projected to grow twice as fast. Well, Medicare spending is expected to grow *four and a half* times faster than the nation's economy.

In 2050, by the most *conservative* estimates, Medicare will have cost a cumulative total of $2.6 trillion, adjusted for inflation, or about the size of the entire federal budget today. By 2079, just the prescription drug benefit of Medicare alone will have cost a total of $8.7 trillion over the years, or more than three times our entire federal budget today.

The Cost of Doing Nothing

Contrary to what some Republicans believe, we won't be able to close the entitlement gap by economic growth alone. Closing the current long-term fiscal gap would require real average annual economic growth of more than 10% a year, every year for the next 75 years. The only major country that's reported double-digit growth in our time is Communist China, but that's because they are starting from a dirt-poor level, whereas we're an advanced economy. (Besides, their statistics are about as trustworthy as other statistics from Communist countries.) During the booming 1990s, the American economy grew at an average 3.2% per year. Ten percent or better for 75 straight years? Get real.

What happens if we do nothing?

Entitlements and debt service take over domestic government. This is already happening. "There's no such thing as a free lunch," as Nobel Prize winning economist Milton Friedman noted. The debt we're accumulating comes with interest attached. The money we pay as interest on the national debt doesn't go to any current government services. It is money down the drain, with only our creditors profiting.

Today we already spend $160 billion a year on our debt interest—$160 billion just to keep this bankrupt system floating a while longer. By 2009 we will be spending more on interest on the national debt than on all discretionary domestic programs in America. And by 2040, all federal revenues will barely cover interest on the national debt.

Entitlements are crowding out discretionary programs. In 1964, two-thirds of total federal spending was discretionary. By 2004, the discretionary portion of all federal spending had shrunk to 39%. And the discretionary share of the federal pie will continue to shrink as a percentage of overall spending.

As this process continues, expect the nastiness in Washington to get nastier. Discretionary programs, after all, are the ones that Congress votes on each session—the goodies, the "bacon" they bring home, the stuff that politicians brag about to their constituents. As the share of the federal pie allotted to these discretionary programs decreases, competition for that diminishing share will become ever more fierce.

America becomes ever more susceptible to foreign economic blackmail. In 2004, over 90% of the new debt that the U.S. issued was purchased by foreigners, and some of those foreigners have agendas very different from ours.

Let's be honest: We're talking about Red China. Right now the relationship benefits both sides: China's Communist government and its front companies buy our debt securities, thus keeping our interest rates lower than they would be otherwise, and we in turn buy massive amounts of consumer goods from them. Because these goods are produced in part by very cheap labor, prices are lower than we'd have to pay elsewhere.

As long as we're willing to finance the Chinese Communist Party, this is a marriage made in—well, not heaven, but at least it's profitable. What happens, though, when the differences between the U.S.

democracy and mainland China's dictatorship come to a head—say, over the separate existence of the Republic of China (Taiwan)?

At that point, China could very well switch a significant portion of its dollar securities to, say, Euro securities. Big trouble could ensue if these foreign investors lost confidence in U.S. securities and decided not to buy them, or, worse, started to sell off their holdings. At one point in 2005, South Korea made ever so slight a switch from the dollar to the Euro, and alarm bells went off throughout Wall Street.

We lose our capacity to handle unexpected events. Being so deeply in debt, in both the government and private sectors, makes us much more susceptible to unforeseen bumps in the road. As Paul Kasriel, chief economist at the Northern Trust Company in Chicago, put it: "We have a very accident-prone economy. We have the most highly leveraged economy in the postwar period, and the Fed is increasing rates. In the past 30 years or so, whenever the Fed has raised interest rates, we've quite frequently had financial accidents."

A heavy debtor is much more susceptible to such economic shocks than someone with sound financial practices and accounts. That's true for both individuals and governments.

Higher inflation. Falling real wages. Higher interest rates. Shrinking or evaporating pensions. Slower economic growth. Higher taxes. Recession. A jolt, even a crash, in stocks and bonds. Any one or combination of these could ruin a deeply indebted man or a deeply indebted country.

Standard & Poor's, the bond rating agency, has warned that American debt issues could become junk bond debt by 2035 because we will have so little financial credibility in the markets.

It is the responsibility of American leaders to ensure that we can respond to future crises, including economic shifts, natural disasters, terrorist attacks, and war. We should not have to worry that, one day, another nation will threaten us, and we will lack the resources to respond.

America moves backward and becomes like Europe. Alison Acosta Fraser of the Heritage Foundation warned that, "Without major changes, federal government spending will continue to increase to unprecedented levels, potentially exceeding 35% of the economy. Historically, it has hovered around 19.6%."

With government commanding more than a third of the economy, our nation would sink into the quagmire associated with Europe's welfare states. The New World will become the Old World, as our market-based economy becomes ever more socialist, as our people become poorer and we lose the American edge in technology, creativity, optimism, and freedom. We will lose our competitive advantage over the rest of the industrialized world.

Government Accountability Office simulations show that balancing the budget in 2040 could require actions as large as—

- Cutting total federal spending by 60%, or
- Raising federal taxes to 2.5 times today's level.

Either option would be devastating, if not unthinkable. Raising taxes that much would sink our economy into another Great Depression, and cutting federal spending that much would require the U.S. government to renege on its entitlement obligations to its own citizens, to say nothing of its obligation to provide a national defense. Either option would result in economic ruin and political upheaval.

Of course, it won't really happen that abruptly. Instead we will likely face death by a thousand cuts—gradually but persistently higher taxes, coupled with an increasingly dysfunctional economy. Our standard of living, and the standard of living for our children and grandchildren, will erode year after year.

So maybe my metaphor is wrong. Maybe the disaster will be less like a Category 5 hurricane, and more like what happens when an animal sinks steadily into a tar pit. Maybe, a million years from now, some scientist will dig out our bones and put us on display.

Republicans Take Action on the Entitlement Crisis, by Making Things Worse

About an hour before sunrise on November 22, 2003 – 5:53 a.m., to be exact – the Republican members of the House of Representatives showed what they were made of. After Republican leaders kept the

House in session through the night, members of Congress finally caved in to pressure from the White House and the GOP leadership, and they approved President Bush's Medicare prescription drug program. The legislation passed the entire House by a vote of 220 to 215 (204 Republicans approving, 25 opposed) and sailed into law.

By that narrow margin, they increased the future indebtedness of the already-bankrupt Medicare program by *$8 trillion.*

This was, in effect, a new entitlement at a time when existing entitlements were already threatening the economic health of the nation, and it represented the largest increase in the welfare state since the Great Society of Lyndon Baines Johnson. This was an abuse of our children and grandchildren, who will be paying for this monstrosity the rest of their lives.

In the Senate, on the key vote that decided whether the program would pass, two Republican senators voted "no." Not 52. Not 42, or 32, or 22, or 12.

Two. John McCain and Chuck Hagel.

President Bush and Karl Rove wanted a Medicare drug prescription bill for one simple reason: to bribe the nation's senior citizens. To their way of thinking, a prescription drug bill, no matter how reckless it was economically, was the way to win over a voting bloc that traditionally has been up for sale to the highest bidder in presidential elections.

The bribery strategy has boomeranged. Discontent with the results of the drug prescription "entitlement" is so intense, it ranks as one of the top reasons Democrats have a chance to take over one or both houses of Congress in 2006 and the White House in 2008. (I am reminded of the Democratic strategists who thought the Clintons' health care plan would seal a Democratic majority for a generation, then watched as the GOP took both the Senate and House of Representatives.)

Back in 2003, Bush's Big Government Republicans were bragging how they had made great strides with the senior community, and as evidence they pointed to the support given by the American Association of Retired Persons, now known simply as AARP. AARP is a corporation that sells insurance and provides discounts and other benefits. It is influential because of its mailing list, its publications, and the fact that some politicians and the media treat it as "the senior citizens' lobby." It is no such thing.

AARP doesn't determine its positions based on the opinions of its members; its high-paid, left-wing Washington staff represents no one but itself. The AARP *Policy Book* touts the group's liberal views on a plethora of issues, including capital gains taxes, the marriage penalty, gun control, a balanced budget constitutional amendment, and—get this!—estate taxes.

The group denies that there is a crisis in Social Security, now or in the near future, and states, "For years, each political party has accused the other of raiding the Social Security trust funds. In fact, no one has raided the funds." As recently as March 2006, AARP provided a letter to Senate Minority Leader Harry Reid, which was read on the floor of the Senate, *opposing* an amendment to the budget bill to require that Social Security surpluses be used *only for retirement purposes.*

AARP is the epitome of Washington corruption, taking its members' hard-earned money and using it for causes they oppose and that are against their best interests. Not surprisingly, AARP stood with Rove in supporting the prescription drug scheme. Not surprisingly, AARP, to which the Bush White House had given great credibility, turned around and played a leading role in quashing Republican efforts to reform Social Security.

What makes Republicans' behavior on the prescription drug issue even harder to accept is the tactics they used to get the measure passed. These tactics included outright lies and even bribery.

Members of Congress were told that the cost of this new welfare scheme would be no more than $400 billion over 10 years ("only" $400 billion). Richard Foster, the chief Medicare actuary, calculated a higher estimate, $534 billion for the first ten years, but he was told he would be fired if he blew the whistle.

Most House votes last about 15 minutes. This one was kept open by House leaders for *three hours* overnight, resulting in that final vote at 5:53 in the morning. Fed by greed for power and by lots of coffee, the GOP leadership kept hammering away at conservative resistance until it got the votes it needed. Conservatives voting "no" were restrained from leaving the floor of the House until they could be pressured into changing their votes. "Door men" were stationed at exits to make sure they couldn't escape. Congressmen Jerry Moran (Kansas) and Charles Norwood (Georgia) managed to outmaneuver them and get away, but Jo Ann Emerson (Missouri) had to hide on the Democratic side, crouching down to avoid being seen by the Republican search team.

I'm not kidding. This is your Republican-controlled House of Representatives I'm talking about.

The lowest point involved strong-arm tactics against Michigan Congressman Nick Smith. Smith was retiring after that session of Congress, and his son Brad was one of five candidates running to succeed him. Majority Leader Tom DeLay offered to endorse Smith's son and raise money for him in exchange for a "yes" vote. According to testimony by a Republican staffer, Rules Committee Chairman David Drier of California offered to find Smith's daughter a job as an actress in Hollywood. (Drier denied this.) Congresswoman Candice Miller, a fellow Michigan Republican, cursed Smith for voting "no." To his credit, Smith stood firm.

Veteran conservative columnist Robert Novak reported that, "after Nick Smith voted no and the bill passed, Duke Cunningham of California and other Republicans taunted him that his son was dead meat. . . . [Other] Republicans voting against the bill were told they were endangering their political futures. Major contributors warned Rep. Jim DeMint they would cut off funding for his Senate race in South Carolina. A Missouri state legislator called Rep. Todd Akin to threaten a primary challenge against him." Duke Cunningham, as you may recall, later went to prison for taking bribes.

(DeMint, by the way, stood firm against the bill, and is now *Senator* DeMint. Akin stood firm against the bill, and was reelected in 2004 with 65% of the vote. They are proof that you don't have to cave in to spending pressure, or "go along to get along.")

Ten months after the vote, following 3,400 pages of sworn testimony and subpoena responses, the House ethics committee rapped DeLay on the knuckles for his "improper" behavior regarding Smith. But the Bush Administration had its prescription drug welfare bill.

Republican Socialism

Just what is it about this Medicare prescription drug scheme that got the White House and the Republican leadership stooping to such depths?

"Republican socialism" is what Congressman Ron Paul of Texas calls it. Congressman Paul is one of the most principled members of the House and a physician. He explains: "The new Medicare drug plan enriches pharmaceutical companies, fleeces taxpayers, and forces millions of older Americans to accept inferior drug coverage..."

Paul adds: "Nothing from the government is free, of course, and prescription drugs will be no exception. . . . In fact, many seniors will end up paying more out-of-pocket under the Medicare scheme than they do now with their private plans. The Medicare drug benefit requires monthly premiums, co-pays, and deductibles, just as private plans do. It also has gaps in coverage that no sensible person would accept if offered by a private insurer. Like all government programs, the Medicare drug entitlement will be shabby, degrading, and inferior to the private sector.

"The vast majority of older Americans already have private prescription drug coverage that they don't want changed, and this 78% of seniors may well lose their good private coverage altogether."

The smoking gun, noted by Paul: "The government's own Congressional Budget Office estimates that at least one-third of all private companies will dump their retirees into the Medicare system as a result of the new bill. Big corporations love the Medicare drug plan, because they want to shift the responsibility for providing drug benefits to their retirees onto taxpayers. Dozens of major companies shamelessly advertised in the *Washington Times* and elsewhere in support of the Medicare bill for this very simple reason. Their pension plans are dangerously underfunded, so naturally they use their lobbying influence to promote a Medicare drug system. In this sense the Medicare bill is a taxpayer-funded corporate bailout for hundreds of American companies."

Once again, we follow the money, and it leads us to one inescapable conclusion—that the Big Government Republicans owe their allegiance to the giant corporations, rather than to the American taxpayer. And they will put their own political interests ahead of the country's—except, of course, when they are wrong about where their political interests lie.

2

THE ERA OF
OBESE GOVERNMENT

"The era of Big Government is over."
– President Bill Clinton in his
1996 State of the Union Address

"After 11 years of Republican majority we've pared it [the federal government] down pretty good."
– House Majority Leader
Tom DeLay (R-Texas), September 13, 2005

If President Clinton and Majority Leader DeLay had been telling the truth, there would be no need for this chapter. But they were not. Not at all.

President Clinton was presiding over a monstrous government, the largest in American history up to that time. He never proposed to pare it down. At most, he cut national defense, and proposed a few cuts in *the rate of growth* of other programs.

(Cutting projected future increases, you see, is what they call a "cut" in Washington. It's like working for an employer who tells you to expect a 5% pay cut next year, then cuts your pay by 4% instead and expects you to thank him for the raise.)

When President Clinton made his claim that "the era of Big Government is over," he knew full well that Big Government was growing and would continue to grow. What he probably didn't anticipate was that, as fast as government grew under Clinton and a Democratic Congress in 1993-94, it would grow much faster under a Republican president with a Republican Congress.

Once Republicans got control of both elected branches of the federal government, the era of Big Government really was over. Because the era of Obese Government had begun!

When President Clinton made his (tongue-in-cheek?) claim, the federal government was spending $1,635.9 billion. Just seven years later, in 2003, the federal government was spending $2,263.9 billion, and matters would get even worse in 2004 and 2005. *The federal government grew more than 38 percent in seven years!* For that we can thank both Republicans and Democrats, but most Democrats don't claim to be fiscal conservatives.

The cancerous growth of the federal government makes it more difficult to apply conservative principles to all the other problems the country faces. How can we provide for the national defense when tax money is being eaten up by wasteful spending? How can we cut the tax burden on working families and promote higher wages and salaries, when the government is consuming more and more of society's resources? Even when there is no apparent connection between the size of government and another issue, there is a connection, because Big Government gives power and influence to the Left and gets liberal politicians elected to office. And the burden of Big Government falls disproportionately on people trying to raise families or start businesses, the core of the conservative constituency.

Meanwhile, justifiable programs—ones identified in the Constitution as within the proper sphere of the federal government— are strangled by this bureaucracy as surely as the unjustified ones.

Every dollar of yours that the government spends is one you cannot spend yourself in the way *you* want to spend it. Who knows better how to spend your money—you, or some bureaucrat in Washington?

Most spending at the federal level is inherently wasteful, because it involves taking money from people at the grassroots, funneling it through Washington, and sending it back. (When you get your own money back, Washington expects your gratitude.) With the exception of national defense and national issues of homeland security such as border control, almost all problems that should be addressed by government should be addressed at the local and state level. That's where individual citizens, and families and communities, have the most impact and influence.

As former Reagan speechwriter Peggy Noonan put it, "Town spending tends to be more effective than county spending. County spending tends—tends—to be more efficacious than state spending. State spending tends to be more constructive than federal spending. This is how life works. The area closest to where the buck came from is most likely to be more careful with the buck. This is part of the reason conservatives are so disturbed by the gushing federal spigot."

The size of the federal government is *the single most important barometer of the health of the American republic.* When domestic federal spending goes up, it's a surefire indicator that something is wrong. And the way spending has been increasing under the Bush administration and the Republican Congress shows that things are *seriously* wrong.

With the solid backing of conservatives, Republicans won the presidency in 2000 and the succeeding election. We gave that Republican president a Republican House in 2000, 2002, and 2004 and a Republican Senate in 2000 (until the defection of Vermont Senator Jim Jeffords), 2002, and 2004. We had every right to expect that *finally* we'd see government spending brought under control, and the size of the federal government cut back.

Instead, the size of the federal government has increased faster under the Republicans than at any time since Lyndon Baines Johnson and the Great Society. At the rate the Republicans are going, with expenditures still zooming, by 2008 they may be responsible for the biggest percentage increases in the federal government since Franklin Delano Roosevelt and the New Deal. That will be George W. Bush's presidential legacy: He'll be the Republican LBJ or FDR!

Let's take a look at all administrations since the time of the Great Society, using data from the Tax Foundation's authoritative handbook, *Facts and Figures on Government Finance:*

Growth in total federal expenditures, adjusted for inflation:

LBJ **32.2%**
Nixon 14.3%
Nixon/Ford 13.9%
Carter 13.1%
Reagan 1st term 13.4%
Reagan 2nd term 6.1%
Bush I 13.4%
Clinton 1st term 4.7%
Clinton 2nd term 3.7%
Bush II **19.2%**

What a stark contrast between the growth of government during the two Clinton terms of office and now, under Bush! The federal government is growing *more than five times as fast* under Bush than it did during Clinton's second term!

What these figures demonstrate is the power of a strong conservative Republican opposition in Congress during the Clinton years. If there ever was a case for divided government, here it is. The lesson for many Americans is that today's Republicans cannot be trusted with the keys to *both* the executive and legislative branches of the federal government.

The Transactional Records Access Clearinghouse (TRAC) at Syracuse University in New York keeps records that show how much the federal government spends on average each year for each man, woman, and child in the country, using Census Bureau data files. Because these figures are adjusted for both inflation and population growth, and because the government was already bloated beyond comprehension at the period of these comparisons, there is no excuse for any increase in TRAC's figures on the size of government.

Cumulative growth in federal expenditures, adjusted for inflation AND population growth:

Clinton (8 years) ....**-1.1%**
Bush (3 years) .... **+15.0%**

Yes, you read that right! Federal expenditures increased relatively modestly during Clinton's two terms of office, as we saw in the first table. But when we look at per capita figures, which means the growth in population is taken into account, the federal government actually spent 1.1% *less* per each man, woman, and child in the U.S. at the end of Clinton's two terms.

With these same per capita expenditures exploding in the first three years of the Bush Administration, can you imagine what the GOP record will look like at the end of eight years if we don't change course dramatically?

During President Bush's first five years in office, the federal budget increased by $616 billion. That's a mammoth 33% jump in the size of the federal government in just his first five years! To put this in perspective, this *increase* of $616 billion is more than the *entire federal budget* in Jimmy Carter's last year in office. And conservatives were complaining about Big Government back then! How can Bush, Hastert, Frist & Company look us in the eye and tell us they are fiscal conservatives when in five short years they increased the already-bloated government by more than the budget for the *entire federal government* when Ronald Reagan was assuming office?

Conservatives believe in taking personal responsibility for their actions. Republicans obviously don't. They refuse to accept responsibility for today's runaway spending, and their excuses are pathetic.

For nearly 50 years, Republicans could blame spending growth on the Democrats, because the Democrats controlled either the White House, Senate, or House—and usually some combination or all of those. Now that the Republicans control all three, apologists for President Bush blame the Republican Congress, and vice versa! None of their excuses hold water.

Now the excuse we hear most often goes something like this: "Federal spending has increased because of the War on Terror. In time of war, spending *has* to increase, just as it did during World War II and the Cold War."

The implication is that you're unpatriotic if you complain about spending a few more dollars, or several hundred billion dollars. This is a total cover-up of the real situation, as I'll now show you.

First, there is an assumption that the Pentagon and Homeland

Security budgets should be sacrosanct. But the Pentagon is spending much of its budget on expensive weapons systems that are unsuited for either the occupation of Iraq or for the kinds of wars we are likely to fight in the foreseeable future. And there are tens of billions in appropriations the Department of Defense cannot account for. As for the Department of Homeland Security, it has quickly become the largest bureaucratic mess outside of the Pentagon, and we saw what we got for our money when Hurricane Katrina struck.

Second, the argument that the increase in federal spending can be blamed on the War on Terror is a smokescreen. For the moment, let's ignore the spending in Defense and Homeland Security. Let's also, for the moment, ignore the imminent crisis in entitlements, chiefly Medicare and Social Security. Let's look only at what's left, discretionary domestic spending. This covers all the other departments of the government, from agriculture and education to human services and the environment and all the rest. These are the areas that take up most of the time on Capitol Hill. Because they are *discretionary* (not entitlements that are automatically paid out by a preset formula) and *domestic* (nothing to do with national defense), they should be the easiest area to cut or freeze.

Not a chance.

Discretionary domestic spending, adjusted for inflation:

LBJ . . . .+4.1%
Nixon/Ford . . . .+5.0%
Carter . . . .+1.6%
Reagan . . . .**-1.4%**
Bush I . . . .+3.8%
Clinton . . . .+2.1%
Bush II . . . .**+4.8%**

When we strip away defense, homeland security, and entitlements, and adjust for inflation, leaving only discretionary domestic spending, *George W. Bush has grown the federal government at a faster pace than Lyndon Baines Johnson.* His record for profligate spending is outmatched (for the time being) only by another Big Government

Republican, Richard Nixon. And when Bush's second term is over, there's every reason to expect that Bush will hold the record as the president who's grown the federal government at its fastest pace in modern times.

Unlike Bush, father or son, Ronald Reagan actually cut discretionary domestic spending in inflation-adjusted dollars. He was the only president to do so since the end of World War II. That's because he didn't follow Lyndon Johnson's so-called "guns and butter" formula of high spending on both military and domestic programs. Reagan knew he had to increase defense spending in order to win the Cold War – a mission that was *really* accomplished – so he insisted on controlling domestic programs to keep the budget on a somewhat even keel. Defense spending went up by 19.2%, but Reagan cut discretionary non-defense spending.

In cutting back on domestic spending during the Cold War, Reagan was following the path blazed by FDR and Truman during World War II and the Korean War. Roosevelt cut domestic spending by 20% between 1942 and 1944, during World War II, even agreeing with Congress to abolish some of his favorite programs, including the Civilian Conservation Corps, the National Youth Administration, and the Work Projects Administration. And after the start of the Korean War, Truman and his Democratic Congress cut domestic spending by 28% in the first year.

Not so George W. Bush. He has followed in LBJ's guns-and-butter footsteps.

Reagan's accomplishment is all the more remarkable given the fact that the House of Representatives – where spending bills originate – was under Democratic control during both of his terms, at one point by more than 100 seats. And Bush's cave-in is all the more inexcusable given the GOP's control of Congress during most of his two terms.

The first tool Reagan used is the same one every modern President —except Bush—has used: the veto. Here's the record for the past 40 years:

President	Total Vetoes
LBJ	30
Nixon	43
Ford	66
Carter	31
Reagan	78
Bush I	44
Clinton	37
Bush II	**0**

Bush apologists give the excuse that it's harder to veto bills that are passed by your own party. Yet LBJ and Carter each cast 30 or more vetoes while their own party controlled Congress.

In fact, the all-time master of the veto was Franklin Delano Roosevelt. He used the veto power an incredible 635 times during his four terms—despite having a Democratic Congress with majorities as lopsided as 75-17 in the Senate* and 333-89 in the House*! Congress overrode his vetoes a mere nine times.

The second tool Reagan and other modern presidents have used— all except George W. Bush, that is—is the power to rescind funds authorized by Congress. This "rescission" power is explained by the House Rules Committee as "a law that repeals previously enacted budget authority in whole or in part. Under the Impoundment Control Act of 1974, the president can impound such funds by sending a message to Congress requesting one or more rescissions and the reasons for doing so."

Here's the record.

Presidential rescissions:

Ford	$ 7.935 billion
Carter	$ 4.608 billion
Reagan	$43.437 billion
Bush I	$13.193 billion
Clinton	$ 6.628 billion
Bush II	**0**

---

*In the 75th Congress (1937-38), there were four senators and 13 representatives who were not members of the two major political parties.

While none of this excuses the Republicans in Congress, of course, it is obvious that George W. Bush has absolutely no desire to cut spending anywhere, anytime.

The Factory-Farming Era of GOP Pork

The best illustration of the corrupting influence of power on the Republicans is the explosion of pork-barrel spending projects since 2000. In Congress-talk these pork projects are called "earmarks." Typically an individual member of Congress inserts an earmark into a spending bill. It hasn't been requested by the President, and it evades the usual procedures for competitive bidding, expert review, and cost-benefit analysis.

"Each one of these," says the *Washington Post*, "as Mr. Reagan understood but Mr. Bush apparently doesn't, amounts to a conscious decision to waste taxpayers' dollars."

In a conspiracy of silence, members of Congress have struck an agreement: "I won't object to your earmark if you don't object to mine." And the leaders of key committees get the lion's share of earmarks. You don't complain about that, either, if you ever hope to get legislation through their committees.

Despite their reputation as skinflints when it came to spending, the Republicans who controlled Congress during the Clinton years weren't exactly bashful about popping in some pork spending for their districts. But since the Republicans took over the White House *and* Congress, the flood of earmarks has become obscene. Let's take a look at some figures compiled by Citizens Against Government Waste.

Number of congressional pork projects by fiscal year, when Bill Clinton was President and Republicans controlled both houses of Congress:

1995: 1,439
1996: 958
1997: 1,596
1998: 2,100
1999: 2,838
2000: 4,326

Number of congressional pork projects by fiscal year, with George W. Bush as President and Republicans in control of Congress (except the Senate during the 'Jeffords betrayal' period):

    2001:..6,333
    2002:..8,341
    2003:..9,362
    2004:..10,656
    2005:..13,997

That's a 121% increase in the number of pork-barrel earmarks in just five years of GOP dominance. And remember, each one of those earmarks represent a conscious decision to spend taxpayers' dollars on a project that benefits only a particular area or interest group. In other words, a conscious decision to waste money on something that is not the federal government's business.

Omnibus spending bills are a favorite place in which to hide these earmarks. The bills are so huge (often thousands of pages in length) and members have so little time in which to consider them (usually a couple of days or less), that no one is likely to discover a piece of pork, not matter how ludicrous, until a congressman brags about it to the folks back home, and then it's too late.

But transportation bills are even worse. The transportation bill enacted in 2005, for example, was the most expensive public works legislation in our nation's history, and printed out at 1,752 pages. It was also laden with no less than 6,373 pork-barrel earmarks. Back in 1987 President Reagan vetoed the transportation bill because it contained 152 earmarks. In 2005 President George W. Bush didn't blink at signing into law a pigsty piece of legislation containing 6,373 earmarks.

Back in the bad old days, when Republicans derided Democrats as tax-and-spend liberals, Senator Robert Byrd (D-West Virginia) was castigated as the king of pork. His state typically receives $2 in federal largesse for each $1 it produces in tax revenue. Today the king of pork indisputably is Don Young, the Republican congressman from Alaska and chairman of the House Transportation Committee. His state gets $5 back for each $1 paid in taxes, thanks to taxpayers in the lower 49 states.

Young, it seems, has no shame. He bragged that the 2005 transportation bill was stuffed "like a turkey" with pork dressing, including a $231 million bridge in Anchorage to be named "Don Young's Way." But the real poster boy in Don Young's pork bill is the now infamous "Bridge to Nowhere."

Congress authorized $223 million to build a mile-long bridge connecting Gravina Island, Alaska (population 50), with Ketchikan, Alaska (population 8,044, with a median household income 9% higher than the national median). It was designed to rise 200 feet above the water, almost twice as high as the 119-foot-high Brooklyn Bridge.

It's not as if the 50 residents of Gravina Island are cut off from civilization. A ferry transports them to Ketchikan in five minutes. And yes, there's a small airport on the island, but anyone in Ketchikan who wants to catch a plane can also use that five-minute ferry ride. Because of the mountainous topography, thus the circuitous route of the highway connecting with the bridge, it will actually take longer to get to the airport via the highway and bridge.

Parade magazine sent a reporter to Ketchikan and Gravina Island to see if there was some urgent need for the bridge that hadn't come to anyone's attention. What he found was this sort of attitude, coming from a local politician: "The general feeling here is that if someone else is paying for it, sure, why not?"

Why not, indeed? Especially when a one-fourth interest in 33 acres on Gravina Island, within a mile of the proposed construction, is owned by a woman named Nancy Murkowski, who happens to be the wife of the Governor of Alaska and the mother of U.S. Senator Lisa Murkowski (R-Alaska). Senator Murkowski, you may recall, took the Senate floor to defend the Bridge to Nowhere project when an attempt was made to use some of the money for New Orleans disaster relief instead.

"Someone else," not the residents of Gravina Island, is paying for the Bridge to Nowhere. *You*, dear reader, are that "someone else." Or, more precisely, your children and grandchildren, since Republicans believe in using deficits to finance bloated government.

Not that Congressman Young has any qualms about this. "I'd be silly if I didn't take advantage of my chairmanship," he told the *Anchorage Daily News.* "I think I did a pretty good job." And: "This is the time to take advantage of the position I'm in."

More congressional pork – wasteful, often unconstitutional

Here are some more examples of what you've been paying for in recent years. Some of these are a total waste of money; others are just not appropriate for the federal government:

- Further extending the nation's longest paved recreational trail, in Minnesota
- Helping Ocean Spray market its white cranberry juice in Great Britain
- A project to provide economic opportunity in areas of low or moderate income—in Coral Gables, Florida, where the per capita income is 19.6% above the national average
- A "prairie parkway" in House Speaker Dennis Hastert's Illinois, even though the state department of transportation won't know for three more years whether it's actually desirable
- Another Dennis Hastert subsidy: to a candy company in his hometown to study caffeinated chewing gum
- An indoor rainforest tourist attraction in Iowa
- Subsidies for the Rock and Roll Hall of Fame in Cleveland, the Paper Industry International Hall of Fame in Appleton, Wisconsin, and the Country Music Hall of Fame in Nashville
- Upgrades to the [Senator] Ted Stevens Airport in Alaska
- A deer avoidance system in Weedsport, New York
- A parking facility for the University of the Incarnate Word in San Antonio
- Production of ethanol at Mississippi State and Oklahoma State universities
- A new subway station for Yankee Stadium in the Bronx, New York
- Burying part of the West Side Highway in Manhattan, which Donald Trump wants to provide better views of the Hudson River from his Trump Place

And the list goes on and on — 13,997 such ways to waste your tax money in 2005 alone.

Hurricane Katrina Blows into Town, and the Pork Barrel Follows

When Hurricane Katrina devastated New Orleans and the Gulf Coast in 2005, Americans witnessed the near-total failure of government at *all* levels—federal, state, and local. Part of the problem was that Katrina hit one of the most corrupt and inoperative states in the country to begin with; as Huey Long famously put it, "One of these days, Louisiana is going to have honest government—and hate it." The larger problem was that President Bush had no idea what to do in a true emergency other than the standard *liberal* response: throw money at it.

How much was he prepared to spend? "Whatever it takes," came his response. Americans were told this could cost $150 billion, $200 billion, or more. In other words, real money, not pocket change.

What's the plan on how to spend it efficiently to get the desired results? There the answers got rather vague. Commit the money first, then we'll figure out what to do with it.

And where is the money coming from? *That* was the question never asked.

The federal government was already spending recklessly, like a drunk with your credit card. This was in what we were told were "good times." Then we were hit with a *true* emergency with no cash and no money in the bank, just IOUs to be paid for by your children and grandchildren. The answer of the president and his compliant Congress was to write more IOUs.

A few courageous conservatives tried to restore some common sense to the process. It was not a matter of being "compassionate"— individual Americans were showing true compassion with their checkbooks and by opening their houses as well to the refugees. It was a matter of restricting the federal government to its proper role, spending the money with a sensible plan and proper oversight, and paying for the federal help in a responsible manner.

In previous natural disasters, the federal government's response under the 1988 Stafford Act was limited to four basic areas: helping clear debris, assisting states with search and rescue efforts, temporary housing and unemployment benefits for the displaced, and rebuilding infrastructure such as highways and bridges. The Stafford Act, accord-

ing to the Congressional Research Service, "does not explicitly authorize the president to provide long-term recovery assistance to communities." And *at least* 25% of the bills—and if possible as much as 75%
—were to be paid by the states and localities.

President Bush set out on a radical departure: the federal government would pay for almost anything that came up, waiving the cost-
sharing requirements. Common sense tells you that if they don't have
to share the cost, those states are going to ask the feds to pay for every
project they're capable of dreaming up. Indeed, President Bush urged
Mississippi officials to "think bold" when planning their raid on your
wallet, but, as could be expected, Louisiana had the boldest politicians
and officials.

A month after Katrina struck, Louisiana's politicians requested
$250 billion in reconstruction funds for their state *alone*. That's
$50,000 for every person in the state, and $1,900 for your household
and every other household in the United States. The 440-page itemiza-
tion was laden with pork projects having nothing to do with hurricane
relief, of course. Even the request for $40 billion in projected Army
Corps of Engineers projects in the state would be 10 times the Corps'
annual budget for the entire nation, and was a corporate welfare wish-
list written by lobbyists representing everyone from shipping firms to
energy companies, and including projects that have *flunked* the Corps'
cost-benefit analyses. Even before Katrina, FEMA was trying to find
out what happened to $60 million in unaccounted funds it had distrib-
uted to Louisiana state emergency offices. Pre-Katrina, Louisiana had
received much more for Army Corps of Engineers civil projects than
any other state during the Bush administration, but somehow that
money wasn't spent on levees or flood control.

Predictably, when President Bush and Congress opened the flood-
gates on "disaster relief," with little or no oversight, there were big
problems involving government bureaucrats and contractors. Like the
$236 million deal with Carnival Cruise Lines to use some of its ships
as refugee centers, even though they remained half-empty. And small
problems everywhere you looked: Hurricane Katrina relief and
rebuilding projects where you, the taxpayer, ended up spending
$25,078 for a laptop computer and accessories, a pizza cutter with a 4-

inch blade for $27.00, steak knives for $92.28 each, a $2,950 wrist watch, and a 3-inch donut cutter for $25.50. But what do you expect when government employees are given government credit cards with a $250,000 limit—100 times the normal $2,500 limit, and 10 times the $25,000 limit during previous natural disaster relief efforts.

Conservatives at the Heritage Foundation and in Congress thought of two obvious places to save money quickly with which to pay for Katrina relief:

- Revoke all the earmarks included in the transportation bill, for an immediate $27 billion that could be spent on Katrina relief
- Postpone implementation of the unaffordable Medicare prescription drug benefit

This would seem to be a start, but President Bush quickly sent out word that he adamantly opposed any postponement of his Medicare expansion. One got the definite impression that if such legislation crossed his desk, he would finally learn how to use his veto pen. How ironic that a President who calls himself a conservative cannot find the will to veto any increase in government spending, no matter how outrageous, but can develop the necessary finger muscles when it comes to threatened cuts or even postponements in federal spending.

For a while it seemed the revoke-the-pork proposal might find some traction. Around the country taxpayers were offering to give up their local pork projects to fund Katrina relief. In Bozeman, Montana, for example, there was a call to refuse the $4 million earmark to pay for a parking garage. One citizen told the *Wall Street Journal:* "We figure New Orleans needs the money right now a lot more than we need extra downtown parking space." (A nice sentiment, but of course it begs the obvious question: What business is it of the federal government to build local parking lots in the first place?)

The reception in Congress was another matter. In the Senate, two staunchly anti-pork senators, Tom Coburn of Oklahoma and John McCain of Arizona, led the fight to revoke the earmarks from the transportation bill, but Alaska Republican Ted Stevens threatened to quit Congress if funding for his beloved "bridge to nowhere" was revoked. "I don't threaten people," he said tellingly; "I promise people."

And in the House, the conservative Republican Study Committee similarly got nowhere in its "Operation Offset" efforts to revoke the pork. Alaska's other pork king, Appropriations Committee Chairman Don Young, called the idea "moronic" and added: "They can kiss my ear. That is the dumbest thing I ever heard." And according to the conservative *Washington Times*, "Appropriations Committee Chairman Representative Jerry Lewis said Republicans already have accomplished spending cuts and Katrina wouldn't force a major change." Which makes you wonder if the congressman is trying to mimic the *other* Jerry Lewis.

Forget revoking pork—so strong is the addiction to pork that Congress wouldn't even consider eliminating pork earmarks on *new* Katrina funding bills. Citizens Against Government Waste proposed a "Hurricane Katrina No Pork Pledge," but the last time I looked, only two Senators (Coburn and McCain, of course) and 15 Representatives had taken the pledge. "We hear the rhetoric that nobody wants earmarks, but the truth is the leadership likes them," says Representative Jeff Flake (Republican, Arizona), who has one of the best records on fiscal responsibility. "They like to get you hooked. They make freshmen believe they are the ticket to reelection."

And remember that the leadership he's referring to is *Republican* leadership. "The Republican Congress's failure to discipline itself is sending us all down a flower-strewn path to financial insolvency," Flake warns. "That the Democrats would get us there faster should be of little consolation to anyone."

"If you had asked me years ago," Senator McCain says (emphasis added), "I would have said that *the combination of war, record deficits, and the largest public debt in the country's history would constitute a sufficient 'perfect storm'* to break Congress out of the spending addiction it is so famous for. I would have been wrong. It would seem that this Congress can weather any storm thrown at it, as long as we have our pork life-saver to cling to."

I have gone into the Katrina aftermath in some detail because it shows so clearly how our government is out of control. And because it served to reinforce, in a strange way, the myth that Republicans are budget-cutting fiscal conservatives who believe in cutting back the size of government. There is bipartisan enthusiasm for spreading that myth.

- Republicans like to perpetuate the myth because that's what the public says it wants: fiscal responsibility and smaller government. And they've been preaching this sermon for so long that most of the public *assume* they mean it.

- Democrats like to perpetuate the myth because it energizes their base and justifies their railings against Republicans for being "heartless" and "against the poor." In other words, the same tired old Democratic song you've heard your whole life.

What Is to be Done About Government Spending

We cannot look to Democrats and liberals for a solution to runaway government. Unfortunately, we have also seen—in the years since 2000—that we cannot look to the Republicans, either, for a solution to runaway government. The only times we have made *any* progress against the growth of Big Government have been under divided government:

- With conservative President Ronald Reagan in the White House forcing the Democrats in control of Congress to cut back on discretionary domestic spending, and…

- With a conservative Republican Congress rejecting the bulk of the spending sprees proposed by President Bill Clinton

If the Republicans don't wake up, and very fast, they are likely to find that Americans have once again voted for divided government. Conservatives will stay at home and liberals will vote for their own big spenders—the Democrats. And at least that's a stop-gap measure until real fiscal reform can be instituted.

But if Americans cannot look to either Democrats *or* Republicans for leadership in controlling runaway government, where are they to turn? There is only one place to turn, and that's to the people who truly believe in fiscal responsibility—conservatives. In turn, conservatives should stop concentrating their efforts on partisan games, and take their case directly to the public. We should stop sparing our criticism of the GOP, even though, in recent years, it is the party that most conservatives have called home. And we have to start from Square One in educating the public about the seriousness of the problem; I hope this book will be a modest contribution to the effort.

Certainly there are plenty of things that can be done to rein in federal spending; conservative think tanks, political groups, and politicians have been developing strategies and specific legislation for years. The problem hasn't been a lack of answers, but a lack of will in Congress. In educating the public, though, we need to bring these ideas and approaches to everyone's attention.

Here are some of the approaches and solutions we need to demand.

Demand that government go on a pork-free diet. The truth is, much bigger cuts than pork need to be enacted, but this is a start that resonates with the public, so it will get our campaign going on a positive tack. And it will cut more than $40 billion from the budget. We must demand an end to earmarks and propose structural reforms of Congress to keep this from being a recurring problem. And we must demand that the President veto any spending bills that include earmarks. Send them back to Congress and tell them you'll sign them into law only when the earmarks are deleted. If a project is worth funding, it can survive the regular legislative process and cost-benefit scrutiny.

A good place to start hunting for pork is the *Congressional Pig Book* published by Citizens Against Government Waste (http://cagw.org).

Cut government waste. This is another no-brainer that resonates with the public. Basic "good government" reforms could save $10 billion a year, but it goes beyond that. The House Budget Committee has identified federal waste totaling $100 billion over 10 years—why hasn't this waste been cut? And Senator Tom Coburn has demonstrated that: "At least $45 billion each year is being wasted on improper payments by the federal government—and that amount only covers a limited number of federal agencies. If the 3.9% rate of known improper payments is applied to the entire federal government, elimination of these improper payments could save taxpayers at least $100 billion a year."

Cut corporate welfare. The federal government has no business protecting businesses from competition and subsidizing them through corporate welfare. These policies are both anti-consumer and unconstitutional. Moreover, these subsidies are actually anti-capitalist, turning businessmen into lobbyists. And eliminating corporate welfare would save taxpayers $75 billion a year, according to Cato Institute estimates. For a primer on this topic, see the *Cato Handbook for Congress* (http://cato.org).

Stop unauthorized appropriations. The rules of Congress require all funded programs to undergo regular reauthorization. The idea is that Congress should audit these programs and determine whether the enabling statutes need updating. As incredible as it sounds, Congress is nevertheless quietly funding some 167 programs whose authority has expired. Congress must be pressured to enforce its own rules and stop funding these unauthorized programs, which receive $170 billion in federal funds.

Pull the plug on failed programs. Each year in the private sector, some 10% of all companies fail. Why shouldn't government programs that fail likewise be terminated? The Program Assessment Rating Tool (PART) is a government initiative to determine whether government programs actually achieve their objectives. Of the first 1,236 programs scrutinized by PART, only 38% were found to be "effective" or "moderately effective," while 40% were found to be "ineffective" or unable to demonstrate results. Congress should terminate these ineffective programs, for a savings of $154 billion.

One way to stop unauthorized appropriations and pull the plug on failed programs is "sunsetting." This process would automatically terminate government agencies and programs after a number of years (usually 10 or 12) unless they are expressly reauthorized by Congress—there would be no discretionary wiggle room for Congress. Programs would be reviewed by a sunset commission before their sunset date, with recommendations to Congress. Such a proposal in the late 1970s, pushed by Senator Ed Muskie (D-Maine), had broad bipartisan support, and another such push should prove even more popular today, when the failures of government are so much more evident.

Enact a simple and legally binding budget. The Family Budget Protection Act, proposed by Representative Jeb Hensarling (R-Texas) and others, would force the president and Congress to commit to the same budget before spending any money that year. It simplifies the current budget by replacing the 20 budget functions with a one-page budget, with spending levels for only five broad spending categories: mandatory, defense discretionary, non-defense discretionary, interest payments, and emergencies. It provides government shutdown protection in case budget agreement is not reached by the legal deadline. It limits growth in entitlement spending to inflation and the growth in population. And it enacts many other reforms to put a lid on federal spending. All of which makes it a worthwhile and attractive act for Congress to pass.

Freeze discretionary spending. Make it extremely difficult for Congress to increase discretionary spending above current levels, taking into account inflation and growth in the population. While actual cuts are needed, this would be added insurance to make certain Congress doesn't return to its addiction to spending.

Shift programs back to the states. This was a favorite in the GOP's "Contract with America" in the 1990s. Today the federal government pays out more than $400 billion in grants a year to states and local governments, which, as we've seen, is ridiculous because billions are lost to the federal government in this round trip of money from the states to the federal government and then back to the states. Instead, transfer all of these programs back to the states and local governments and reduce federal taxes accordingly.

Privatize, privatize, privatize. The postal service is private in welfare-state Germany, air traffic control is privately run in welfare-state Canada, and private space exploration is making headway in Russia. So why not privatize NASA, air traffic control, and the U.S. Postal Service? Just for starters.

The budget ax has just started to chop away. One good place to find programs to eliminate is Taxpayers for Common Sense (www.taxpayer.net). Its "Operation Offsets" would save $201 billion over five years. The conservative Republican Study Committee's "Operation Offset" would save close to $1 trillion over 10 years. Even more ambitious is the Citizens Against Government Waste report, *Prime Cuts 2005*, which recommends some 600 cuts that could save taxpayers $232 billion in fiscal year 2006 alone, or $2 trillion over the next five years.

Start adhering to the Constitution. The U.S. Constitution lists specifically what the federal government is authorized to do, and says simply and clearly that all other powers reside with the people or their state and local governments. Most of today's federal government expenditures are therefore unconstitutional, as James Madison, Benjamin Franklin, Alexander Hamilton, and the other Founders would have no trouble understanding. (After all, they *wrote* the Constitution!) A good place to start is eliminating the Education, Commerce, and Energy departments of the federal government—all clearly unconstitutional, and targets for elimination by Republicans in the 1990s. Back to the future!

Finally, consider some constitutional amendments—specifically, a balanced budget/tax limitation amendment and an amendment to give the President line-item veto power. The time has come to bind the politicians and bureaucrats down with the chains of the Constitution.

The Big Picture

Our nation cannot continue indefinitely to spend indiscriminately and lay the cost on our children and grandchildren. This is political child abuse. The day of reckoning is coming ever faster, especially with the Republicans' reckless expansion of Medicare in 2003. To really bring the federal government under control, we need serious spending cuts, tax reform, "entitlements" reform, and structural reform. We conservatives have our work cut out for us!

3

TAXES:
THE POWER TO DESTROY

"The power to tax involves the power to destroy"
— Chief Justice John Marshall

"Only the little people pay taxes."
— Leona Helmsley
(quoted by her housekeeper)

How would you like to live in a country where a person might never run into, or hear from, a tax man? ...where a person's salary is considered his or her own and not the government's, and no deductions are taken out before a person gets paid? ...where someone can live an entire life without tax liens, audits, or any income tax or payroll tax at all?

There has been such a country. It was known as the United States of America.

As the U.S. Department of the Treasury noted, in its "Fact Sheet on the History of the U.S. Tax System": "For most of our nation's history, individual taxpayers rarely had any significant contact with federal tax authorities as most of the federal government's tax revenues were derived from excise taxes [levied on businesses, not individuals], tariffs, and customs duties."

Makes you wonder how our country survived, much less grew to be the world's freest and most prosperous nation! Certainly a modern-day liberal, transported back in time to America in 1782, or 1810, or 1857, or 1902, or almost any other year before 1913, would recoil in horror at what he saw. "No safety net! No Social Security! No benevolent government organizing everything! These people are barbarians, and certainly won't last long!"

Well, this was then: "Prior to the enactment of the income tax, most citizens were able to pursue their private economic affairs without the direct knowledge of the government," the Treasury Department noted. "Individuals earned their wages, businesses earned their profits, and wealth was accumulated and dispensed with little or no interaction with government entities. *The income tax fundamentally changed this relationship, giving the government the right and the need to know about all manner of an individual or business' economic life"* (emphasis added).

Yes, today the government has first dibs on your income and accumulated wealth, and you are expected to be grateful to the government for whatever it leaves you. You essentially have no right to privacy left. The feds can snoop on you, pore over every detail of your private life (because everything in life has an economic component), and haul you into court and jail at the whim of some bureaucrat.

The Founders would be ashamed. The British taxes they fought against were tiny compared to what our own government takes from us, and we don't utter much more than a peep in protest. Perhaps the cruelest irony is that the average American citizen pays more in taxes today than the citizens of Russia or most of the former Soviet bloc of nations in Eastern Europe. *We* are the ones left living under policies suggested by *The Communist Manifesto:* the "graduated" income tax and the death tax ("inheritance" tax).[1]

Conservatives and Taxes Today

Government has legitimate functions that must be funded, of course. Conservatives believe that each of us has a duty as a citizen to pay for

---

[1] In *The Manifesto of the Communist Party (The Communist Manifesto),* Marx and Engels wrote that, in most "advanced countries" – that is, countries advancing toward communism – 10 policies would be put into effect. Numbers two and three on the list were "a heavy progressive or graduated income tax" and "abolition of all rights of inheritance."

the legitimate functions of the federal government, which are those enumerated in the Constitution. We recognize that returning the federal government to its legitimate functions is a project that will take many, many years. And, in the meantime, all Americans have a duty to pay taxes that are lawfully assessed, even those we disagree with, while we work though the democratic process to reduce or eliminate those taxes.

That doesn't mean, however, that we have to accept the present tax system. From a conservative perspective, there are compelling reasons the system is morally bankrupt and economically counterproductive:

- The present system enables the federal government to spend, and to waste, too much money, much of it on functions not allowed by the Constitution. Conservatives believe in small, limited government, and we realize that high taxes are the oxygen that feeds big government. As President Reagan put it, "The problem is not that people are taxed too little; the problem is that government spends too much."

- The current tax system makes tax slaves of American citizens for a considerable portion of our lives. Each year the Tax Foundation calculates the date each year when we've made enough money to pay that year's federal taxes—in effect, the date when we've finished working for the federal government and start working for ourselves. In 2006 this "Tax Freedom Day" was April 26. Think about it: You spend the equivalent of nearly four months, every year, to support our bloated, inefficient government! During that time, you fit President Reagan's definition of the taxpayer as "someone who works for the federal government but doesn't have to take the civil service examination."

- The current tax system makes you a slave in another way as well: You are legally responsible for complying with a Tax Code so enormous and convoluted that even IRS agents cannot understand it. Indeed, the U.S. Tax Court was created because taxes are so complicated *federal judges* aren't expected to understand it. *You* are, though, and that puts you at the mercy of the IRS. Moreover, you are forced to keep detailed records and make decisions based on tax consequences, not on what is best for you and your family.

- Similarly, the current tax system contradicts free-market principles by pushing individuals and businesses to make spending decisions based on tax "incentives" rather than the most productive use of capital. That distorts the economy, reducing growth and destroying (or preventing the creation of) jobs. And the current system fosters the culture of lobbying and corruption, as Big Business and other special interests seek tax breaks for themselves. The higher taxes go, and the more complicated they are, the greater the incentive for special interests to seek tax breaks, and the more they're willing to spend to get those breaks.

Who benefits from the present system?

(1) The federal bureaucrats themselves, who in essence don't have to worry whether their jobs are needed or whether they make a real contribution to the national welfare. The system of ever-bigger government is on auto-pilot thanks to the tax system.

(2) Members of Congress, who build their taxpayer-funded fiefdoms by acting as ombudsmen for individual taxpayers and businesses, and who grant favors to the special interests that fund their campaigns.

(3) All the lobbyists and tax lawyers who have a vested interest in keeping taxes as high as possible and as complicated as possible. The current system—with its complexity, its unfairness, and its unconscionable burden upon working people, small business people, and the economy in general—pays for their mansions and country club memberships. A simple, fair, flat tax system would force them to get real jobs.

We need a much fairer system and a much simpler system—if for no other reason, to protect us from these people.

What Is to be Done

Maybe someday we'll be able to repeal the Sixteenth Amendment that created the federal income tax, and we can substitute some other system of collecting revenue that's better than the present corrupt system.

Before coming to power, many Republican leaders talked seriously about repealing the income tax and substituting another system such as a value added tax (similar to a sales tax). At the very least, they were expected to make the tax system fairer by getting rid of special-interest deductions and exemptions while lowering rates and simplifying the system for everyone. But once Republicans were in power, they merely tinkered with the system, and as time passed they talked less and less about fundamental reform.

After getting control of Congress in the 1994 election, Republicans did nothing to stop the income tax system from being used to distribute welfare in the form of refundable tax credits, and they even added a government subsidy for children to the income tax system. Later, when they got the White House, they passed a small tax cut, half as big as Reagan's.

Let's be clear: Conservatives favor tax relief for working people and small business people and for families. But it is *not* a tax cut when the government simply uses the tax system to hand out welfare payments or subsidies for having children. Republicans don't do the country any favors when they imitate Bill Clinton; Clinton claimed falsely to have cut income taxes when what he actually did was to increase spending on the earned income tax credit program, a welfare program administered by the IRS.

A real tax cut improves the condition of the economy and makes life better for all Americans, not just for those who qualify for special treatment. A real tax cut leaves people more of their own money, and decreases the power of government over their lives.

"Conservatives have increasingly become just like liberals on tax policy in an important philosophical way," economist and commentator Bruce Bartlett said recently. "Neither liberals nor conservatives really care about the structure of taxation any more." He noted that the Republicans, once in power, "liked being able to add special provisions to the tax code to benefit their friends and did so with abandon."

In just the first three years of the Bush administration, the number of pages of federal tax rules increased from 45,662 to 54,846. That's a 20 percent jump in three years, from the party that supposedly wants to cut back on government regulations! If we go back to 1995, when the GOP first took over Congress, the number of pages of federal tax rules has risen by 35 percent.

The Bush administration and the Republican Congress deserve credit for passing tax cuts, flawed as they were. The cuts helped limit the depth and length of the Clinton recession, and helped shore up the economy in the aftermath of the 9/11 attacks. But the cuts were temporary, and even with extensions enacted recently will expire in what could be a Democratic administration.

As Nobel Prize-winning economist Milton Friedman said, "I never met a tax cut I didn't like." He also said, "I am in favor of cutting taxes under any circumstances and for any excuse, for any reason, whenever it's possible."

Why? "Because I believe the big problem is not taxes, the big problem is spending. I believe that government is too large and intrusive, that we do not get our money's worth for the roughly 40 percent of our income that is spent by government. . . . How can we ever cut government down to size? I believe there is one and only one way: the way parents control spendthrift children, cutting their allowance. For government, that means cutting taxes."

That makes great sense to me, but given the sad state of affairs today, not even all who call themselves conservative will agree. I'm referring to so-called Big Government conservatives. For example, Kevin A. Hassett, the director of economic policy studies at the American Enterprise Institute, said Bush should give up on making his cuts permanent.

"Until now," Hassett said, "Bush has said he wants to make the tax cuts permanent, and then have 'revenue neutral' tax reform. . . . Bipartisan reform is impossible down that path. Democrats oppose the extension of the tax cuts too strenuously. But if Bush gives up the first step, he could easily accomplish the second. . . . In order to sweeten the pot, he should offer to make this tax reform revenue neutral under current law – giving up his effort to make the tax cuts permanent."

By way of explanation, the term "revenue neutral" means that the so-called reform will not require a reduction in government spending. So Hassett is calling on the president to raise taxes and enact "reforms" that won't require the government to cut spending—in order to appease the Democrats! Is this why voters elect Republicans, to enact the Democratic platform? This is a sure path to Republican defeat—the path that George W. Bush's father took when he reneged on his promise of "no new taxes."

Two Tax Reform Movements

Since Republicans in Washington have lost interest in serious tax reform, if they were interested in the first place, it is up to political outsiders to get the job done. Most of those tax reform advocates fall into one of two camps.

The first camp, supporting a so-called Flat Tax, is led by former presidential candidate Steve Forbes, editor-in-chief of *Forbes* magazine and author of Flat Tax Revolution. Former House Majority Leader Dick Armey (R-Texas) is also a prominent supporter of a Flat Tax. Under such a system, the number of deductions, credits, exclusions, etc. would be strictly limited. All income above a certain amount per family member would be taxed at the same rate. For example, a family of four might pay a 17% tax on all income after the first $36,000. (Because of the exemption, higher-income people would pay a higher percentage of overall earnings than lower-income people.) Such a system would enable a person to file his or her annual tax return on a postcard.

Another approach, the so-called Fair Tax, was described in *The FairTax Book* by Neal Boortz, a syndicated radio talk show host, and Congressman John Linder (R-Georgia). The book, which debuted at the No. 1 position on the *New York Times* best seller list in 2005, proposed a repeal of the income tax, along with an end to payroll taxes such as the Social Security tax. Under this plan, the federal government would be financed mostly by a national sales tax.

Each plan has problems. The Flat Tax plan would require people to give up many deductions that they hold dear and based on which they have made significant decisions. For example, people have bought houses in part to take advantage of the mortgage interest deduction, and they have taken employer-paid health insurance in lieu of salary because they don't have to pay taxes on the health insurance. Also, a danger inherent in a Flat Tax is that politicians could simply ratchet up the rate any time they wanted an increase, or they could refuse to adjust the exemption for inflation, resulting in an automatic tax increase each year.

(That sort of automatic tax increase has happened before. In fact, it's happening right now. The Alternative Minimum Tax (AMT) was enacted in 1969 to prevent the richest taxpayers—only 155 people—

from using so-called loopholes to avoid paying income tax entirely. In effect it created a parallel income tax, and a taxpayer would be hit with the regular tax or the AMT, whichever was higher. In the beginning, that wasn't much of a problem, because the tax only applied to wealthier people. But as inflation has pushed incomes up, and more and more people have been hit by the AMT. Increasing numbers of middle-class people are considered "rich" by the government's definition, even though the purchasing power of their incomes has not increased. The AMT ensnared 3.8 million Americans in 2005, and according to the Treasury Department, this is due to increase to 20.5 million Americans in 2006.

As for the Fair Tax, the plan would require a complex system to keep track of, the increased value of a product at each stage of production and sale. Modern computer technology makes such a system more feasible than ever before, but there are still many areas where problems could arise. For one thing, in order to replace current taxes, the Fair Tax would have to start at 30 percent! And, as long as the Sixteenth Amendment—the income tax amendment—remained part of the Constitution, Congress could restore the income tax and simply add it on top of the Fair Tax.

Nevertheless, either plan would be far better than the mess we have today.

Even without a Flat Tax or a Fair Tax, real tax cuts are possible. President Kennedy understood that high taxes on the rich simply push those individuals into tax shelters instead of productive, job-creating investments, so he cut the top individual tax bracket from 91 to 70 percent. President Reagan followed up by cutting the top individual tax bracket from 70 to 28 percent. Each time the economy prospered as a result of those tax cuts. However, with the reckless level of spending by Republicans in Washington, any tax cuts are likely to be minimal. In fact, we'll be lucky if taxes aren't hiked.

It's time to hold politicians responsible for a tax system that gets more burdensome and more complicated each year. It's time to apply basic conservative principles for tax reform, and use these principles as the standards by which politicians are judged on the tax issue.

Principles for Tax Reform

> Taxes should be as low as possible. The total burden of taxes, compared to the size of the economy, should be smaller each year than the year before, or, at least, smaller from one decade to the next. The trajectory of the tax burden should be downward. (Don't worry that taxes will get too low. There are too many well-funded, politically powerful, special-interest groups to ever let that happen.)

> Another measure of the tax burden is the marginal tax rate for the average family headed by a working person or small business person at the height of his or her earning power. (The marginal rate is how much a person loses, in extra taxes and lost benefits, for each additional dollar he or she makes.) By this measure, too, the tax burden should be in continual decline.

> Tax cuts should always be made across-the-board, so that everyone gets the same percentage tax cut. If an adjustment is to be made in the relative burden of different income groups, that adjustment should be done only after a tax cut has been implemented.

> Taxes should be kept as simple as possible.

- The total number of tax brackets (different rates for different people) should be as low as possible – preferably, a single bracket for everyone, as in the Flat Tax.

- Special-interest tax breaks should be methodically eliminated. In the case of a tax break that affects large numbers of people, each taxpayer should be given a choice: take the deduction and pay the old tax rate on what's left, or decline the deduction and pay a lower rate. That way, no one is worse off than he or she was before.

- The total number of words and pages in tax regulations should be significantly smaller each year than the year before.

> *To use the tax code in an attempt to control people's behavior is a violation of everything this country stands for.* Therefore, to the degree possible, the tax laws should be neutral as to whether a person spends or saves, whether someone buys a house or rents an apartment, whether an employee gets paid in dollars or in benefits, whether a high school graduate goes to college or gets a job, whether someone

eats healthy food, drives a certain type of car or uses a certain kind of fuel, etc.

Ultimately, our goal should be to create a tax system so simple and fair that we can abolish the income tax itself, by repealing the Sixteenth Amendment. That sounds like an impossible dream, but many generations of Americans lived their lives without an income tax. Life without the income tax is something we had, and something we can one day have again.

We know from painful experience that the politicians in Washington will put their hands on everything they can grab. We know from our experience in the past few years that Republicans, while passing tax cuts, will nevertheless make the federal government grow —and we know that all government spending is eventually paid for, either through taxes or inflationary deficits that cause higher prices for everything we buy.

Conservatives must organize and speak out on taxes, and stop depending on politicians to kick the tax-and-spend habit on their own.

What works for junkies, works for Washington politicians: The first step to curing an addict is to take away his drug.

A Nation of Immigrants, But a Nation Nonetheless

Today our very identity as a sovereign nation is under attack.

When a few in Congress try to do something about this problem, proposing useful legislation, hundreds of thousands of protesters file into the streets in Los Angeles, Atlanta, Milwaukee, and other cities across the country. They don't even *pretend* to be in the tradition of previous immigrant groups that wanted desperately to be Americans; they come from organizations with names like The Race (La Raza) and Mexicans Without Borders, and they wave Mexican flags. As a nation, America has sometimes struggled to assimilate waves of immigration, but these protesters aren't interested in assimilation. And they aren't trying to protect the idea of *legal* immigration.

Traditional immigrants wanted desperately to be accepted just like "native Americans" (the term that was used for anyone who was born in this country). Traditional immigrants worked hard to learn English, not so they could give up their own culture but so they could add it to the mix that helped make the United States the first universal nation. Almost all came here legally. And they were welcomed.

I don't deny that immigrants sometimes faced bigotry. Planned Parenthood was created in large part to fight what its founder, Margaret Sanger, called the "mongrel races," including Italians and Poles. For decades, immigration laws were used harshly, notably against people of Asian origin.

Conservatives are proud of our collective identity as a nation to which freedom-loving people came from all over the world. Conservatives celebrate stories of immigrant journeys to America.

Conservatives recognize that it's one thing to be lucky enough to be born in the United States; it's something else to journey in a rickety boat across dangerous seas; learn a completely foreign language; work hard at what may be a menial job; do everything possible to avoid taking public assistance; instill in their children a strong ethic of education, work, and accomplishment; and become a citizen. It is for such immigrants that conservatives reserve a tremendous amount of respect and admiration. Such people are, in every sense, "real Americans."

Conservatives do not feel animosity or bigotry toward the current wave of immigrants from Latin America. Indeed, conservatives believe Latinos/Hispanics are overwhelmingly hardworking, God-fearing, freedom-loving, and culturally traditional, with family and church as centerpieces of their lives—exactly the kind of people we admire, and exactly the kind of people who vote conservative.

The problem is that many of today's immigrants are different from the legal immigrants who have come before. They are radical and criminal. They want to stay here illegally without serious consequence for breaking the law. They want access to the government services such as schools, health care, and welfare checks that American citizens and legal residents have paid for. They want to elect politicians who will simply ignore immigration laws, so that more and more illegals will come until it is simply impossible to do anything about the problem. We may already be at that point, with at least 11 million illegal aliens in the U.S.

(By the way, this controversy reveals what was really behind efforts by the Left to use statistical "sampling" in the U.S. Census, a practice which the Constitution would suggest is illegal. When "sampling" is used, illegal aliens can be more easily counted to determine the size of congressional and other legislative districts. Even if these illegals cannot vote themselves—and the 2000 election showed that illegals often *can* vote—others who live in the same area get representation based on total population, including illegals. So, for example, one area with 300,000 citizens might get one state senator, while another area with 100,000 citizens and 500,000 illegals would get two state senators.)

Illegal immigration is a tough issue to deal with. In individual cases, Americans empathize with those who come to this country seeking a better life for themselves and their children. The problems begin when the number of illegal aliens grows, when they start to overwhelm the capacity of schools and hospitals and law enforcement, when they force local communities to raise taxes on citizens and legal residents to pay for services for this new underclass, and when, unlike earlier immigrant groups, they segregate themselves behind a wall of language.

Because they are illegal and fear deportation, undocumented workers are of the mercy of employers who do not have to pay the minimum wage or provide state-mandated benefits or deal with the stifling bureaucracy that serves as a crushing burden on legal business activity. These requirements have made it too difficult and expensive to hire teenagers and unskilled workers for many jobs that traditionally served as an entry to the labor force. Illegal workers fill that void.

(It should be noted that allowing illegal workers to fill the void lessens the pressure on businesses to help defeat bad legislators – that is, legislators who pass anti-hiring laws such as a high minimum wage, high payroll taxes, and mandatory employee benefits. If businesses aren't willing to help clean house of anti-worker/anti-business liberals, they should face the consequences instead of simply going outside the law.)

The same factor that allows illegals to fill low-skill jobs leaves them vulnerable to exploitation. Some illegals are, if not exactly in a state of slavery, closer to that state than our society should tolerate. They can't call in the authorities if an employer pressures them to provide improper favors or commit a crime. They live in a world where law enforcement is ineffective or nonexistent. The presence of large numbers of off-the-books people, speaking a language other than English and cut off from the justice system, creates entire communities where gangs rule the streets. That's why some cities have a policy against police turning in illegal aliens.

Meanwhile the wealthy rely on illegals to provide them with nanny and gardener services and otherwise to act as low-paid servants. Many businesses employ illegals, avoiding another layer of rules and regulations that would require them to do a citizenship/residency check on each employee. So a major portion of the political elite—including the wealthy and many business people—opposes any meaningful immigration reform.

The result is that politicians, Republicans especially, have ignored this issue for year after year until it is almost unmanageable. The longer they wait, the harder it will be to solve the problem—not only in terms of illegals who are simply too numerous to be rounded up and deported, or who have children born in the U.S. (therefore, U.S. citizens), but also in terms of business's reliance on illegals and the political clout of illegals.

It's often said that Republicans protect illegal immigration because they want the cheap laborers, and Democrats protect illegal immigration because they want the voters. Of course, in the long run, the side with the most voters wins.

The low end of the estimate of the number of illegals, 11 million, comes from a March 2005 study by the Pew Hispanic Center, a research foundation. The group relied largely on statistical data from the U.S. Census Bureau, which itself estimates the growth of the illegal population at around 500,000 per year.

A Virtual Invasion

Half a million a year. That means that, each year, a city full of people is added, illegally, to the population of the U.S. – a city with the population of Atlanta or pre-Katrina New Orleans.

A nation with that little control over its borders is asking for trouble, ranging from economic dislocation to terrorism. This current system of porous borders makes a mockery of the rule of law, and it is unfair to virtually everyone.

- It's unfair to the illegal immigrants themselves, who must lead a life of existence in the shadows. Their illegal status makes them fair game for all sorts of unscrupulous people, and results in the horrifying images of mass deaths in the desert or in sealed trucks, not to mention sexual exploitation of women. It is far more compassionate to turn them around at the border, rather than to return them after they've already endured threats like these.

- It's unfair to all our *legal* immigrants, including the legal immigrants from Latin America, who got in while following the rules. That's why so many of our Latino/Hispanic citizens also feel the need to bring the situation under control. Arizona's Proposition 200, requiring proof of citizenship in order to vote and valid ID before applying for benefits, passed with the support of 47 percent of Arizona Hispanics and 59 percent of Arizona's Republican Hispanics. (The overall vote in favor was 56-44. Unfortunately, enforcement was enjoined by a federal judge—one appointed by President George W. Bush!)

- It's unfair to the more than four million eligible foreigners currently waiting patiently for years, and sometimes decades, to be legally admitted to the United States. Illegal immigration, when condoned by doing virtually nothing to stop it, makes a mockery of their adherence to our rules and procedures.

- It's unfair to our poorest and least educated native citizens, often members of minority groups, who need and want jobs. They are the first to be displaced by the illegals, and the wages offered them go down in "competition" with the illegals.

- It's unfair to American taxpayers in general, who have to pay for a wide range of social services to take care of this illegal population—everything from classrooms and teachers to subsidized housing, emergency medical care, and expanded police services. And, in turn, American taxpayers must put up with poorer quality themselves because of the strain on these services.

- And it's unfair to our 50 state governments and thousands of local governments, which have to grapple with these problems and finance them because of a failure to enforce *federal* law. Even on those rare occasions when the feds make a partial reimbursement, payment is cents on the dollar.

We're paying the price for losing control of our borders. These burdens result in part from the massive amount of illegal immigration, and in part from the fact that many of the people coming into the U.S. illegally are criminals in other ways, too. The overwhelming majority of immigrants, even illegal immigrants, are good people, but when the border of an attractive country become porous, the less-worthy crowd on the other side of the border takes it as an invitation.

An open door policy for terrorists: The horrible events of 9/11 remind us what happens when the federal government abandons its responsibilities to control internal immigrants and visitors. As the 9/11 Commission reported: "It is elemental to border security to know who is coming into the country."

Yet years after 9/11 and billions of dollars later, we still don't know who is coming into the country. We know they're not all Mexicans: The Department of Homeland Security says more than 70,000 non-Mexicans were caught trying to enter the U.S. through Mexico in 2004. Those are only the ones who were caught, and for every illegal that is caught, at least two get through undetected. These 70,000 came from Brazil, Syria, Pakistan, Indonesia, Iraq, China, and 120 other nations.

In 2005, Admiral James M. Loy, former Deputy Secretary of Homeland Security, told the Senate Select Committee on Intelligence that information gathered from ongoing investigations and detentions suggested that Al Qaeda leaders were considering using our Southwestern border to get their operatives into the U.S.

The same smugglers and the same tunnels that are used for illegal immigration can be used for other things, too. Massive illegal immigration makes it easier to smuggle in drugs, terrorists, and weapons of mass destruction.

Criminals who break more than our immigration laws: The federal Bureau of Prisons estimates that nearly 30 percent of its prisoners are aliens. The percentage is undoubtedly higher in many local jails, and 40 percent of these alien criminals are caught committing more crimes after they are released from jail. You might ask, if they're in this country illegally and have served time for a crime, shouldn't they be deported upon their release? How naïve! In places like Los Angeles, fewer than half are deported, and the rest are simply turned loose on the streets again. Congressman Tom Tancredo (R-Colorado) has noted that the Bureau of Immigration and Customs Enforcement cannot locate nearly 100,000 criminal aliens who had been ordered deported but instead have "absconded." And these are just the ones we know about.

Alien gangs are becoming increasingly violent, as happens when gangs' membership and territory grow. The Justice Department estimates that there are more than 750,000 alien gang members in the U.S. A report published in the Manhattan Institute's *City Journal* gives an example of why they're not stopped: "In cities where the crime these aliens commit is highest, the police cannot use the most obvious tool to apprehend them: their immigration status. In Los Angeles, for example, dozens of members of a ruthless Salvadoran prison gang have sneaked back into town after having been deported for such crimes as murder, assault with a deadly weapon, and drug trafficking. Police officers know who they are and know that their mere presence in the country is a felony. Yet should a cop arrest an illegal gang [member] for felonious reentry, it is he who will be treated as a criminal, for violating the LAPD's rule against enforcing immigration law."

Yes, you read that right. In many localities, including Los Angeles, there are "sanctuary laws" that direct local law agencies *not* to cooperate with federal immigration officials or report illegal aliens to them. Such laws are found in San Francisco, New York, Austin, Houston, San Jose, and other cities. This practice is supposed to be against federal law, but breaking this federal law carries no penalties so it is unenforceable.

Congressman Tancredo tells of one case involving the sanctuary law: "In New York, four people raped, brutally raped, a woman. And at least two of the four, perhaps three, were actually people who had been in the past detained, found out to be here illegally, but not given over to the INS and therefore not deported. So there are people being affected by this in the most horrible ways. The story I just told is replicated hundreds, if not thousands, of times across this country."

This willful disregard of federal law and the safety of our citizens is itself criminal and must be stopped immediately, but you won't see the Bush Administration lifting a finger.

Adding to the woes of already overburdened taxpayers: Illegal aliens are picking your wallet with the burdens they place on local schools, subsidized housing, medical facilities, law enforcement agencies, and welfare programs. A study by the National Academy of Sciences on the costs of immigration found that the taxes they pay do not begin to cover the costs of the services they receive.

A government study of illegals who were granted amnesty in the 1980s showed that 80 percent had used taxpayer-supported health services. Dr. Madeleine Pelner Cosman says 84 hospitals in California have had to close because of the high cost of treating illegal aliens. In the *Journal of American Physicians and Surgeons*, she reported that illegals are bringing increases in multiple drug-resistant tuberculosis, chagas disease, dengue fever, polio, and hepatitis A, B, and C. "Certain diseases that we thought we had vanquished years ago are coming back," she wrote, "and other diseases that we've never seen or rarely seen in America, because they've always been the diseases of poverty and the third world, are coming in now."

The Federation for American Immigration Reform (FAIR) estimates that "the net cost of illegal immigration to our society totals more than $24 billion every year." These costs are spreading all through the nation, but the burden falls heaviest on citizens and other legal residents of states with the highest influx of illegals. FAIR has done four state studies counting only the costs for education, health care, and incarceration. In Florida, illegal immigration costs $4.3 billion a year, or about $575 per Florida household headed by a native-born resident. In Arizona, the figures are $1.3 billion and $700 per household. In Texas, $4.7 billion and $725 per household. And in California, a whopping $10.5 billion and $1,183 per household.

Now, if our present system is so unfair to the illegal immigrants themselves, to our *legal* immigrants, to eligible foreigners waiting to become legal citizens, to our poorest and least educated workers, to American taxpayers in general, and to our state and local governments, why is it still in existence?

The answer can be found by looking at the other side of the coin: Who *gains* from the present system? Follow the money and it becomes clear that the biggest beneficiary is Big Business, and especially Big Agribusiness. Our present system of illegal immigration lets Big Business and Big Agribusiness dramatically cut its major cost, which is labor. Sure, some of that cost-saving trickles down to us consumers. We may pay a few cents less each time we go to the grocery store, but that doesn't begin to make up for the added taxes we pay. In effect, illegal immigration is a transfer of wealth from the American taxpayer to the Big Business and Big Agribusiness corporations.

This helps explain why the U.S. Chamber of Commerce has fought hard to block serious penalties for employment of illegals.

It also helps explain why virtually nothing has been done by the Bush Administration to stop this flood of illegals, despite the pledge by candidate Bush, in two presidential campaigns, to tackle the issue. Instead, President Bush has proposed a guest-worker scheme that is a thinly camouflaged amnesty. In conservatives' struggle with Big Business for control of the GOP, this administration has taken sides, and it's not with the conservatives.

Look at what happened right after the 2004 election. As reported by Phyllis Schlafly, "The way President Bush steamrollered the Intelligence bill through Congress this December, demanding that the House abandon its sensible provisions for border security, indicates that he may be willing to split the Republican Party. . . . Rep. James Sensenbrenner (R-Wisconsin) emerged a hero in the legislative battle because he fought all the way to include strong border security and a prohibition against granting driver's licenses to illegal aliens, finally saying that the failure to include this 'will keep Americans unnecessarily at risk.'"

It certainly cannot be a matter of money and budgetary restraints —not with *this* spendthrift presidency and *this* spendthrift Congress. As California Governor Arnold Schwarzenegger noted: "It is not a lack of money. When we can afford the war in Iraq, we can afford to control our own borders."

Another excuse given for the Bush Administration's being AWOL on illegal immigration is its desire to attract the Hispanic vote. That wouldn't be the first time a politician has put vote pandering above the Constitution, but it doesn't even make sense as political strategy. As I noted, Arizona's Proposition 200 was supported by 59 percent of the state's Hispanic Republicans, and 47 percent of all of the state's Hispanic voters overall. It really comes down to *how* you want to gain votes—by pandering and dishing out pork, or by appealing to the constituency's conservative principles. Do you attempt to buy off the organized lobbies and media "gatekeepers" that claim to represent an ethnic group, or do you appeal directly to the members of that ethnic group based on principle? The Bush Administration is strongly opting for pandering and buyoffs.

Certainly it's not necessary for the GOP to favor either amnesty or the present don't-ask-don't-tell immigration policy in order to gain Hispanic vote share. As Congressman Tancredo pointed out, "President Bush increased his share of the Latino vote from around 32 percent [in 2000] to 40 percent [in 2004] – without using the [soft-on-illegal-immigration] issue." The issues Bush used "to attract Latino voters were economic empowerment, educational opportunity, and traditional moral values." (I would add strong support for the military and on national security issues in general.) Said Tancredo: "Not a single Bush-Cheney campaign ad mentioned Bush's guest-worker proposal or liberalized immigration rules."

Recently, the Bush Administration and its allies have been trying to isolate Congressman Tancredo and the conservative base of the Republican Party that wants stronger immigration controls and border security. Its vehicle is a front called Americans for Border and Economic Security, which offers membership to business lobbies at levels ranging from $50,000 to $250,000. This isn't my conspiratorial imagination at work. The *Los Angeles Times* interviewed its leaders and reported that they "said the new group's message would seek to isolate players such as Tancredo, who leads a House caucus that backs stiff border restrictions. Tancredo [has] succeeded in dominating the debate, [they] said, because of an echo chamber of conservative talk radio and other advocates for limiting the influx of Mexicans across the border."

So, what it comes down to is that the Bush Administration was elected and reelected in large part due to the efforts of that "echo chamber of conservative talk radio and other advocates," but once safely in power seeks to *counter* those voices through its Big Business front. Tancredo denounced the effort and noted that his own legislation cracking down on illegal immigration "won't require a multi-million dollar sales pitch. The grassroots are already on board."

Tancredo issued a further warning of the activities of people like George Soros: "Liberals are investing millions of dollars to build a media empire to match the one the conservative movement created over the last generation. If the GOP leadership tries to disconnect the party's direct line to the base, we'll be kicked out of here faster than you can say 'minority party.'"

Conservatives have had it, and anyone in touch with the Republican Party's conservative base knows it. That's why, at the 2005 Conservative Political Action Conference (CPAC), former House Speaker Newt Gingrich proposed that the U.S. completely seal off its borders with Mexico and Canada, deport illegal aliens within 72 hours of their arrest, and exclude U.S. courts from reviewing such deportations. Gingrich appears to have presidential ambitions, or at least seeks to continue to be seen as a significant leader, and he knows a critical issue when he sees one.

Bill O'Reilly, the Fox News commentator, is a conservative on most issues and a populist. He proposed recently a plan for dealing with the problem: Move the National Guard to the border. Detain and immediately deport anyone caught crossing the border illegally. Levy large fines (first offense) and jail time (second offense) on business people who hire illegals. Give illegals 60 days to register and get temporary working papers, with a $3,000 fine deducted from paychecks over the next three years. If the illegal fails to register in 60 days, he would be guilty of a felony with mandatory jail time. Allow a registered illegal to file for citizenship in three years, getting in line behind legal immigrants. Finally, set up a guest worker program in which the other country provides a list of applicants for jobs. Immediately deport any illegal who evades taxes.

Then there's Hillary Rodham Clinton. Americans for Better Immigration gave her a grade of "F," and she recently suggested that Jesus would have helped illegal immigrants break the law. But with Republicans in disarray on the immigration issue, it's questionable whether they will be able to take advantage of Hillary's position on the issue.

A Conservative Agenda on Immigration

The contradictions and entanglements of our immigration laws are not there by conscious design, but are the result of a lack of immigration *policy*. Without knowing what we want to accomplish, we have no vision or coherent goals. Year after year, every imaginable pressure group gets some of its agenda added to the concoction, the bureaucracies get larger but accomplish less, and the result is the unworkable mess we have now.

We need to get back to first principles, and design a new system that will move us in the direction of eliminating illegal immigration. The principles of conservative immigration reform: No amnesty. Border control. Inclusion of all guest workers in a database that includes identifying information such as fingerprints. An end to requirements that government forms such as ballots be in languages other than English or that providers of government services speak other languages. No driver's licenses or other government-recognized IDs for illegals. Jail time for repeat employers of illegals.

As for amnesty – been there, done that.

Amnesty of any shape or form should be off the table. As used in relation to immigration, the term "amnesty" means granting legal status to people who are in the country unlawfully. We tried that in 1986, with the Simpson-Mazzoli Immigration Reform and Control Act, which granted amnesty to some 2.7 million illegal resident aliens. The result was a dramatic *increase* in additional illegal immigration, as relatives flocked in to join the newly legalized residents. That was supposed to be a one-time-only event, but actually Congress has approved additional amnesty legislation six times since then, with the results we see today. Enough is enough.

Actually we don't need new laws; we just need enforcement of the existing laws. How can politicians and law enforcement justify selective enforcement of the law – only enforcing the laws they like?

A blanket amnesty rewards illegal behavior, encourages others to emulate the illegals who got rewarded, and adds to the taxpayers' burden, since illegal aliens given legal residence become eligible for additional tax-funded services. Morally it's the equivalent of a blanket pardoning of criminals because that's easier than capturing them. For over 200 years the United States granted no blanket amnesties, only individual amnesties due to exceptional circumstances. That worked, and it's time to return to that system.

Control our borders: I would like to say *seal* our borders, but that's probably an impractical goal in the near future, given our thousands of miles of border with Mexico and Canada. Nevertheless, we can take immediate steps to control at least the major holes in our borders, steps such as these:

— Congress has already passed legislation increasing the size of the Border Patrol by 2,000 agents a year for the next five years. That's not enough.

— Look to alternative sources, such as the ranks of former and retired military, for help in patrolling the borders. In congressional testimony the Department of Homeland Security has said it costs $179,000 to train a new Border Patrol agent. That seems ridiculously high on the face of it, but using former military personnel should dramatically lower that cost.

— Congress should give the Border Patrol whatever high-tech surveillance gear the U.S. has, and the Border Patrol needs, to increase the effectiveness of its job. Certainly our armed forces must have a variety of hardware that could be put to use along our borders. Bureaucratic walls have to be broken down when it comes to the military and border control agencies, just as with our intelligence agencies.

— There is one branch of service that is semi-military and is used in border operations, and that's the U.S. Coast Guard. The Pentagon tends to prefer its high-tech combat toys and relegates leftover crumbs to the Coast Guard. This has to stop, and Congress has to provide the funding to modernize this service so it can enforce our immigration laws at sea, in coastal areas, and at coastal ports of entry.

— Allow and encourage ordinary civilians to help, through projects like the Minuteman patrols in Arizona and California. Despite liberal nightmares of vigilante action, the Minutemen have proven to be both lawful and effective.

— It's time for a new attitude in the Border Patrol. Their mindset seems to be one of winking at most infractions in order to concentrate on a few selective goals, and it's easy to see how they got there, given the enormity of the problem and their limited capabilities. But as we revitalize the Border Patrol with more personnel, material, and funding, its attitude must correspondingly change and become more proactive.

Implement a 3-step program to promote business responsi-bility: Businesses should not be required to do the government's work, such as determining what constitutes proper identification for legal workers. Nor should they have to *guess* at what the rules are. But once those rules are made clear and simple, businesses should be held accountable and pay a fine that hurts if they don't follow the rules.

Step 1: Create a responsible guest worker program that is NOT an amnesty. Such a program would authorize an alien to work in the United States *for a limited period of time*, subject to a background check that establishes no criminal background and no terrorist or drug-smuggling ties. Renewals would be subject to a repeat back-ground check to establish the person's clean record while in the U.S. And the worker would have to sign an affidavit that he understands issuance of temporary work permits in no way will lead to amnesty— to legalization of his residence in the U.S. after the stated period of time, or to citizenship.

Step 2: Establish and require proper identification for legal guest workers. To get a temporary work permit, an alien would have to produce a passport or birth certificate. Social Security cards, Individual Taxpayer Identification Numbers (ITINs), and especially foreign consular cards, such as Mexico's, would not be sufficient. Once the worker obtains a temporary work permit, that alone should serve as his ID allowing him to work in the U.S. for the stated time period.

Step 3: Severely punish any person or business that employs an alien without a proper temporary work permit. The fine has to be heavy enough to ensure that the business rigorously follows this rule. One possibility is to make the employer responsible for the financial cost of deporting an illegal worker to his country of origin. Unlike in our present situation, inspections have to be frequent and the law enforced.

Close loopholes: Currently we have pregnant aliens sneaking into the United States right before the birth of the child, so that the child is born an American citizen. Such an "anchor baby" opens the floodgate to taxpayer-financed benefits. The law should be modified, to establish that a child born to an alien during his or her stay in the United States will not be granted such automatic birthright citizenship. Legal scholars disagree as to whether a simple statute could accomplish this, so it will probably require a Constitutional amendment.

Also under current law, the first instance of entry without inspection (illegal entry) is a misdemeanor, and becomes a felony only upon repeated violations. The result is that U.S. attorneys will rarely prosecute a first-offender; a misdemeanor offense is not worth their time. And to get a felony conviction, they have to prove prior illegal entry, so this becomes a Catch 22 situation. The law should be changed to make illegal entry a felony from the first time on, punishable by a fine and/or imprisonment.

Play hardball with Mexico: I'm not picking on Mexico unfairly, since something like 70 percent of our illegal immigrants come from Mexico, and many others come to us *through* Mexico.

Senator Jon Kyl (R-Arizona) has pointed out that Mexico obviously could do more to stem the tide of illegal entry to the United States, if it wanted to. Mexico has a government-sponsored agency, Grupos Beta, which patrols its border with the U.S. and aids Mexicans stranded in the desert. (Grupos Beta defines its mission as "minimizing harm to U.S.-bound migrants without explicitly discouraging their exodus." Well, at least you have to give them some credit for honesty.) During the Minuteman patrols they would advise Mexicans where the patrols were located, so they wouldn't cross the border there.

"Mexicans didn't come across there," Kyl said. "What that demonstrates obviously is that the Mexican government could be very effective in helping us stem illegal immigration if it wanted to, but obviously they have not wanted to do that."

The government's official excuse is that Mexican citizens have freedom of movement within its borders, and once they're over the border they are no longer under Mexican jurisdiction. Very convenient, but that freedom-of-movement argument hasn't stopped the Mexican government from arresting smugglers who thrive in its northern deserts.

Instead of trying to stop the flow of migrants into the U.S., Mexico has printed 1,500,000 copies of a 32-page comic book-style handbook telling them how to make the trip across the border safely, and, once they're in the U.S., how to avoid detection by law authorities. "A foreign government is teaching their citizens how to break our laws," responded Carlos Espinosa, a spokesman for Congressman Tancredo. "It's pretty shocking. It's like saying that a lot of people are dying from drunk driving, so we're going to teach you how to drive drunk better."

Even more insulting are the threats of high Mexican government officials against American citizens who are only seeking to protect our system of government. Typical of this type of meddling in our internal affairs are the statements from Mexican Foreign Secretary Luis Ernesto Derbez. He calls the Minutemen "migrant hunters" who "hunt illegals" and says they should be prosecuted, and he has asked a group of U.S. lawyers in Los Angeles to put together a legal strategy against them. "We are going to attack by all legal means," he vowed.

Another target of this meddling Mexican official is Arizona's Proposition 200. If the U.S. courts do not declare it unconstitutional, he said, "of course we would file an international lawsuit." What especially galls him, he said, is that almost half of Arizona's Hispanic citizens voted for Proposition 200. "It's sad," he lamented, "and it gives an idea of how we have to work to educate even our own Mexican-Americans about why it is important that these proposals are not accepted."

"Our own Mexican-Americans"? Pardon me, Mr. Foreign Secretary, you don't own them, you have no jurisdiction over them, and they are American citizens like the rest of us. What business do you have criticizing how American citizens vote and what *our* requirements should be for obtaining welfare?

"The threat by Mexico that, if the courts of this country do not do what Mexico wants, it will haul the U.S. before the United Nations is odious," said William Perry Pendley of the conservative Mountain States Legal Foundation, which represents Proposition 200's backers. "Our courts respond to the requirements of our Constitution, not to the arrogant demands of foreign countries."

The response of the Bush Administration to all this interference in our domestic affairs is a cowardly silence. And President Bush's response is to push again for the "A" word he dare not speak—amnesty. When he did this at a joint press conference with Mexican

President Vicente Fox, the microphone was given to Fox for his response. Not surprisingly, he was all smiles. "What else can we wish?" he said.

The United States gives Mexico more than $30 million a year in foreign aid. Until the Mexicans stop promoting illegal immigration and stay out of U.S. affairs, we should cut off the spigot.

In fact, we should redirect that money so that it goes only to projects that help grassroots Mexicans build a free market economy and an honest political system. We will never really solve the illegal immigration problem as long as Mexico—which, based on resources and location, should be one of the world's richest countries—is mired in socialist poverty and hobbled by one of the most corrupt governments on earth.

Promote assimilation: America's immigration problem isn't confined to the massive flood of illegal aliens I've been discussing. We are also departing from our historic traditions and creating a Balkanized America by encouraging our alien workers (legal and illegal) as well as our new citizens to pursue public life in their native language rather than English.

Of course all previous waves of immigrants continued to talk largely in their native tongue at home and in their social life—while they learned English. They, and especially their children, learned English because government instructions were posted only in English, school instruction was in English, and you had to know English in order to perform your work.

The goal was full assimilation of the new immigrants and citizens into a cohesive American society. As former Reagan Attorney General Ed Meese and Matthew Spalding put it, "a successful immigration policy is only possible by means of a deliberate and self-confident policy to assimilate immigrants and educate them about this country's political principles, history, institutions, and civic culture. *This may be a nation of immigrants, but it is more accurate to say that this is a nation where immigrants are Americanized.*"

Today we seem determined to make it as easy as possible for immigrants and aliens *not* to have to learn English, even though studies show the ones who don't will almost always fall behind in income and advancement on the job. Bilingual recorded telephone messages are so common they're the butt of late night comics. Government documents are published in multiple languages.

For example, in 2003, ballots, voter information, forms and instructions for voting, and other election materials in Los Angeles were printed in seven languages at a cost of $3.3 million. This sort of practice is dangerous to our democracy, because each separate version of election materials increases the chance that voters will receive incorrect or misleading information or that people will be able to vote illegally.

Besides: How can one make an informed decision about political issues in the U.S. without the ability to read the (usually very simple) English on a ballot? So much for a common basis for citizenship!

Even safety concerns don't stop the trend. Some 38 states offer drivers license exams in languages other than English, with California leading the way with 30 languages. So they pass the exam. What if they can't read the road signs? What do they do when they're in an accident and can't speak English like (in most cases) the other driver, the police and EMTs, the witnesses?

At this writing, a crane operator is suing the State of California, demanding a safety test in Spanish! (He doesn't speak English despite the fact that he's been in the United States for more than two decades.) He has filed this suit despite the fact that crane safety manuals are in English and that English is required for such basic tasks as dealing with management and reporting safety violations.

And a retired Army colonel recently suggested that our military forces should take care of their recruitment shortfalls by allowing Spanish entrance exams. Would you want the soldier in the foxhole next to you to not know English as he's handling his weapons and attempting to communicate with his commanders and fellow soldiers?

Enough is enough. Assimilation requires a common language. As Alexis de Tocqueville noted, "The tie of language is perhaps the strongest and the most durable that can unite mankind." Yet today we are headed in the opposite direction, the wrong direction. U.S. English, Inc., an advocacy group, reports that by 2000, 11.9 million U.S. residents were "linguistically isolated." That was an increase of

more than 53 percent from 7.7 million in 1990. In the cities of Los
Angeles, Houston, Miami, and Dallas, more than a third of the illegal
residents are not proficient in English. Labor studies document that
this will sentence them to lower wages and fewer opportunities, and
that's the sort of cauldron that erupts eventually in resentment, the
politics of scapegoating, and even violence, as we saw in the French
riots of 2005.

We are familiar with the stories of how Miami is more of a Spanish-
speaking city than an English-speaking city. A poll conducted in South
Florida found that 83 percent of Hispanics agreed that "it's easy to get
along day in and day out without speaking English well or at all." But
this situation is spreading to communities where we least expect it,
like Hartford, Connecticut. Over 40 percent of its population is
Hispanic. About a quarter of that segment speaks English "not very
well" or "not at all," and half of the city's Hispanic business owners do
not speak English. Bakery owner Freddy Ortiz noted: "In the bank,
they speak Spanish; at the hospital, they speak Spanish; my bakery
suppliers are starting to speak Spanish. Even at the post office, they
are Americans, but they speak Spanish." Mayor Eddie Perez said,
"We've become a Latin city, so to speak. It's a sign of things to come."

It's also a sign of impending disaster, if steps aren't taken immediately to integrate and assimilate Hispanics into the general American
culture through the common use of English in our civic and educational life. In recent years we've had two very clear and alarming examples
of what bilingualism and cultural segregation can do to a society. In
Canada, English-French antagonisms nearly split the nation in two.
And throughout Europe, unassimilated Arab and South Asian enclaves
are proving to be a breeding ground for terrorism.

Bilingualism, even multilingualism, is a most worthy goal to attain
for yourself and to seek for your children. As former Senator S. I.
Hayakawa (R-California) put it, though, "Bilingualism for the individual is fine, but not for a country." English literacy must be a require-
ment for citizenship, for dealings with government at all levels, and for
advancement in schools. These are not only needed policies, but policies that are wanted by the vast majority of Americans. A national
Zogby poll found that 84 percent of Republicans and 72 percent of

Democrats favored requiring schools to use English immersion. And in 1998, Californians approved Proposition 227, outlawing bilingual education, by a landslide 61 percent. Requiring proficiency in English is both the right thing to do and the popular thing to do.

Countless Origins, but One Nation

Any sovereign nation, including the United States, has the responsibility and obligation to set conditions for immigration, naturalization, and citizenship, and then enforce those conditions. Yet today, at a time when the federal government is involved in a multitude of unconstitutional activities, it is failing to fulfill its constitutional obligation to protect our borders.

The result is a tidal wave of illegal immigrants and a rapidly deteriorating social structure. Our open borders are giving the green light not only to illegal workers, but to terrorists and criminals as well. The entire patchwork system is unfair to the illegal aliens themselves, to legal immigrants, to would-be immigrants who abide by our rules and regulations, to the American taxpayer, and to local and state governments. It's unfair, in fact, to everyone except businesses that exploit this system in order to cut their major cost, the cost of labor. The entire scheme is a subsidy of certain businesses by the American taxpayer.

It must stop. President Bush and his administration have shown themselves unwilling to defy these law-breaking businesses and tackle this problem, while liberals worship at the altar of internationalism rather than respecting sovereignty. It's up to conservatives to do the job. Our present laws have to be enforced and new safeguards put in place. Instead of amnesty, which rewards lawbreaking, we need to take whatever steps are necessary to control our borders and stop the flow of illegals, to make it highly unprofitable for businesses to hire them, and to close numerous loopholes in the present system. It's also time to play hardball with Mexico, taking strong measures when they don't respect our sovereignty and forcing them to stop the illegal flow on their side of the border.

We also need to pressure Mexico to get rid of its corrupt, socialist government that keeps people poor, and we need to encourage it to build a free market economy that lifts people up from poverty.

The other necessity is to reverse the present trend toward cultural Balkanization of the United States. We conservatives take pride in our nation's role in welcoming and assimilating countless waves of immigrants over two centuries, but today we're not assimilating them. Assimilation requires a common language, and for the United States that is and will remain English. Government activities and forms should be in English only. Educational advancement should require proficiency in English. And even in the private sector, conservatives should use their influence to advance English as the sole language of the public square.

Assimilation has always been the American goal and the American tradition. George Washington welcomed immigrants "if by decency and propriety of conduct they appear to merit the enjoyment" of citizenship. But he was also aware of possible pitfalls. As he put it in a letter to Vice President John Adams in 1794 (and with punctuation modernized), "the settling of [immigrants] in a body may be much questioned, for, by so doing, they retain the language, habits and principles (good or bad) which they bring with them. Whereas by an intermixture with our people, they, or their descendants, get assimilated to our customs, measures and laws: in a word, soon become one people."

One people. From all over the world, with every type of cultural background. But one people.

E pluribus unum. Out of many, one.

RESTORING THE RIGHT TO LIFE

"It is a poverty to decide that a child must die so that you may live as you wish."

—Mother Teresa

Abortion on demand is a plague that has killed almost 50 million Americans in the years since *Roe v. Wade.* That's roughly 3,600 abortions each day, about 150 each hour, or one baby aborted every 24 seconds.

It violates the principle, enshrined in the Declaration of Independence, that all are endowed by their Creator with the right to life.

It turns traditional American values on their head. Abortion is defended as a matter of rights and choice, even though it depends on the absolute violation of another person's rights. In that sense, it is like slavery, which was perversely defended as a property right.

Its most well-known proponent, taxpayer-funded Planned Parenthood, is a remnant of the eugenics movement, which sought to improve the human race by selective breeding. Jews, Italian-Americans, African-Americans, and others were "mongrel races," said Planned Parenthood founder Margaret Sanger, who published, in the organization's magazine, the writing of the Nazi minister of racial purity.

Opposing abortion was one of the reasons many suffragists worked so hard to get women the vote. Women's rights proponents believed that the savagery of abortion would never be permitted in a society in which women could vote.

Today, even many of the most vocal proponents of abortion-for-any-reason and abortion-up-to-and-including-the-moment-of-birth acknowledge the harm it does to society. Even Senator Hillary Clinton suggests that there are too many abortions, and, along with her husband, says that abortions should be "safe, legal, and rare." (Of course, that viewpoint doesn't prevent them from supporting partial birth abortion, in which the baby is killed while being born by having its skull punctured and its brains sucked out. It's a process that has no possible medical rationale.

The Alan Guttmacher Institute, the research arm of Planned Parenthood, keeps an astonishing record of abortion's legacy. According to Guttmacher, some 42 percent of abortions in the U.S. are performed after the nine-week point, and some 1.5 percent – 19,500 in a typical year – are performed in the late second or third trimester. These late-term abortions – the ones often referred to as "extremely rare" by the abortion movement – would, since *Roe*, equal the population of the state of Vermont.

Ironically, there have been so many abortions since Roe that some political analysts talks of a "Roe effect" in politics: So many children of pro-abortion parents have been aborted that pro-lifers have a significantly greater percentage of the population than they would have had otherwise.

The excuses for abortion are standard by now, and tiresome.

1. **"It's my body, so it's my choice."** Obviously, abortion is not an act on a woman's body alone; it is a destructive act on *another's* body, that of the unborn child.

2. **"The baby will be better off."** This is a particularly dishonest euphemism that conceals selfishness. When an abortion advocate says, "The baby will be better off," what she is really saying is: "*I* will be better off." Actually, the baby will be dead.

3. **"It's not really a baby. It's a clump of cells."** From the

instant of conception, the complete genetic endowment for a unique human being is completely in place. In 1966, Lennart Nilsson and Lars Hamberger published what would become a perennial bestseller, *A Child Is Born*, showing the world for the first time breathtaking color photographs of the unborn child at every stage of development. Today, technology allows parents to see their baby's face before it is born – and, not surprisingly, support for abortion-on-demand is falling with every 3-D ultrasound.

4. **"I'm not ready for a baby."** This is a little more honest version of "The baby will be better off," but the fact that an admission is honest does not make it right. In life, things *happen*. Whether it's winning the lottery or finding out one has a dread disease, a person has to deal with events as they occur – ready or not. When a child comes down with a fever in the middle of the night, the parent can't send the child away because mom or dad "isn't ready" to deal with it. The situation requires attention *now*. A parent-to-be does not relinquish responsibility for a negative outcome of his or her choice just because doing the right thing is inconvenient.

5. **"I can't afford to have this baby."** This excuse has gained currency in a culture in which our high standard of living has been taken for granted. To many Americans, the poverty level begins when they cannot afford cable television and a cell phone. Luxuries that did not even *exist* a generation ago are now thought of as necessities. Inconvenient children cannot be allowed to affect one's lifestyle. In infamous comments in a 2004 *New York Times Magazine* article, abortion advocate Amy Richards of Manhattan casually detailed her reasons for "selective reduction" – killing two of three triplets before they were born: She would have to move to Staten Island, a decidedly working class borough in no way as "hip" as her East Greenwich Village address. She would not be able to fly in an airplane for the last half of her pregnancy. And, she complained, if she had had the triplets she would "have to start shopping only at Costco and buying big jars of mayonnaise."

6. **"I don't like abortion, but it is always going to be with us, so let's make it safe, legal and rare."** Lots of unspeakably bad things will always be with us: wife abuse, child abuse,

and murder, to name a few. Should these acts be made "safe, legal and rare"? This is a very fatuous line of reasoning that can be used to protect any injustice. Pro-slavery arguments, recall, often revolved around the specious claim that slavery represented a permanent, immovable American custom.

Roe was born in ignorance: Nothing in the Constitution gives one person the right to end the life of another. Arguments to the contrary died with slavery.

Roe was born in confusion: Warren Burger, the Chief Justice named by Nixon, wrote that the court was legalizing early abortions only. However, *Roe* legalized abortion for all nine months when the mother's emotional, psychological, or "familial" health might be endangered—conditions so vague as to remove nearly all restrictions on the practice.

Roe did not even do what most reporters say it did. Contrary to what one hears or reads in the news media, abortion was already legal in much of the country. (To his great regret, Ronald Reagan had, as governor, signed the nation's most liberal abortion law, in California.) What the Court did was to overturn all abortion laws in all states, removing the issue from the democratic process and putting it in the hands of unelected judges. Abortion, which was never contemplated by the Founders, was made more of an absolute "right" than any of the rights specifically listed in the Bill of Rights!

This power grab by judges was so far-reaching that even many advocates for the "right" to abortion find the reasoning of *Roe* indefensible. Timothy Carney assembled some of the points made against *Roe* by "pro-choice" law professors and other scholars:

- "As a matter of constitutional interpretation and judicial method, *Roe* borders on the indefensible...The problem, I believe, is that it has little connection to the constitutional right it purportedly interpreted. A constitutional right to privacy broad enough to include abortion has no meaningful foundation in constitutional text, history, or precedent..."—Edward Lazarus, former clerk to Justice Harry Blackmun

- *Roe v. Wade* and *Bush v. Gore* "represent opposite sides of the same currency of judicial activism in areas more appropriately left to the political processes...Judges have no special competence, qualifications, or mandate to decide between equally compelling moral claims...(C)lear governing constitutional principles...are not present in either case," Alan Dershowitz, professor at Harvard Law School

- "What is frightening about *Roe* is that this super-protected right is not inferable from the language of the Constitution, the framers' thinking respecting the specific problem in issue, any general value derivable from the provisions they included, or the nation's governmental structure," the late John Hart Ely, former dean of Stanford Law School and one of the most widely-cited legal scholars in U.S. history

- "One of the most curious things about *Roe* is that, behind its own verbal smokescreen, the substantive judgment on which it rests is nowhere to be found." – Laurence H. Tribe, professor of constitutional law at Harvard Law School and who, over recent decades, has been mentioned more than any other person as a potential Democratic appointment to the Supreme Court

Most "pro-choice" advocates do not want to admit that *Roe* legalized abortion on demand for any reason, from financial hardship to disappointment at conceiving a girl when one or both parents wanted a boy. They prefer to portray *Roe* as a defense of abortion in cases that involve the "health of the mother." How did the health-of-the-mother issue expand *Roe* from what its author intended—a "right" to early abortion only—to encompass abortion throughout pregnancy, including abortion during birth?

The answer lies in *Roe*'s companion case, *Doe v. Bolton*, in which the Supreme Court created a bizarre definition of a woman's health. It was a definition that, it turned out, included almost any reason a woman would want an abortion! All she has to do is find a doctor—any doctor, including the abortionist himself—who will find a reason in his "medical judgment"! The Court noted:

> [M]edical judgment may be exercised in the light of all factors –

physical, emotional, psychological, familial, and the woman's age relevant to the well-being of the patient. All these factors may relate to health.

As Planned Parenthood declared in a press release:

> The health exception must allow the physician to exercise reasonable medical judgment, even where medical opinions differ. The court made clear that the exception cannot be limited to situations where the health risk is an "absolute necessity," nor can the law require unanimity of medical opinion as to the need for a particular abortion method.

In other words, the term "medical judgment" meant the stated opinion of a single abortionist, as long as he is "reasonable"—that is, as long as he can point to other physicians (including abortionists) who would support his judgment.

Thus, "the health of the mother" became a loophole through which any abortion can pass. When Bill Clinton said he opposed partial birth abortion except to protect the health of the mother, his statement was nonsensical. How could killing the baby during a live birth protect the health of the mother? Only if one uses a *Doe*-type definition of health, that health is what the abortionist says it is.

Most schoolchildren have heard this famous line: *"When I use a word, it means just what I choose it to mean — neither more nor less."* This quotation comes from Lewis Carroll's *Alice in Wonderland*, but it reflects the logic of *Roe* and *Doe*.

> *"The question is," said Alice, "whether you can make words mean so many different things."*
>
> *"The question is," said Humpty Dumpty, "which is to be master – that's all."*

How Callousness Infects a Culture

When Planned Parenthood was caught distributing T-shirts that read, "I Had an Abortion," the organization's Web site explained: "The *'I Had an Abortion'* T-shirt is intended to **challenge the taboo that cloaks abortion in silence. The t-shirt is an affirmation that abortion is not shameful.**" (Emphasis in the original.) In Planned Parenthood's view, elective abortion isn't even a wrongful act. Some feminists have made similar slogans, stating that, "If men could get pregnant, abortion would be a sacrament."[1] Peter Singer, a world-renowned professor at Princeton University, has justified the killing of unborn children and of many infants and disabled people, including people with Alzheimer's, on the ground that they are non-persons. (Singer, it should be noted, is a strong proponent of legal rights for apes.)

U.S. Senator Daniel Patrick Moynihan, a Democrat from New York, wrote in 1993 about the problem of "defining deviancy down."

How does society come to accept behaviors formerly considered wrong? Moynihan wrote that societies decide among themselves what level of crime and deviant behavior is acceptable—whether the actions involve violence such as robbery or murder or are seen by some as "victimless crimes" (prostitution, drug abuse). When the number of deviant acts increases, Moynihan wrote, society can deal with it in two ways: it can increase enforcement and incarceration. or it can re-classify some crimes and deviant acts so that, by definition, crime and deviancy declines to an acceptable level. It is through this process that "criminal aliens"/"illegal immigrants" become mere "undocumented workers."

Moynihan asserted that modern culture has chosen to keep crime at an "acceptable" level by "defining deviancy down." What was once illegal or stigmatized as immoral and unacceptable behavior – out-of-wedlock pregnancies, living together outside of marriage, pre-marital sex, open homosexuality, gay "marriage," abortion – has become "normal." Simply by re-defining what it means to be moral, society can maintain the illusion of an acceptable level of crime and immorality.

This, of course, is a very childish and delusional way of addressing deviancy, as if expunging the idea of morality and repealing all laws could turn us into a crime-free society of perfectly behaved mortal angels. Facts, as the saying goes, do not cease to exist because

---

[1] The story about Planned Parenthood's T-shirt reminds me of another story about that group. In 2004, Planned Parenthood sponsored a poster-making contest for children. Emblazoned at the top of the rules was this warning: *Kids, if you're under 18, be sure to get permission from your parent or guardian before sending in your entry!* If those same children wanted an abortion, Planned Parenthood would fight to the death (of the baby, that is) to keep the parents in the dark. But such is the logic of liberalism.

humans choose to ignore them. Crime does not disappear if we choose to take criminal codes off the books, any more than bad education disappears if we choose to junk test results.

Abortion is of a piece with this larger erosion of morality and common sense. It is both a symptom of that erosion and a cause of it, for normalizing abortion has undermined society's fight against lesser evils. We must never forget that the abortion debate is real and not rhetorical. Real human lives are lost in abortion. Country-club Republicans complain that there is too much talk about abortion, as if the loss of life is a frivolous source of conversation. They are wrong. One baby is aborted every 24 seconds, every hour, every day. Conservatives should make no apologies for speaking for these victims who do not have a voice of their own.

Partial-Birth Abortion: Infanticide by Another Name

(**Note: This paragraph contains graphic language.**) The grisly character of abortion is revealed most starkly in partial-birth abortion, a procedure so brutal it gives some members of the Left pause. The procedure entails the delivery through the birth canal of all but the head of the infant. While gripping the child by the legs, the abortionist inserts scissors into the back of the baby's skull, spreading the tips of the instrument to make a hole. The scissors are then removed, and the abortionist uses a catheter to suck out the contents of the skull and collapse the skull. At this point and only at this point, the head may be removed from the body of the mother.

A great deal of attention is paid to the technically insignificant matter of leaving the baby's head inside. Why? Because if the abortionist removes the baby completely from the birth canal, the person executing the procedure can be charged with murder.

The difference between abortion and infanticide, then, is a matter of inches. Abortion advocates are quick to sweep such inconvenient details under the rug. Look at how the procedure is described by Planned Parenthood:

> The fetus and other products of conception are removed from the uterus with surgical instruments and suction curettage.

Why, it's just removing the "products of conception"! If the pro-abortion side supports letting a woman make an informed choice either way, why do they skip over such critical details? And why does the pro-abortion movement oppose requiring parental permission and even parental notification? Could it be that they are not pro-choice but really pro-abortion? Could it be that abortion is too profitable a business to risk an honest presentation of its details?

Were Planned Parenthood driven by compassion for women and families, as it claims, it would provide all abortions for free. Instead, it generates profits from them. (An associate of mine, Art Kelly, estimates Planned Parenthood's 2004 profit from abortions at approximately $28.4 million.) Giving potential customers all the facts about abortion is the last thing *Planned Parenthood* wants to do.

The partial-birth abortion debate of the late 1990s and early 2000s has been very valuable to the pro-life movement, for it has laid bare the true agenda of much of the "pro-choice" movement: abortion on demand, for any reason, at any time during pregnancy, up to and including the moment of delivery.

President Bill Clinton, who claimed that he preferred abortion to be "rare," twice vetoed bans on partial-birth abortion. It took President George W. Bush to sign the ban into law. But how long will the law remain in effect? After all, abortion-rights supporters say the law is unconstitutional under the 5 to 4 *Carhart* decision of 2000, the Supreme Court opinion that used a ridiculously broad definition of "threat to the mother."

My prediction is that the Supreme Court will uphold the ban, but just barely, thanks to recent additions to the Court by President Bush. If the ban had been brought before the Court prior to the ascension of Chief Justice John Roberts and Associate Justice Samuel Alito (and prior to the departure of the swing vote in *Carhart*, Justice Sandra Day O'Connor), the ban probably would have been discarded.

Helping Women and Their Babies

Protesting peacefully at clinics, working on lawsuits, and educating the public about choices other than abortion—those are all important and vital efforts in the pro-life movement. Those who commit their time and resources to this work deserve our gratitude and our support. But pro-life one-on-one work with women in crisis gets little attention, even though it is some of the most positive, life-saving and life-enriching work taking place today.

One of the most effective efforts to help unwed mothers-to-be is the Liberty Godparent Home in Lynchburg, Virginia. My friend Dr. Jerry Falwell helped establish this Home, whose motto is "Changing lives two at a time!" For nearly two decades, women who are unwed and pregnant have been welcome there. They can receive housing, high-school and college-level education, parenting education, counseling, pre-natal classes, and adoption service. In short, a woman who is pregnant and feels she has nowhere else to turn always has a place to turn with the Liberty Godparent Home.

Fighting for the Right to Life

It's time to sweep abortion-on-demand onto the ash-heap of history. Here's how:

Pass the Human Life Amendment banning abortion. As welcome as reversing *Roe* would be, that alone will not achieve this goal; it would only allow the states to regulate abortion as they see fit. In fact, the mere reversal of *Roe*—without added legislation or a constitutional amendment—would probably have only a small impact on the number of abortions. Only a Human Life Amendment to the U.S. Constitution would eliminate the loopholes that judges always "discover" to circumvent abortion regulation.

Oppose all federal support for pro-abortion groups and programs. When the government funds sex-education programming that promotes abortion, we must oppose it. When government provides funds to groups like Planned Parenthood, we must demand that our elected officials stop it. These groups invariably say that such funding is not for pro-abortion programming. But the fact is that giving taxpayer dollars to those efforts allows these groups to funnel money in various directions that frees up resources which end up being used for abortion.

Save lives in the interim by enacting pro-life policies. The First Amendment right to protest at abortion clinics must be preserved absolutely, and protected from liberals who have tried to make an exception for pro-life speech. We should press for informed consent laws, requirements that women considering abortion be fully informed as to the risks and consequences. And let's remember that when such laws were passed at the state level in the 1990s, the abortion rate went down, proving that we can make a difference, and that not everything we do must be conducted at the federal level.

It is impossible to be at once a sincere conservative and in favor of abortion-on-demand. At the core of our conservatism is the principle that life is sacred and that the innocent must be protected from harm. Causing harm to others for the sake of personal convenience can never be reconciled with conservatism.

RESTORING THE
CULTURE OF LIFE

It's a matter of life and death.

A society is measured by its respect for life at all stages, from beginning to end. This is an especially tough test for Americans in the 21st Century, because medical technology in our country today is advancing at lightning speed. It seems that a new question of life and death is raised every year.

In the old days, it was thought that an unborn child became alive when the mother could feel it move. Thanks to modern technology, we know better.

In the old days, when a person's heart stopped, he or she was dead. Now, sometimes, we can bring such a person back, sometimes to full functionality. And, sometimes, we can keep a person alive indefinitely, even with severe brain damage that raises, in many people's minds, the question of whether that person is truly alive or dead.

In the old days, a diagnosis of cancer was a death sentence. Doctors used to debate whether even to tell a patient that he or she had cancer, since nothing could be done. Premature babies, if born before a certain point, were a lost cause, and even if they survived were likely to suffer severe disability throughout life. Today, most people with cancer can be saved, and most preemies can be saved without impairment, but sometimes this can be done only at the cost of a lifetime's earnings. If it *can* be done, it *must* be done, but someone has to pay, so who will it be?

In the old days, we didn't have to face issues such as embryonic stem cell research, because such a thing existed only in the realm of science fiction.

We live in a complicated world, and it's only going to get more complicated.

Modern medicine allows us to hasten or deny birth, to postpone death, and to modulate pain for the years in between. How do we apply the principles of our society—those based on our Judeo-Christian heritage and on the reasoning of this country's Founders—in this new world?

The first step to dealing with these issues is to accept that God, not man, sets the boundaries of life.

This is the only reasonable approach to take. Without some concept of God—without the Creator who, the Declaration of Independence declared, endowed us with the right to life—there are no boundaries on what one person can do to another. If the only test is, say, the greatest good for the greatest number, then what's to stop medical experimentation on condemned prisoners, or even on innocent people if such experiments could help save many others or prevent suffering? At the end of such a line of reasoning, there stands the Nazi Dr. Mengele.

The temptations of modern science are great in a culture that has lost its moral bearings. Life is painful? End it. Birth is inconvenient? Prevent it. The body is defective? Exploit other, weaker lives to repair it. We must reject this crass utilitarianism, this idea that the end justifies the means.

We must help those who cannot help themselves. The degree to which the vulnerable are protected is a reliable standard for measuring the health of a civilization. And, as Vice President Hubert Humphrey (D-Minnesota) noted, "the moral test of government is how that government treats those who are in the dawn of life, the children; those who are in the twilight of life, the elderly; and those who are in the shadows of life, the sick, the needy and the handicapped."

We must restore what Pope John Paul II called the culture of life. Speaking to journalists near Denver in 1993, he denounced abortion and euthanasia, and declared that, "The culture of life means respect for nature and protection of God's work of creation. In a special way, it means respect for human life from the first moment of conception until its natural end." In 1995, in the encyclical *Evangelium Vitae* (*Gospel of Life*), he noted: "In our present social context, marked by a dramatic struggle between the culture of life and the culture of death, there is need to develop a deep critical sense capable of discerning true values and authentic needs."

Let's examine some of the issues we face that are related to building a culture of life: embryonic stem cell research; euthanasia; the equation of human and animal life; and the death penalty.

Embryonic Stem Cell Research

A stem cell is a kind of cell that can develop into any specialized part of the body, such as a skin cell or heart cell or nerve cell. In theory, any body part can be created from stem cells.

Scientists do not fully understand the mechanism that turns an undifferentiated stem cell into a part of the liver or kidney or brain, and they do not know how to *make* it happen in a predictable, controlled manner. But they believe that, with enough research, they will eventually be able to use stem cells to cure such diseases as Alzheimer's disease, muscular dystrophy, and diabetes.

So far, so good. The problem is: Where do you get the stem cells? You can get them from a child's umbilical cord blood (which is why many parents now store these cells in case the child needs them later). Or you can get them from adult cells that have been stripped of their differentiation—that is, turned back into stem cells.

Or you can get stem cells by destroying an embryo, an unborn child in an early stage of development. To put it bluntly: To get embryonic stem cells, you have to kill the baby. Then you harvest—that's the word, *harvest*—the cells.

By the time President Bush announced his policy on this research, some of the harvesting had already been done. These embryonic stem cells had been multiplied in the laboratory, creating various "lines" of stem cells. President Bush's policy was hardly radical; it allowed federal funding (taxpayer funding) of research on the lines that already existed, but denied federal funding for research on new lines.

The policy did not prohibit embryonic stem cell research. It did not prohibit state, local, or private funding of such research. It did not prohibit federal, state, local, or private funding of adult stem cell research—a far more promising area of inquiry, since adult stem cells can be taken from a patient's own body and do not present the same risk of cancer or of rejection by the body. The Bush policy did not even prohibit federal funds for embryonic stem cell research, as long as the research was on cell lines that already existed.

Most advocates of embryonic stem cell research and most journalists covering the story seemed unable to understand the nuances of the Bush policy. Most seemed unaware of the difference between adult and embryonic stem cells, and of the moral issues involved. To hear them tell it, the Bush policy was inexplicable. In the simplistic, liberal view, the issue was presented this way: In restricting embryonic stem cell research, is Bush following instructions from religious fanatics, or just cruel? Why in the world would he deny scientists the ability to make Christopher Reeve walk again?

Think I'm kidding? On October 11, 2004, at a rally in Newton, Iowa, Democratic vice presidential nominee John Edwards told a crowd, "If we do the work that we can do in this country, the work that we will do when John Kerry is president, people like Christopher Reeve are going to walk, get up out of that wheelchair and walk again."

Columnist Charles Krauthammer is a medical doctor who has been a quadriplegic since a diving accident in 1967. He knows the very real obstacles to repairing the injuries of someone like Christopher Reeve. Regarding John Edwards, he wrote: "In my 25 years in Washington, I have never seen a more loathsome display of demagoguery. Hope is good. False hope is bad. Deliberately, for personal gain, raising false hope in the catastrophically afflicted is despicable."

Still, we must avoid making utilitarian arguments on embryonic stem cell research, or abortion, or euthanasia, or other issues of respect for life. In other words, we shouldn't base our arguments on whether a given practice will *work.*

You could argue, as some economists do,[1] that abortion-on-demand

---

[1] See, for example, *Freakonomics: A Rogue Economist Explores the Hidden Side of Everything,* by Steven D. Levitt and Stephen J. Dubner.

has lowered the crime rate by reducing the number of people in the age group most likely to commit crime. So what? Some argued that slavery in the U.S. was part of an efficient economic system, that the slaves were better off than if their ancestors had stayed in Africa, etc. etc. blah blah. So what? Abortion is wrong. Slavery is wrong. So is the killing of the elderly, the sick, and the disabled, no matter how much some claim our society would benefit from such a practice.

Killing unborn children, at any stage of development, to harvest their bodies for medical research, is wrong. No medical experiment that involves the exploitation of another human being can ever be just. Unjust research does not cease to be unjust once it is productive.

It is unwise for conservatives to argue primarily that a wrong thing is wrong because it doesn't work. What then would we say if it *did* work?

This debate is about the killing of an unborn human being, for the purpose of medical research, funded by the taxes of people who abhor such a practice—and done despite the fact that adult stem cell research offers far more hope for "miracle" cures. South Korea's cloning hoax should give pause to anyone inclined to believing the fantastic claims of advocates of embryonic stem cell research.

The true argument rests on a principle not subject to compromise. Conservatives are not against science. We are against wrongs committed in the name of science.

Euthanasia

They came for Terri Schiavo, and they're coming for you next.

Terry was 26 years old in 1990 when, under mysterious circumstances, she apparently collapsed at home in St. Petersburg, Florida, and suffered respiratory and cardiac arrest. She was in a coma for 10 weeks, and had severe brain damage. Although he had initially supported efforts to keep her alive, her husband in 1998 petitioned the courts for permission to remove her feeding tube and cause her to die, slowly, by dehydration and starvation. That began a legal battle that lasted until Terri's death in 2005.

Over the years, as it became clear that the courts would not provide relief, some elected officials sought to intervene. Florida's legislature passed "Terri's Law" in an attempt to save her. Later, as Terri's family ran out of options at the state level, they turned to Washington, where, for once, Congress and the White House got something done. They passed a law requiring the federal courts to take a fresh look at the matter, which the courts simply refused to do. Terri died on March 31, 2005.

The Left seized on the opportunity to spin the story, to blame the controversy on meddling Republicans who are (of course) Taliban-type religious extremists. For example, according to the *Los Angeles Times*, Howard Dean, national chairman of the Democratic Party, said at a "gay rights" breakfast in West Hollywood that "We're going to use Terri Schiavo later on. . . . This is going to be an issue in 2006, and it's going to be an issue in 2008 . . . The issue is: Are we going to live in a theocracy where the highest powers tell us what to do? Or are we going to be allowed to consult our own high powers when we make very difficult decisions?"

Terri Schiavo was not brain-dead. She was not in pain. She was not dying. She had not left instructions for someone to "pull the plug" in such a situation. Her family, except for her estranged husband, was unanimous in support of Terri's right to life. None of the usual "justifications" for killing a sick person applied in this case.

(I say the husband was "estranged" because he was living with another woman and had fathered two children by her. Without regard to the rightness or wrongness of his involvement with the other woman, it certainly constituted a conflict of interest and should have disqualified him as the sole decider of Terri's fate. All he had to do was divorce her, and he could have walked away—yet he chose to fight for the power to kill her.)

In the 1920s and 1930s, people who considered themselves "progressives" sought to limit the supposed burden on society created by the people they considered parasites. No less an authority than the U.S. Supreme Court, in the Carrie Buck case, authorized forced sterilization. Carrie Buck, a rape victim who became pregnant out of wedlock, was involuntarily sterilized by the authorities of Virginia, as were her mother and her daughter. Though the victims were of normal intelligence, advocates of selective breeding falsely painted them as deficient. "It is better for all the world, if instead of waiting to execute degenerate offspring for crime or to let them starve for their imbecility, society can prevent those who are manifestly unfit from continuing their kind," wrote Justice Oliver Wendell Holmes Jr. "Three generations of imbeciles are enough."

One of the most famous books of the 1920s promoted the sterilization (or worse) of "parasitic" people such as the disabled. It also promoted white supremacy. The book was *A Civic Biology*—that is, a political biology—by George William Hunter. Don't recognize the title of the book? It was the textbook that John Thomas Scopes used to teach Darwinism, and the use of which the American Civil Liberties Union defended in the Scopes "monkey trial."

Racist groups like the American Birth Control League (Planned Parenthood), which survives to this day—thanks partly to taxpayer support—put forth the idea that some people were more worthy of life than others.[2]

Now, you might think the fate of the Nazis would have prevented these ideas from resurfacing, but resurface they do, on a fairly regular basis.

In 1982 in Indiana, a child was born with Down Syndrome and an improperly formed esophagus. Rather than correct the esophagus problem, the parents and physician decided to have the baby starve to death. Years later, in an obituary for Ronald Reagan, Dr. James Dobson

---

[2] Planned Parenthood denies that its founder, Margaret Sanger, was a racist, yet the organization, on its own Web site, admits the following:

"Although Sanger uniformly repudiated the racist exploitation of eugenics principles, she agreed with the 'progressives' of her day who favored

- incentives for the voluntary hospitalization and/or sterilization of people with untreatable, disabling, hereditary conditions
- the adoption and enforcement of stringent regulations to prevent the immigration of the diseased and 'feebleminded' into the U.S.
- placing so-called illiterates, paupers, unemployables, criminals, prostitutes, and dope-fiends on farms and open spaces as long as necessary for the strengthening and development of moral conduct"

In fact, those terms, such as "feebleminded," "people with untreatable, disabling, hereditary conditions," and even "dope-fiends" (as in the *New York Times* term, "Negro cocaine fiends") were common euphemisms for people in various supposedly inferior groups such as African-Americans, Asian immigrants, and Appalachian folk.

wrote about the case, known as the Baby Doe case, and about President Reagan's response.

"[Reagan aide] Gary Bauer shares a story that occurred during one of his regular lunch meetings with the President. Each senior staff member was given an opportunity to raise an issue or two with 'the boss,' after gaining prior approval from the Chief of Staff. Without asking anyone, Gary discussed a problem that he knew would make his superiors uncomfortable. He told the President about a little girl in Bloomington, Indiana, who was suffering from severe life-threatening complications associated with Down Syndrome. Apparently, the child's parents had received terrible medical advice and instead of seeking treatment, had the baby rolled into the corner of the hospital nursery where a sign was hung on the crib that said, 'Do not feed.' A Christian nurse observed this barbaric situation and called the White House, wondering if there was any legal recourse available. As Gary spoke, he noticed that his colleagues flinched because this story was not the kind of topic that is worthy of the President's time. Then he looked at Mr. Reagan and saw that he had tears in his eyes. He had been deeply moved by Gary's account of the hurting child. He ordered that the Justice Department seek to protect her from those who would allow her to die. Incredibly, the judges who are able to find legal justification for killing unborn babies could not figure out how to preserve the life of 'Baby Doe.'"

More than 50 couples offered to adopt Baby Doe, but it didn't matter. The Indiana courts had their say, and the child was killed for having Down Syndrome.

Where is this headed? The *Sunday Times* of London reported on March 5, 2006: "Each year in Holland, at least 15 seriously ill babies, most of them with severe spina bifida or chromosomal abnormalities, are helped to die by doctors acting with the parents' consent. But only a fraction of those cases are reported to the authorities because of the doctors' fears of being charged with murder. Things are about to change, however, making it much easier for parents and doctors to end the suffering of an infant. A committee set up to regulate the practice will begin operating in the next few weeks, effectively making Holland, where adult euthanasia is legal, the first country in the world to allow 'baby euthanasia' as well."

Once it starts, so-called mercy killing doesn't stop. More and more groups are added to the list of what the Nazis called "life unworthy of life"—those who would supposedly be better off dead. C. Everett Koop, who was Surgeon General in the Reagan Administration, noted: "My great concern is that there will be 10,000 Grandma Does for every Baby Doe."

In *National Review Online*, Wesley J. Smith noted a *San Francisco Chronicle* article about Web sites that help people—including troubled teenagers—kill themselves. "First, they bestow moral permission. Then, they teach the self-destructive person how to do it. Finally, they keep the suicidal person company until the deed is done. It is the modern version of the howling crowd yelling, 'Jump! Jump!' at the suicidal person standing on the skyscraper window ledge."

Smith also reported that, in the Netherlands, reasons for "assisted suicide" have included grief over the deaths of a woman's two children, and a young woman's fear that her anorexia will recur.

The editor of *National Review Online*, Kathryn Jean Lopez, reported that the pro-suicide Hemlock Society has supported the development of a suicide pill by a doctor who said he hoped the pill would be available to "anyone who wants it."

Assisted suicide and euthanasia are often just cases of killing for convenience. Sometimes these practices are described as being conducted for the good of someone who is in physical or psychological pain. Often, though, there is not even a pretense of caring for the suffering; the emphasis is on the needs of society, or on the desires of the next of kin (desires which may be selfless or selfish).

As conservatives, we must support people who are suffering, or who are caring for the suffering, while at the same time insisting on the value of human life even under such trying circumstances. We must do what we can to alleviate that suffering and to ease the burden of the caregivers, even as we reaffirm the sanctity of life. We must recognize that the temptation to end life can sometimes be very strong and can cloud judgment and moral sensibility.

As Marvin Olasky has pointed out, euthanasia quickly expands beyond cases in which a seemingly rational person makes a voluntary decision to end his or her life. If we adopted rules allowing "consensual" euthanasia, "bullies would soon give them preferred status or make them compulsory. If 'voluntary euthanasia' became common, the pressure would grow on the elderly or the disabled to get out of the way rather than use up resources. If infanticide under 'strict' conditions were legalized, the conditions would soon be loosened, reporters would discover inequities where it was allowed in some circumstances and not others, and soon infanticide on parental demand would become standard. That's what happened with abortion."

As conservatives, we must speak up for those who cannot speak for themselves.

The Equation of Human and Animal Life

Most people want animals to be treated humanely. Even animals that are raised for food should be treated with kindness and should not be subjected to unnecessary suffering. But "animal rights" advocates seek nothing less than to equate the lives of animals with the lives of human beings. As Ingrid Newkirk, president of People for the Ethical Treatment of Animals (PETA), put it:

"A rat is a pig is a dog is a boy." In other words, one is the moral equivalent of the other.

Newkirk once said that, "Even if animal research produced a cure for AIDS, we'd be against it."

Peter Singer, a professor of Bioethics at Princeton, is the author of the 1975 book *Animal Liberation* and is considered the father of the animal liberation movement. As Marvin Olasky described Singer in *World* magazine: "He has consistently tossed aside the Declaration of Independence concept that all of us are created equal. Instead, the worth of a life varies according to its rationality and self-consciousness, with no essential divide between animals and humans. For example, given a choice between keeping alive an adult chimpanzee and a human infant, the chimp should beat out the child."

Singer has expressed the belief that the United Nations should recognize great apes as persons, and that "mutually satisfying activities" of an intimate nature may sometimes occur between humans and animals. No, I'm not making this up.

As he elevates apes and other animals to the moral level of humans, Singer advocates the legalization of infanticide—human infanticide, that is—though he admits to a preference that parents kill their children as soon as possible after birth rather than waiting.

As bizarre and dehumanizing as these ideas are, what makes the animal rights movement especially troublesome is its advocacy and commission of violence.

- At a July 2001 animal rights conference, PETA official Bruce Friedrich said, "[O]f course we're going to be blowing things up and smashing windows. . . . I think it's a great way to bring about animal liberation, considering the level of suffering, the atrocities. I think it would be great if all of the fast-food outlets, slaughterhouses, these laboratories and the banks who fund them exploded tomorrow. I think it's perfectly appropriate for people to take bricks and toss them through windows."

- The radical Animal Liberation Front (ALF) claimed responsibility for a January 2006 attack on the home of a drug company executive in Britain. "Next time it won't just be wet paint we leave on his doorstep," ALF threatened in a Web site statement.

- In January 2006, federal prosecutors indicted 11 alleged eco-terrorists for 17 attacks that caused $23 million in damage to western lumber companies, meat plants, a ski resort and other facilities. ALF and the Earth Liberation Front (ELF) claimed responsibility for the violence.

- PETA's Dan Matthews said he admired Andrew Cunanan, the murderer of designer Gianni Versace, because the killing stopped Versace from using fur in his fashions.

Some mainstream liberal environmentalists are sympathetic with groups such as ELF, ALF and PETA, and in some cases are even providing funding to defend violent offenders and to support property destruction. (See documentation at AnimalScam.com.)

Animals should be treated humanely. Conservatives should

oppose cruel farming practices such as force-feeding and severe over-crowding, and buy farm products only from farms where animals are treated compassionately.

But we must oppose those who would twist a caring concern for animals into an equation of humans and animals. That will only weaken the concept of a human being's sovereignty over his own person—a human being's right to life, liberty, and the pursuit of happiness.

The Death Penalty

To some people, this will be the most controversial argument that I make in this book: Conservatives should give up their support for the death penalty.

I understand why so many conservatives want to impose the death penalty on those who have taken the lives of others. It is the old idea of an eye for an eye, a life for a life. I understand why they make a logical distinction between those who are innocent, such as unborn children who deserve life, and those who are guilty of heinous crimes and deserve death. Anyone who follows the news can think of numerous examples of people who, it seems, deserve such punishment.

But a lifetime of imprisonment can be a far greater punishment than death. The criminal has day after day after day to contemplate what he's done, and the effect of his actions on his victims, his own family, and himself. If he sees himself as a martyr, as in the case of the terrorist Zacarias Moussaoui, giving him the death penalty is doing him a favor. Why not sentence such monsters to, say, life at hard labor in Alaska, as commentator Bill O'Reilly has suggested?

And, as we have learned from the results of DNA testing, miscarriages of justice do occur, far more often than we once thought. The death penalty allows no correction for mistakes.

My opposition to the death penalty, though, is based less on the weighing of pros and cons than on principle. It stems from the idea that our lives are granted by God and cannot rightly be taken by man except to save the lives of innocents.

When people were ruled by kings, a person's life belonged to the government – or, at least, that's what people thought. The head of the government, the king, was supposed to be God's agent on earth.

The rise of Christianity gradually changed this understanding of leadership. Joseph (Jody) Bottum, editor of the religious magazine *First Things*, writes that Christianity "demythologized the state," making people realize that government is a product of man and not the agency of God. Eventually, we Americans came to believe in the idea expressed by Thomas Jefferson and Benjamin Franklin that "Rebellion to tyrants is obedience to God."

Today, we do not regard governments as divine instruments. Consequently, government's authority to execute a person rests on a much shakier foundation. The power to take life is not a power we should reliably entrust to secular governments run by fallible men. The death penalty presupposes a level of divine wisdom that secular governments do not possess.

Killing a person can be justified in certain circumstances: in the case of a just war conducted justly, or in a case of direct defense of oneself or of innocents. But if we apply conservative principles consistently in all areas, we must oppose the killing of a person, no matter how evil, who is not a threat. Once the evildoer is captured and is locked away for the rest of his life, he no longer constitutes such a threat.

Finally, we must oppose the death penalty because support for it undermines our arguments against abortion, euthanasia, and related practices. Even if you disagree with me regarding the underlying principle, you should see that many conservatives' inconsistency on the sanctity of life drives away people who might otherwise support conservative positions on life-related issues. Even if you think conservative support for the death penalty is a good idea in theory, you should see that it is a bad idea in practice, because our loss of credibility on life issues is not worth the (very rare) execution of a criminal.

There. I said it.

A Seamless Garment

The late Joseph Cardinal Bernardin suggested that the approach to various issues, including abortion, the death penalty, war, and poverty, be seen as a "seamless garment"—a reference to Jesus' robe or tunic, for which soldiers cast lots so they would not have to tear it (John 19:23). The metaphor represented a consistent ethic of life, an ethic of respect for life from conception to natural death, or, to put it another way, a culture of life.

Now, some have used the concept to rationalize the welfare state and other evils. Some advocates of the concept act as if they can ignore science, economics, and political reality. They suggest that supporters of a culture of life should support a "catastrophic man-made global warming" theory, no matter what the scientists say. They suggest that we should support anti-hiring laws such as minimum wage laws, which, when combined with payroll taxes and mandatory benefit laws, hurt unskilled workers more than anyone else. They suggest that we should support so-called universal health care, even though every country that has ever implemented such a scheme has done so by denying care to the old, to the supposedly (but not necessarily) "terminal," to premature babies, and to people with less-common conditions such as AIDS.

During the Cold War, some "seamless garment"/culture of life advocates suggested that the U.S. should unilaterally disarm in the face of the Soviet Empire, and they opposed—as extreme, reckless, and a threat to the survival of the world—Ronald Reagan's policies that peacefully freed hundreds of millions of people from totalitarianism.

And they continue to suggest that prosperous countries should give up the policies that have made them prosperous, because it's unfair that some countries are prosperous while others are poor. They decry the "distribution" of wealth in the world, as a smokescreen for the fact that most impoverished countries are kept that way by oppressive, corrupt, socialist governments whose wealthy rulers actively prevent the people from improving their situation. (One person's poverty is not caused by another person's wealth, any more than one person's sickness is caused by another person's health, and one country's poverty is not caused by another country's prosperity.)

The willingness to examine all the consequences of a given policy – not just the *intended* ones – is part of what makes us conservatives. We know which road is paved with good intentions. We do not give up this quality of healthy skepticism when we adopt the principle that a proper role of politics and policy is to help make people's lives better and to care for those who cannot care for themselves. We do not give up our common sense when we make a belief in the sanctity of life the cornerstone of the conservative philosophy.

As Alicia Cohen wrote in the *New York Sun:* "Most pro-choicers accuse us of having a love affair with the fetus. This is true, and we also love the zygote, embryo, preemie, infant, toddler, teenager, adult, and senior citizen. We respect life in all its stages, and when human life is treated as dispensable in any of its developmental stages, it also becomes cheap at any stage."

Love and respect—pretty good bases for a political philosophy, don't you think?

7

FIGHTING THE CULTURE WARS

We are engaged in a struggle between traditional values and moral relativism; between morality and humanism; between a belief that the universe is built by God on absolute truth, and the belief that life is meaningless, accidental and random.

This war—and it is a war, make no mistake—is far greater than any of its individual battles. This is not just an argument about what kinds of TV shows we will have and how important the family will be in American life. It is a struggle between a world of perpetual conflict (the liberal vision) and a world of cooperation based on tradition (the conservative vision).

In the liberal world, life is viewed as a constant struggle for power between oppressors and the oppressed. By this light, you can easily see why liberals always speak in terms of victims and refuse to concede even the slightest progress against poverty and racism.

In the conservative world, life is viewed as often unfair, but ultimately as a series of opportunities. By respecting immutable definitions of right and wrong, men and women are able to support their families and not be dependent on others, but they know the community will help if they face unforeseen hardship. The idea of self-determination is balanced with the idea of compassion, and competition is tempered by caring.

For liberals to win this battle of world views, they cannot simply promote their own. For the idea that "the world is struggle" to make sense, liberals must inculcate in people the idea that they are oppressed. If there's no oppression, there's no fight.

More than ever before, American politics is based on a struggle between two philosophies of life. This struggle has become known as "the culture wars," pitting privileged elites against regular Americans on issues ranging from abortion to gun control; from funding of government-approved art, to the mixing of politics and science in schools; from "pulling the plug" on disabled people, to the public celebration of Christmas.

A New Kind of Politics

There were times when a person's politics was based mostly on factors that were determined at birth. One's politics was usually rooted in the status of one's parents in economics (unskilled laborer, skilled laborer, white collar, professional, "silver spoon" wealthy), education, region, religion, or ethnicity, or how long one's family had been in the U.S. At least 80% of Americans stayed in one political party, and in a particular faction of that party, from their first vote to their last.

Today, although those factors continue to play a role, the crucial division in our society is based more on culture. We are divided between liberals (who would use the power of government to overturn traditional values) and conservatives (who support the right of families and individuals to live according to traditional values).

The original culture war—Germany's Kulturkampf against Catholics—was based on religion, and so it is with today's culture wars, in which radical secularists would deny religion and religious-based values any place in public life.

Consider the issue of "gay marriage." The Left is not content to argue that, say, instituting state-recognized "gay marriage" would be good for society, or that it would be fairer than the current system. Rather, the Left is trying to use its domination of the courts to impose "gay marriage" on society, without a vote, against the will of the vast majority of Americans.

The Left sought for years to find some court, anywhere in the country, that would legalize "gay marriage" in a given state, thus requiring all states to recognize that marriage under the Full Faith and

Credit Clause of the Constitution. (This was tried first in Hawaii, before it succeeded in Massachusetts.) This scheme was thwarted by the Defense of Marriage Act, without which a single state court could have legalized such unions throughout the country.

Similarly, the Left is not satisfied that people who practice homosexuality have the same rights as other Americans. It attempts to make it illegal to ostracize anyone on the basis of homosexual practices, or to "discriminate" based on such practices even when such distinction is practical and reasonable. So the Left would use the heavy hand of government against a "discriminating" private employer (including a religious organization), or someone renting out the basement of a house, or even the U.S. military, within which the possibility of same-sex relationships would put lives at risk. The Left has even gone after the Boy Scouts, seeking to ban them from public facilities.

In one area after another, the Left seeks to impose its views on society with the help of government. As part of its culture wars, it seeks to ban guns even from areas where police are ineffective or where the nearest police station is a hundred miles away, because it sees gun owners as ignorant ghetto-dwellers and backward rednecks. To stop voucher programs, it promotes legal concepts such as the "separation of church and state."[1] It seeks to apply anti-Mafia laws to groups that peacefully oppose abortion, and to have the IRS take away the non-profit tax status of any church that supports or criticizes the views of political candidates. When most members of Congress supported efforts to save the life of Terri Schiavo, the Left sided against her family and with her estranged husband (who could easily have divorced her, leaving her in her family's care, but chose to pull the plug instead).

The Left uses the government school system to promote its

---

[1] Contrary to the belief of many people, the term "separation of church and state" does not appear in the U.S. Constitution. As a legal concept, the "separation of church and state" (based on an out-of-context phrase quoted misleadingly from a letter by Thomas Jefferson) was created by Supreme Court Justice Hugo Black in the 1947 case, *Everson v. Board of Education.*

agenda. It opposes, as "teaching religion," the teaching of criticism of Darwinism, even when that criticism comes from renowned scientists who happen to be atheists or agnostics. And much of "sex education" in government schools is, in fact, indoctrination, in which homosexuality is presented as just another lifestyle choice; sex outside of marriage is detached from morality; abstinence is portrayed as naïve, ineffective, or both; and love is portrayed as incidental to a physical relationship.

Morality vs. Amorality

On one side of the conflict stand members of the Left who argue for a new morality, one that broadly rejects traditional understandings of right and wrong. Many of these extreme liberals can be described as "moral relativists" because they see morality as relative, subjective, and arbitrary. They do not see morality as based on rules handed down from the Creator, nor do they see morality as the result of thousands of years of human experience boiled down to the rules on which any successful civilization must be based.

On one side of the culture wars is amorality (that is, an absence of morality). On the other side is the morality based on Judeo-Christian beliefs and on millennia of accumulated wisdom. On one side is law made by the powerful to bend society to its wishes. On the other side is Natural Law such as described in the Declaration of Independence.

Perhaps no one has provided a clearer statement for the liberal combatants in the culture war than Supreme Court Justice Anthony Kennedy. To the dismay of mainstream Justice Antonin Scalia, Kennedy declared in the case of *Casey v. Planned Parenthood* that, "At the heart of liberty is the right to define one's own concept of existence, of meaning, of the universe, and of the mystery of human life." Scalia calls this Kennedy's "famed sweet-mystery-of-life passage," marking Kennedy's attempt to enshrine moral relativism in the Constitution.

Some see the culture wars as a series of skirmishes over relatively unimportant matters. When taxpayers are forced to pay for artwork that depicts the Virgin Mary covered in elephant dung, or when a broadcast TV show slips in nudity and foul language for the sake of ratings and the riches that come with ratings, or when a CD glorifies cop-killers and depicts women as "bitches" deserving of violence and exploitation, it doesn't seem like a big deal. So what if chain stores change "Merry Christmas and Happy Hanukkah" to "Happy Holidays," and schools close for "The Winter Holiday" on December 25th?

These things matter because every war is made up of countless small conflicts, each of which contributes to the outcome. In the Revolutionary War, a British sniper had George Washington in his sights, but hesitated—and the course of history was changed. Little things mean a lot.

The War Against Christianity

In the world of arts and entertainment, Christianity is fair game. Rapper Kanye West, famous for declaring (during a charity fundraiser) that George W. Bush "doesn't care about black people," appeared on the cover of *Rolling Stone* as Jesus Christ wearing a crown of thorns; there was little protest. Andres Serrano depicted a crucified Jesus in urine in his "Piss Christ." And Terrence McNally's play about Jesus as a "young gay man" having "sexual adventures with his 12 disciples" was seen by large crowds in New York.

(This contrasts with the attitude toward Islam. As of this writing, the *Washington Post* and most other major news media have failed to publish the Danish cartoons ridiculing Muhammad that sparked anti-Western riots in Muslim countries. At CNN's Web site, a remarkable editor's note appeared at the bottom of a story about the cartoons: "CNN has chosen to not show the cartoons out of respect for Islam." This from CNN, whose founder, Ted Turner, called Catholics "Jesus freaks" and said Christianity was a "religion for losers.")

Likewise, the courts have waged war on Christianity.

- A federal appeals court judge ruled that New York City public schools can ban a Christian nativity scene while permitting a display of the Jewish menorah and the Islamic star and crescent.

- Federal judges in Kansas and later in Colorado ruled that Washburn University was not engaged in hostility toward religion, which violates the Establishment Clause of the Constitution, when it used publicly-owned property to display a statue of an angry Catholic bishop wearing a miter shaped like a penis.

- The 9th U.S. Circuit Court of Appeals in San Francisco ruled that a California school was not practicing religious indoctrination when teachers forced seventh graders to pretend to be Muslim for three weeks. Students were required to pray to Allah, memorize verses from the Koran and play "jihad games." The judge ruled that this program was devoid of "any devotional or religious intent."

- The ACLU threatened to sue the Los Angeles County Board of Supervisors if they did not remove a small cross from the county seal. The county capitulated and removed the cross, one of nine symbols on the seal including the Hollywood Bowl and a Roman goddess (whose status as "goddess" did not seem to disturb the potential plaintiffs).

Some liberal Democrats in Congress have suggested that traditional Catholics should not be allowed to serve as judges, because the Church opposes abortion.

What the states feared at the time of the Constitution's writing has largely come to pass: the federal government, via courts, is imposing upon them a view of religion—in this case, secularism. Ronald Reagan saw it coming: "The frustrating thing is that those who are attacking religion claim they are doing it in the name of tolerance, freedom, and open-mindedness. Question: Isn't the real truth that they are intolerant of religion?"

This is a deep and all-encompassing struggle that will determine the future of our society. If conservatives win the culture wars, the country will rest stably on the foundations of "ordered liberty" the Founding Fathers conceived. If they lose it, the country will drift toward the moral chaos that George Washington predicted would result if America lost its Judeo-Christian moorings.

The Left has already collected many victories in the culture wars, sometimes with the acquiescence of conservatives who are afraid to be "judgmental." Most alarmingly, one casualty has been the traditional family. Since the 1960s, the Left has sought to liberate Americans from the traditional ethos surrounding marriage, and they have succeeded beyond their most ambitious plans. What does "liberation" look like? We now know: one in three children born outside marriage; $150 billion in annual government spending to subsidize single-parent homes; the normalization of cohabitation; and easy divorce, leaving millions of children without two fulltime parents and emotionally scarred and damaged.

Liberals cast the last fifty years of American social life as "progress." Is it? Yes, we have made progress in some areas such as the elimination of official segregation. But we have also seen the disintegration of the traditional family, which is the cell of civilization. In that regard, this period has been a regress into a dark past. Indeed, the Left's vision for America's future looks not so much like a plan for ennobling the republic but a return to the decadence of pagan antiquity.

Cultural erosion spills over into every area of society, including business, military life, and education. Once the idea has permeated a culture that morality is relative, cheating becomes acceptable. We are seeing the results in everything from the Enron scandal to the now-common practice of teachers "helping" students by giving them answers. If much of the success of Western society has been the result of institutions that encourage people to trust and cooperate with one another, what will happen when the dog-eat-dog ethic of moral relativism becomes the norm?

A weakened culture will ultimately produce a weakened economy and a weakened defense. Historians like Edward Gibbon have observed that countries fall from within and without. External enemies are not the only threat to a country's existence. The internal weaknesses of a country's culture can contribute to its demise as well.

The Founders, steeped in learning, understood the factors that bring about the rise and fall of civilizations. They knew that a system of self-government would last only as long as an internal culture of self-restraint did.

Restoring the Family to its Rightful Place

People want to be led. They do not want to be told what to do; that's something else entirely. But throughout history, people have sought from their communities and nations institutions and individuals to help set the tone for behavior.

If we intend to fight back against the spectacular progress the liberals have made toward winning the culture wars, we have to convert our beliefs into action. I suggest these steps:

Enact tax policies that reward fulltime homemakers and single-income families. With all the emphasis on subsidizing single parenthood and making the system "fair" for two-income families, our elected leaders pay little attention to encouraging traditional families with a mother who does not work outside the home and those families that choose to live on one income. For instance, parents who pay for daycare get a tax break—a financial incentive—for doing so. In this way, the government actually discourages parents from staying home to care for their own children. How fair is that? More important, how wise is that? Conservatives should press for a fairer, flatter tax code that ends the use of tax regulation for social engineering.

Supplement funding for government schools with school-choice voucher options for all parents. The government should allow parents to take the money designated to pay for their children's education and put it toward private education. Government monopoly schools are immune from market forces and are therefore only as good as their staffs choose to be. They are only going to get worse as long as they are controlled by unions. Children deserve better, and competition and parental choice will improve all schools.

Recruit teachers from fields other than "education." Too many teachers have been trained in "teaching methodology" rather than the subjects they actually teach, such as math or science or history. We should make it easier for mathematicians, scientists, historians, and others with special expertise to get certification to teach in government schools.

Place responsibility for school curriculum and policy at the local level. End federal influence. Nationalized curricula ignore local concerns, impose one-size-fits-all standards, and encourage teachers to "teach to the test" instead of teaching the material. In almost all matters of public policy, the more localized the control, the better. In no area is this more true than in education.

Allow local schools to celebrate the local culture and traditions, and to enforce standards of decency as they see fit. If a community wants to celebrate its traditions and character, it should be free to do so. If the people in a town want to display a crèche on the town square, then that should be their right. After all, a government should reflect the beliefs of those it represents. Of course, the federal government is not now and never should be allowed to coerce any citizen to engage or finance those traditions in any way. But today anti-Christian hostility is for many liberals a religion in itself, and the government in many cases has institutionalized it.

End government funding for abortion-providing organizations and re-direct those funds toward support for unwed mothers during pregnancy and in the early childhood of their offspring, and for adoption services. If abortion is a choice, as the liberals say, then adoption is a choice, too. The government should create tax incentives for the permanent adoption of older children (who are often difficult to place) and those children with physical or emotional handicaps.

Support wholesome, moral, pro-family entertainment. Avoid supporting entertainment with anti-family themes. Changing the popular culture is not easy but there are things each of us can do. I am not calling for a boycott, because those require more coordination and, frankly, more willpower than most people will have. Our power to influence our neighbors is far greater than Hollywood's influence on them.

A long time ago, it took a lot of fortitude for Hollywood to promote sexual promiscuity and vulgarity in the movies. Today, however, those things are standard elements in entertainment. And, outside of "Seventh Heaven" and "The Simpsons," good luck finding a primetime TV reference to a family regularly attending religious services. Today it takes fortitude to make a TV show that portrays Christians in a realistic or even kind way, to show people making moral choices and benefiting from them, to depict business people as generous and honest, or even a half-hour sitcom that doesn't glorify sex outside of marriage.

Just as the entertainment world changed once, so it can change again. Imagine how much more powerful your word and your example can be against something someone sees a stranger say or do in a movie. Our strength can be contagious, but we have to begin by showing that strength to the world. When it comes to anti-Christian, anti-conservative values in entertainment, the answer begins this way: Just say no.[2]

But it will never be enough for conservatives to simply write off popular culture—movies, TV, music and now the Internet—and declare that we are *in* the world but not *of* it. That's a kind of emotional segregation that might be fine for buttressing our own character, but it's a worse-than-useless way to influence the rest of the world. Conservatives must organize to *produce and distribute* wholesome entertainment, and entertainment that promotes our values, not just support the occasional good book or movie after it comes out.

Pass a constitutional amendment establishing marriage as the union between one man and one woman. Marriage and the nuclear family are part of the foundation of Western civilization and of order itself. Marriage is between a man and a woman, and it always has been. God, not man, established marriage. Therefore, man cannot unmake it. This obvious truth now needs to be enshrined in the Constitution. It's a shame something so reasonable would have to be written down in the Constitution, but that's what the culture war has come to; common sense is under constant assault from the armies of "tolerance." Many homosexual activist groups—really radical groups operating in the name of homosexuals—have spent the past few decades trying to tear down the traditional family one step at a time. We must stop them.

Conservatives must oppose legal recognition of so-called civil unions, which are "marriages" in everything but name. Conservatives

---

[2] The same principle, by the way, applies when radical secularists and their allies try to rewrite our history and reconfigure culture to remove references to religion. The most egregious recent example was what's been called the War on Christmas. This ranged from school calendars referring to a mysterious "Winter Holiday" on December 25, to Christmas-season advertising campaigns talking about the "holiday season" without mentioning Christmas or Hanukkah, to the actual re-writing of Christmas songs such as "Silent Night" to remove religious references—a practice that was lampooned on "Saturday Night Live." These things were the result of the fact that, until recently, secularists were more likely to complain about Christmas references than Christians were to complain about the *lack* of Christmas references. The lesson is that, in the culture wars, the squeaky wheel gets the grease.

do support humanitarian measures such as allowing people to designate whomever they wish to visit them in the hospital. But with regard to "gay marriage," it's time for conservatives to say, *Enough is enough.*

Restoring Traditional Morality

Finally, conservatives must take a leadership role to restore traditional morality in the world around us. Political involvement alone is not enough. We must lead by setting an example.

No one alive today is perfect. But there is a difference between failing to live up to the highest standards, and denying that such standards exist, should exist, or could exist. The latter is the view of the Left. That's why members of the Left delight in pointing out "hypocrisy" every time a prominent conservative is discovered to have moral failings.

An idea that has taken hold among many is a twisted concept of tolerance—not simply the recognition that everyone is entitled to believe as they wish, but the insistence that no set of values is better or worse than any other. Stretching tolerance into moral blindness produces devastating outcomes for individuals and for society: adultery, the number one cause of rising divorce rates; out-of-wedlock pregnancies; the belief that ethics and morals vary with the situation; the rejection of absolute right and wrong; excuse-making for incivility and dangerous behavior; and even the decline of art and entertainment.

The mentality that "tolerance" (that is, this distorted version of tolerance) is a great virtue and "hypocrisy" the greatest sin leads to unfortunate behavior, such as parents who fail to warn their kids about drugs because they tried marijuana themselves when they were in college and they don't want to be "hypocrites."

We must never let the Left's bizarre view of "hypocrisy" stand in the way of doing what is right. Even if we are sinners ourselves—and *every* person is a sinner—we must speak out fearlessly on issues of morality.

Members of the clergy such as priests, ministers, and rabbis have a unique position in society. They are expected to speak out on how members of their flock and how people in general ought to behave. Yet our clergy mostly stay quiet on the great moral issues of our time, especially when it comes to personal behavior.

Why don't members of the clergy speak out against sex outside of marriage? My travels take me coast to coast and overseas every year, and, as a Catholic, I have attended Mass in towns great and small—yet, in the last 45 years, I can count on my fingers the number of sermons I have heard on divorce, sex outside of marriage, illegal drug use, avoiding immoral TV shows and movies, treating spouses and children properly, and, in general, conducting ourselves in a moral way both in public and at home.

If we truly believe that promiscuity, infidelity, homosexuality, and drug abuse are related to areas of decline of American life—such as the acceptance of abortion and easy divorce—why in the world aren't we saying something about it?

The clergy, as well as the rest of us, have an obligation to speak out for what we believe, speak against what we oppose, and to live by example. If we don't do these things, we really can't complain. The liberals use the platforms they have. We ought to be using ours.

Is it sometimes difficult or embarrassing to broach these subjects? Of course it is. It's always easier to "go along" than to stand up for a point of view that some people will find "old-fashioned" or, to borrow the liberals' language, oppressive, bigoted, or politically incorrect.

Yet the example of our lives and the words we speak are for many of us the only tools we have. Fortunately, they can also be the most effective tools, because nothing influences another person more than a personal example.

If conservatives want to change the culture, we have to begin by speaking up for our own point of view. And don't tell me it's too hard. If the highest price we pay for our beliefs is a few snickers from our opponents—especially when so many people in the world are imprisoned or executed for speaking the same truths—then we should consider ourselves most fortunate.

Hollywood's war on American values

The Left seeks to turn popular entertainment into propaganda for its cultural views. So a character who was an obnoxious government official might be changed to an obnoxious businessman. Today, high-tech millionaires put their money behind movies that are propaganda from the first frame to the last, and these movies are showered with praise by the Hollywood elite.

In 2006, the slate of Oscar nominees proved this point. Not all of them were blatant propaganda, and most had some artistic merit, but the overarching theme was an attack on traditional values and on America itself. "Crash" focused on racism in Los Angeles, "Brokeback Mountain" depicted the plight of homosexual cowboys, and "Capote" was a story about a famed writer who was a homosexual.

Also nominated for Best Picture was "Munich," which exposed the evil that results from terrorism—not the evil of the terrorists themselves, but the evil of the people who *fight* terrorism!

The fifth nominee was "Good Night, and Good Luck," about a TV journalist's crusade against Senator Joseph McCarthy. McCarthy was an anti-Communist U.S. Senator in the 1950s. That's right: The movie's villains weren't the Communists, who murdered 100 million people. The villains weren't the hundreds of Communist agents who —as we now know from the Venona intercepts—penetrated Washington at the highest levels, including the State Department, the Treasury Department, and the White House. No, the movie's villains were people who *fought* the Communists.

All five Best Picture nominees released in 2005 made less money *combined* than a single Christian-themed film released the same year—"The Chronicles of Narnia."

Other movies nominated for top awards included one in which chemical companies murder people, one in which corporations and the U.S. government murder people for oil, and one in which a company sexually harasses a woman until she turns for help to lawyers (the good guys). Sexual harassment is bad, sexual slavery is acceptable: This year, the motion picture academy selected, as Best Song, a little ditty about how tough life is when you're a pimp.

George Clooney, accepting the Best Supporting Actor award for the murder-for-oil movie, addressed the charge that Hollywood is out of touch with America: "We are a little bit out of touch in Hollywood every once in a while. I think it's probably a good thing. We're the ones who talked about AIDS when it was just being whis-

pered, and we talked about civil rights when it wasn't really popular
. . . [T]his group of people gave Hattie McDaniel an Oscar in 1939
when blacks were still sitting in the backs of theaters. I'm proud . . .
to be part of this community, and proud to be out of touch."

Clooney's acceptance speech was about as historically accurate
as his propaganda movies. Hollywood waited about ten years before
addressing the AIDS issue in a major film. In some cases, actors who
were, or were considered, homosexuals lost roles because people
were afraid of working with them and catching the disease.

As for civil rights, it is true that some movie and TV figures such
as Charlton Heston and Robert Dornan marched with Martin Luther
King. But for decade after decade, Hollywood produced movies like
"Birth of a Nation," which inspired the rebirth of the Ku Klux Klan,
and "Gone With The Wind," which glossed over the evils of slavery.
For decades, Hollywood edited movies to please racists—for example, by removing a Lena Horne song from the version of a film to be
shown in some parts of the country. As for Hattie McDaniel: After
winning her Oscar, she never appeared in a movie except as a ser-
vant.

Indeed, with the possible exception of the academic world, no
place in America discriminates more blatantly than Hollywood.

And no place in America cares less about the 100 million people
who died under Communism. Countless Nazis have died in Hollywood
movies, but it's hard to think of a movie with a Communist as a villain.
A Communist in a Hollywood movie is more likely to be a good guy, or
at worst a misguided person who means well, than a villain. Just as
most elites ignore genocide in places like the Sudan, Hollywood
ignores mass murder when it's committed by the Communist Left.

Hollywood presents almost all Christian ministers as hypocrites
and con men, while going to ridiculous lengths to avoid offending
Muslims. For example, when Tom Clancy's *The Sum of All Fears* was
made into a movie, a top Hollywood executive involved in the production promised that under no circumstances would the movie feature
Muslim villains, as the book had. Thus, in a movie that came out short-
ly after 9/11, the villains attacking the U.S. with an atomic bomb were,
implausibly, European "right-wingers" rather than Muslim terrorists.

JUDICIAL ACTIVISM, JUDICIAL TYRANNY

"The Constitution, on this hypothesis, is a mere thing of wax in the hands of the Judiciary, which they may twist and shape into any form they please."
— Thomas Jefferson, on the idea of judicial activism

"If the policy of the Government upon vital questions affecting the whole people is to be irrevocably fixed by decisions of the Supreme Court, the instant they are made, the people will have ceased to be their own rulers."
— Abraham Lincoln

Anyone who surveys the world scene can see that the Rule of Law is a rare and precious thing. For people to lay down their arms and agree to settle disputes through a legal system, they must respect it. They must believe it is fair, that two people in the same circumstances will be treated the same, that the rules will be applied equally. For such a system to work, the law must be clear and predictable, so that people can look at the rules themselves and determine the likely outcome of a dispute. That way, it's far less likely such disputes will arise in the first place, and people are more likely to cooperate and enter into binding agreements, and a prosperous and free society is possible.

The greatest danger to the Rule of Law is judicial activism – that is, the idea that judges should insert their own preferences into the law without regard to what the law actually says. Activist judges feel entitled to ignore the actual Constitution and write from the bench a new "Living Constitution" that advances their philosophy. Even after the successful nominations of John Roberts and Samuel Alito, at least five Supreme Court seats – a majority – are held by judicial activists, and those activists are able to veto any legislation they don't like, or take away any constitutional right they find inconvenient.

Liberals call judicial activism "progress." Americans should recognize it as tyranny.

To call this tyranny is not an overstatement. Look at the perverse sweep of the Supreme Court's reach: it prevents the American people from getting laws that restrict abortion; it protects racist "affirmative action" discrimination; it silences political speech by approving McCain-Feingold-type laws; it takes away the power of local communities to control obscenity; and it allows the confiscation of private property under eminent domain.

The Constitution is usually pretty clear. For example, under the Fifth Amendment, private property can be taken by the government only for "public use" such as a road or a public park. Yet the Supreme Court, in the *Kelo* case, allowed homes to be seized so they could be replaced with hotels, on the ground that this would somehow raise the value of the property and bring in more tax money, and therefore it was a "public use." I'm not kidding.

Now, the Framers of the Constitution wrote extensively and debated practically every word in the Constitution. Before creating the Constitution, they studied every governmental system known to history, to discern and apply the basic principles by which mankind should live. We have volume after volume of the Framers' commentaries, including the *Federalist Papers*, which were written to persuade Americans to support the proposed system of government. We have volume after volume of the writings of ordinary Americans on the issues that were raised. And the Framers knew they were creating a document for the ages, for a system that they hoped would last for all time.

In those instances when the Constitution should be changed—for example, to outlaw slavery or ensure women the right to vote—there is an amendment process involving the people's chosen representatives. When the speed of travel and communications made it possible for a new president to take office in January instead of March, and after the Great Depression exposed a need to shorten the length of a president's time as a lame duck, the Inauguration was moved. But it was done by amendment, not by some judge who decided to update the Constitution. The courts have no role in the amendment process. A judge has no more right to change the Fifth Amendment or the Ninth Amendment because the world has changed than he has the right to alter the ratio of House members to Senators because he thinks small states have too much, or too little, power in the electoral college.

Judicial activists show contempt for the very document that gives them authority. Don't they realize that with each new brazen ruling they saw off a little more of the branch on which they sit? If the words of the Founding Fathers can be so easily ignored by judicial activists, why must the American people pay attention to theirs?

Judicial activists also show contempt for the American legal system itself. Recently, the Supreme Court has taken to citing foreign law as rationale for its decisions. This bizarre practice is another way of doing an end-run around American democracy and around the Constitutional protections that Americans have. Why look for justification for your political opinions in American law, when you can look to the law of Europe (home of monarchy, fascism, and communism) or the Muslim world (home of Sharia law, under which people can be beheaded for converting to Christianity)?

As I recall, Americans fought several wars to make sure we would *not* live under the laws of other countries.

Recently, Justice Ruth Bader Ginsburg attacked efforts to prevent the Court from using foreign law, or even to criticize the Court for this horrific practice. The proposals weren't likely to pass, but that didn't stop Ginsburg from declaring (at a conference in South Africa) that "it is disquieting that they have attracted sizeable support. And one not-so-small concern—they fuel the irrational fringe."

Yes, Ginsburg, who used to work for such groups as the ACLU and the National Organization for Women, said such efforts fuel an "irrational fringe." She cited an Internet posting—a single posting—as evidence that critics of the Court encourage extremists who kill people. Someone in a chat room had called on unnamed "commandoes" to make sure that Ginsburg and Sandra Day O'Connor "will not live another week."

It's an old technique: Find some loon, and suggest that he is typical of your political opponents and that they are responsible for his actions. Blame every anti-Vietnam War protester for the actions of someone who bombs a government office, or blame every pro-life activist for the shooting of an abortion doctor. Former Senator Bob Packwood (R-Oregon) used to express fear for his life after conservatives said they were "targeting" him; of course, they were "targeting" him for defeat, not for physical harm.

Ginsburg's comments, which were posted on the Supreme Court's taxpayer-funded Web site, reflect the degree to which judicial activists have disdain for the Americans they seek to dominate. And she has used foreign law in her decision-making. For example, her 2003 opinion in *Grutter v. Bollinger* rationalized racist practices by noting that the so-called International Convention on the Elimination of All Forms of Racial Discrimination permits the "maintenance of unequal or separate rights for different racial groups." She also cited the so-called Convention on the Elimination of All Forms of Discrimination Against Women—a treaty the U.S. has not ratified, as she knew. (She later said that, "Sadly, the United States has not yet ratified it." Note the word "yet.")

Regarding this issue, Ginsburg in 2003 declared her happiness that "Our 'island' or 'Lone Ranger' mentality is beginning to change." She called for more Supreme Court citation of the UN's Universal Declaration on Human Rights—some provisions of which are worthwhile but redundant to the U.S. Constitution, other provisions of which are absurd (for example, the right to vacations, or that "No one shall be subjected to . . . attacks upon his honour or reputation"), and which, in any event are universal only in the sense that they are universally ignored.

Justice Sandra Day O'Connor, before she retired, said that, "We will find ourselves looking more frequently to the decisions of other constitutional courts" such as those in other countries.

Justice Anthony Kennedy's majority opinion in *Lawrence v. Texas* in June 2003, which struck down laws against homosexual practices, illustrated the shamelessness of this approach. Kennedy rested it on, among other things, a 1967 vote in the British Parliament in favor of legalizing homosexual acts and a 1981 European Court of Human Rights ruling that those acts are enshrined as rights under the European Convention on Human Rights. In explaining his ruling, Kennedy said that "the right the petitioners seek in this case has been accepted as an integral part of human freedom in many other countries." Yes, and in some countries homosexuals are hanged or thrown to the street from rooftops. Would Kennedy have us emulate those monstrous practices, or does he use other country's laws only when it suits his purpose?

Kennedy's hypocrisy on this issue is reminiscent of liberals' hypocrisy on respect for previous decisions, or, as it's called, *stare decisis*—"to stand by things decided." Liberal Senator Arlen Specter (R-Pennsylvania) lamely refers to the idea of "super-duper precedent." Under this principle, as liberals put it forth, conservative decisions can be overturned—the Earl Warren court disregarded 63 prior decisions, the Warren Burger court junked 61 decisions—but liberal decisions must be respected even if it turns out they were wrong.

Stare decisis has its place, of course. Conservatives accept the principle that radical change is to be avoided unless there is a very good reason for the change. Antonin Scalia has noted that "Courts do not have the time to reconsider every legal issue anew, and citizens cannot confidently plan their actions if what the Supreme Court has said a statute means today is not in all probability what the Supreme Court will say it means tomorrow." But liberals' version of *stare decisis* reminds me of that old quip, "What's mine is mine and what's yours is negotiable." Their version would enshrine liberal mistakes as the law of the land, forever, while making progress impossible. It's like the old Brezhnev Doctrine—once the Communists took a country, it could never be freed, no matter what—only applied to the courts.

The effort by Supreme Court liberals and radicals to replace the law with their own vision for society constitutes a naked grab for power. Thomas Jefferson anticipated that the Supreme Court would exercise this incremental totalitarianism over the American people by "sapping and mining slyly and without alarm the foundations of the Constitution." By this method, he wrote, the justices "can do what open force would not dare to attempt."

When judicial activists wage war on the Rule of Law, they make the law unfair, unclear, and unpredictable. When Sandra Day O'Connor was on the Supreme Court, she apparently decided each case on the basis of which side she wanted to win, rather than on the basis of which side was right. Then, after she decided who she wanted to win, she would come up with a justification for her decision. This practice, which was celebrated by the media as "moderation," made her the swing vote between the mainstream and radical factions on the Court. But it left the law in a state of confusion. Under what circumstances, if any, can abortion be restricted? Good luck figuring it out, with O'Connor on the Court.

Standing up for the Rule of Law are a few jurists such as Antonin Scalia and Clarence Thomas. They represent "originalism," the idea that the words of the Constitution should be followed, as the words were understood at the time a given provision was adopted. Some on the Left accuse originalists of supporting the original 1789 Constitution without any changes at all, as if Scalia and Thomas would allow slavery, or the denial of the vote to women, or the election of Senators by state legislatures! But that's absurd: Originalists support the Constitution *with its amendments*. Their position is that of any rational person who respects the Rule of Law: that the law means what it says and says what it means.

Some have wondered why Supreme Court nomination hearings nowadays involve much hysteria and over-the-top atmospherics. The reason is obvious: As long as Supreme Court justices can rewrite the law on a whim, as long as the Supreme Court acts as a sort of ongoing Constitutional Convention, Americans will fight to ensure that Supreme Court seats are filled by people who represent their views.

Every Supreme Court seat is precious. Scalia and Thomas believe in the Rule of Law, and most people expect that new members Roberts and Alito do, too (although we've been disappointed time and again with justices who change their minds once the power goes to their heads). If those four members do vote together on most issues, it will take only one more appointment to bring the number of mainstream jurists to five, a majority. If the five stick together, they will be in a position to outvote the Court's radicals.

What litmus test should conservatives apply to Supreme Court (and lower court) nominees and potential nominees? It is not, repeat *not*, whether they agree with us on policies such as taxes or national security or even abortion. It is entirely possible for a judge to believe that abortion-on-demand is a good thing, yet overturn *Roe* and allow states to restrict the practice. It is also possible, vice versa, for a judge to oppose abortion yet believe that *Roe* was rightly decided.

This is a difficult concept for many people to understand, but let me give an example: I believe O.J. Simpson is guilty and that his acquittal was a travesty of justice. But, if I were a judge, I would not allow him to be tried again, because the Constitution protects people from being tried more than once for the same crime. To me, the Constitution must prevail, even when the immediate result makes me feel sick. The Rule of Law is more important than any individual case or individual issue.

So, given a choice between a judge who's "personally" pro-life (but believes in judicial activism) and one who "personally" supports abortion (but supports originalism), conservatives must support the second choice – the one who would help overturn *Roe* and otherwise restore the authority of the Constitution.

Confusion over this issue is one reason that many commentators fail to understand the case of Harriet Miers, briefly President Bush's nominee for the Supreme Court. President Bush assured you she was pro-life, the commentators say, and shouldn't you believe him? The answer: It didn't matter, because her pronouncements over the years indicated that she would succumb to the lure of judicial activism – or, at least, that she lacked the fortitude and intellectual ability of Scalia or Thomas (or Janice Rogers Brown, another potential nominee), qualities necessary for someone to stand up effectively to the judicial activists.

Most conservatives were opposed to the Miers nomination even before she was caught telling a Senator that her favorite justice was

"Warren," which she said meant Warren Burger. (Some believe she actually meant Earl Warren, but suddenly remembered that conservatives didn't like Earl Warren and changed her answer to Warren Burger. I'll take her word that she really meant Burger—the ineffectual, befuddled Chief Justice appointed by Richard Nixon.) Then old remarks and writings of hers were discovered. In some of them, she was simply incoherent. In others, she was entirely accepting of the liberal rationale for such policies as "affirmative action" discrimination.

Sadly, the Miers nomination was nothing new. Fortunately, the conservative reaction, which killed the nomination, represented a new independence, a new willingness to confront President George W. Bush when he is wrong. Too often, conservatives have settled for less-than-stellar Supreme Court nominees. Between 1968 and 1993, every single nominee was selected by a Republican president, and Republican appointees eventually filled all but one seat on the Supreme Court, that of the moderate Byron White. Even today, seven of the nine justices are Republican appointees. Yet *Roe* remains intact, and judicial activism has reached unseen heights. What happened?

Well, Nixon named a single moderate-conservative to the Court, William Rehnquist, whom Reagan elevated to Chief Justice. Reagan named a single conservative, Antonin Scalia, although one can assume that unsuccessful nominees Robert Bork and Douglas Ginsburg would have been conservative. George H.W. Bush named one conservative, Clarence Thomas. Unfortunately, during that period, Nixon also appointed Lewis Powell, Harry Blackmun, and Warren Burger; Ford appointed radical John Paul Stevens; Reagan appointed Sandra Day O'Connor and Anthony Kennedy; and the elder Bush appointed radical David Souter. Thus, by the time Bill Clinton named radical Ruth Bader Ginsburg and extremely liberal Stephen Breyer, the Court was tilted heavily to the Left.

Of course, justices don't always do what an appointing president would like them to do, or what they're expected to do. Sometimes that's the result of politics: Eisenhower picked liberal Earl Warren for the Court because he had promised Warren, the governor of California, the first available Supreme Court seat in return for his support for the 1952 Republican presidential nomination. Sometimes it's the result of a mistake: Eisenhower named radical William Brennan to the Court after Brennan delivered a conservative speech on behalf of another judge, who was unavoidably absent. Often, the problem is that a justice simply lacks the intellectual firepower to stand up to a Ruth Bader Ginsburg-type ideologue with a political agenda, or to the legal and political establishment that hands out honors to justices who "grow" (become liberals) in office.

Democrats aren't shy about applying litmus tests to nominees. Bill Clinton said he would never appoint a justice who would overturn *Roe*. It's time for Republicans to start using the same sort of tests to screen out judicial activists from the judiciary and ensure that all Republican appointees support the Rule of Law, are able to explain why they do so, and have a demonstrated record of fighting for conservative legal principles.

9

CONGRESS:
THE U.S. HOUSE OF LORDS

W e knew something was rotten a few years ago when we realized that a member of the U.S. Congress had a greater chance of holding onto his seat than a member of the USSR's governing body, the Supreme Soviet. Today, the situation is even worse. Since the fall of the Soviet Union, the turnover rate for congressmen has actually declined.

Today, no matter how bad his or her record, a member of Congress has something like a 98% chance of getting reelected.

In 2004, we might as well have cancelled the congressional elections and saved taxpayers some money. That year 407 of the 435 members of the House sought reelection, and all but five won. That's a reelection rate of about 99%. In the Senate, 25 out of 26 were reelected, for a reelection rate of 96%.

As this is written, the *Cook Political Report* lists only 12 seats in the House as toss-ups for 2006 – that is, as races in which either party has a good chance to win. That's a mere 2.7% of the total number of seats in the House. Even the highest published estimate of the number of vulnerable House members amounts to less than 10% of the total, so at least 90% of House members might as well be unopposed.

Some people point to 1994, the year Newt Gingrich and his band of freshmen Republicans gave the GOP control of the House for the first time in 40 years, as an example of how the people can rise up and "throw the rascals out." Well, some rascals did indeed get thrown out, but not nearly enough. Even in that relatively tumultuous election year, nearly 90% of House incumbents who sought reelection (314 of 348) were successful, as were 92% (24 of 26) of the Senators who sought reelection. The GOP takeover of the House was dramatic, but it was hardly a mass revolt against incumbents.

Contrary to all that the Founding Fathers intended, our Congress has turned into the equivalent of Britain's old House of Lords. In the American version, you don't directly inherit a seat in the House or Senate—although a disturbingly high number of members are, in fact, the children of politicians. But once you win an election to Congress, you have a very good chance of keeping your position, if you so desire, until you retire or die.

Capitol Hill is like a feudal country with 535 fiefdoms, one for each of 100 Senators and 435 Representatives, and Congress has built castle walls to protected itself from the citizenry.

Opponents of reforms such as term limits sometimes make the argument that elections themselves serve as term limits, so no such amendments are necessary. Certainly, that's what this country's Founders thought. Term limits weren't necessary in their day because the federal government was so small and had little insulation from the general public. In the 20th Century, though, government grew in size and intrusiveness to a degree the Founders couldn't imagine.

When government is as obese as Washington is today, it is simultaneously intrusive into every aspect of your life, and impervious to your pleas for relief. Somebody has to act as mediator between the ruling bureaucracy and its subjects. Businesses hire an army of lobbyists and lawyers to handle that job. Individual citizens are pretty much left to the mercy of their Representative and Senators in Congress.

Former Congressman Tony Coelho, a California Democrat who resigned from Congress beleaguered by scandals, once explained the power of incumbency in an interview with the Capitol Hill newspaper *Roll Call*: "When I was DCCC [Democratic Congressional Campaign Committee] chairman, we undertook an incumbent protection strategy and we lost very few incumbents. I felt very strongly that no incumbent should lose. You have tremendous, tremendous tools you can use that a challenger cannot use."

Let's look at some of those "tremendous, tremendous tools."

Constituent Service

Constituent service is the most important tool available to incumbents and not available to their challengers. Staffers on Capitol Hill and in district offices spend far more time on constituent service than on any other task. Sometimes it's a request for a flag that flew over the Capitol or some other service of little consequence, but the most important and frequent requests are for help in dealing with the government bureaucracy.

Constituent service, as a type of incumbent protection, works. If a congressman helps an elderly constituent resolve her problems with the Social Security Administration, she will remember that the next time she votes. She'll tell her friends and relatives what a great job Congressman X did for her, even though the work was actually done by a staffer on the taxpayers' payroll.

When a congressman takes a principled stand on a controversial issue, he risks alienating many of his constituents. But nobody objects to having that congressman solve their problems with the bureaucracy. That's why, when senior congressional staffers were asked in a survey to identify the most important factor in boosting their boss's political support, 56% said constituent service was most important, compared to only 11% who cited his legislative record.

"You're elected to be a legislator," explained one of the staffers, "but casework and projects *keep* you elected."

In 1988 political scientist George Serra worked with a House member, who remained anonymous, to see whether this intuitive wisdom was true in fact. The congressman gave Serra two lists, totaling 419 people, of constituents who had benefited from the congressman's casework and constituents who had not. The results: Even constituents from the opposite political party who had benefited from casework had a significantly higher opinion of the representative than constituents from his own party who had not benefited from casework.

Not surprisingly, constituent service helps when the congressman seeks reelection. An American National Election Survey found that when constituents contacted their representative for ombudsman service and reported being "very satisfied" with the results, 64.7%

voted for the incumbent in the next election and only 3% voted against him. Interestingly, 32.3% did not vote. We might surmise that many of them were from the opposite political party and couldn't bring themselves to vote for the incumbent, but felt guilty about voting against someone who had helped them, so they stayed home on election day. So even when constituent service fails to persuade someone to vote *for* the incumbent, it helps prevent that person from voting *against* the incumbent.

Can you see the conflict of interest here? A congressman can win points for supporting new programs that provide goodies for constituents (at the expense of the nation's taxpayers in general). Then, when constituents run into problems with the bureaucracy administering that program, the congressman wins more points by intervening for them. This is why ever bigger government is the natural ally of incumbents.

It's a political Stockholm Syndrome, in which a hostage forms a bond with the captor who has taken him hostage (think of Patty Hearst). Congressmen create the problem, then earn your gratitude, even affection, for helping you survive it.

The most recent example was the 2003 Medicare prescription drug "entitlement." It may help bankrupt the nation, but the White House and GOP congressional leaders strong-armed Republican congressmen to vote for it as a bribe to get the senior vote. Then, when the program actually went into effect, constituents started complaining about how difficult it was to sign up for the program, and the Republican National Committee advised GOP incumbents to set up buses to tour their districts and help constituents with their sign-ups. All too often our representatives win by creating the problem, and then win again by "solving" the problem they created.

Pork-Barrel Spending

If new national programs help an incumbent win reelection, pork-barrel projects for the home district or state are even more likely to do so. After all, many of your constituents may be against the new national program, but few are going to be perceptive enough and principled enough to be against federal spending right at home. This ability to shower federal dollars on local projects is an advantage obviously not shared by an incumbent's challengers.

A group called the Congress Project examined this issue in the 1970s. It grouped first-term congressmen according to the amount of federal dollars flowing to their districts. The result? "Those with the least federal spending added 4.6% to their original victory margins when they sought reelection. The next group, with more federal spending, received a 6% hike in the victory margin. The lucky ones who procured the most local public works added a whopping 8.9% to their share of the vote."

Similarly, a later study by Robert M. Stein of Rice University and Kenneth N. Bickers of Indiana University concluded that "voter awareness of new projects in their district increases the probability of voting for the incumbent House member by 9.7%."

A follow-up study by Stein and Bickers focused on congressmen most recently elected in an open seat race by a narrow margin—those incumbents who should be the most vulnerable. They found that it was most important for these vulnerable incumbents to secure pork early in their term of office as a way to dissuade "quality challengers" from contesting them in the next election.

Of course, none of this pork helps if the constituents don't know about it. But you can bet that constituents will be told about it, over and over and over again. By press secretaries, who get paid by taxpayers.

"Visibility" – at Taxpayer Expense

Name recognition is extremely important, whether you're selling soda pop or yourself as a candidate for office. Incumbents start off with a name recognition advantage because of their previous, successful campaigns. They then fortify that advantage by maintaining their "visibility" at taxpayer expense throughout their term of office.

Here's how they do it:

Direct mail: Members of Congress may use free mailings to constituents for "official business." And since fiscal year 1999, they may use any portion of their official budget for these mailings. This is commonly called the franking privilege, or just "the frank."

Radio and television: Members of Congress have free use of audiotape- and film-preparation facilities.

Internet Web sites: Taxpayer dollars are used to develop these Web sites, and tax-supported staffers maintain and update them.

Long-distance telephone: Members of Congress may put the tab for unlimited telephone service on taxpayers.

Travel to the home district or state: Members of Congress may include travel expenses in their overall expense account.

All of this "visibility" promotion pays off. A 1994 study found that 63% of voters received mail from incumbents, while only 25% received mail from challengers; 33% heard the incumbent on the radio, while only 18% heard the challenger; 61% saw the incumbent on television, while only 34% saw the challenger; and 14% received a phone call from a member of the incumbent's staff, compared to just 5% who had talked to someone working for the challenger.

Today, congressional incumbents use sophisticated taxpayer-funded direct mail (out of their generous office budget) targeted to voters with a known particular interest in a subject. They can also use taxpayer funds to employ professional outside help to make their mailings as effective as possible.

Dane Strother, a partner at D.C.-based political consulting firm Strother-Duffy-Strother, is blunt about the advantages of using expert outside help: "I'd use a political consultant who knows the difference between direct mail and a whole lot of government talk. There are guys who move from office to office to show them how to put out cleaner pieces. If you have a legislative assistant doing a lot of the writing, you're missing a golden chance to have a professional polish them up."

And in election years, an incumbent may actually spend more on taxpayer-supported direct mail to constituents than his or her challenger spends on the entire campaign. In the first 18 months of the 1993-94 election cycle, for example, House incumbents spent $51 million on the frank. "By comparison," the National Taxpayers Union noted, "the Federal Election Commission reported that the 1,041 challengers had raised just $40.8 million over that same period for their entire campaigns."

In an article in *Roll Call* in the year 2000, a former House press secretary, John Solomon, revealed how this franking privilege is used: "I
have never seen a newsletter that positioned the elected official in
anything but the best possible light. The purpose of these mailings has
become little more than to remind citizens of who their elected officials are before they vote. It's an unfair perk of incumbency. That's
why many congressional offices accelerate the number of mailings as
the election draws closer. It's surely not because of all that summer
legislative activity."

This is especially true with incumbents facing a tough reelection
challenge. A survey of 12 vulnerable House members, for example,
revealed that they spent nearly three times as much on mailings to
their constituents in election year 2002 as they did in 2001.

One could argue that the franking privilege was justified when it
was first instituted because most of the population lived in rural areas,
far from any city, and the only form of communication available to
them was postal service. Without mail from their representatives, they
had few options for learning what was going on in Washington. But
that certainly isn't the case today. No matter where he or she lives, an
individual now is likely to have access to hundreds of newspapers and
magazines, dozens of radio stations, 100 or more TV channels, and the
Internet, all bombarding him or her with political news.

Congress Spends Money on (Surprise!) Itself

How much does Congress spend on salaries, office expenses, and
the like? You might think that that information would be readily available, but no. While I was investigating this issue, the spokesman for
one Washington think tank said that they tried to figure out the total
but gave up because it was too hard to get the information. Another
staffer at a taxpayer watchdog organization said they'd never even
tried. The most recent report on congressional expenses is a study
from the National Taxpayers Union, which covered the year 2001 and
was published in 2003. (As this is written, an updated study is in the
works but not yet available.)

For that study, the NTU had to utilize an outside contractor, who
went through some 4,000 pages of materials – materials that, even in

this Internet age, are not available in electronic form – in order to esti-mate eight categories of spending for each member of the House. It is necessary to do this on a quarterly basis, as there are constant "adjust-ments" in the members' accounts.

As difficult as this was for the House, you can forget trying to do

National Taxpayers Union slams Congress

Excerpts from an April 17, 2003 press release by the nonpartisan National Taxpayers Union, about its difficulties in researching a study of House of Representatives expenses:

"'Despite the zeal for campaign finance legislation in the last Congress, many incumbents have taken advantage of loose restrictions on mass mailings to boost their chances for reelec-tion,' said study author David Keating, who is Senior Counselor for NTU. . . .

"NTU found the most egregious data inconsistencies in House mass mailing expenses. A reform law requires accurate disclo-sure of mass mailing expenses, but this law is clearly being flout-ed by many offices. . . .

"'The House's recordkeeping for mass mail makes a mockery of the law, and raises the question of whether some Representatives are evading disclosure by failing to make accurate reports,' Keating said. . . .

"[S]pending figures for each office were tough to pinpoint, because of the thousands of 'adjustments' for a given year's costs that appear in subsequent reports (in some cases up to two years later). 'The House spending disclosure reports are, simply put, a mess,' Keating observed. . . .

"'The House's bookkeeping makes it difficult for citizens to mon-itor Congress . . . ,' Keating concluded."

this for the Senate. The House gives you thousands of pages of paper-work, and leaves it to you to try and figure out what it all means. The Senate's attitude is that it's none of your business at all.

My staff and I supplemented the valuable information from the National Taxpayers Union by consulting the appendix to the budget of the Office of Management and Budget; the Office of Personnel Management; the Congressional Research Office; and the

Congressional Management Foundation. This is what we found.

The Office-Budget Money Advantage of Incumbency

The first major advantage incumbents have over challengers is their generous taxpayer-funded budgets for their office operations.

Today more than 30,000 people work in the Capitol Hill bureaucracy, the majority of them as staffers for members of Congress. Their job is to make their bosses look good, mostly through constituent services and by raising their "visibility" in the ways I've mentioned. In 2006, these staffers are being paid salaries totaling more than $390 million. That's a $390 million money advantage not enjoyed by their bosses' challengers. Challengers have to get their money to pay staff from private sources.

Each Representative is entitled to 18 fulltime staffers for Capitol Hill and home district offices. That figure does *not* include the many employees of House committees and subcommittees. It's common for many of them to spend more of their time helping out the congressman who sponsors them than on actual committee work.

Then there are those other expenses that help the incumbent congressman get reelected, such as taxpayer-funded offices back in the home district, taxpayer-funded postage and printing allowances for direct mail to constituents, and taxpayer-funded allowances for travel between Washington, D.C. and the home district.

Putting them all together, we get these taxpayer-funded advantages:

> $392 million for staff salaries
> $45 million for district offices (other than salaries)
> $45 million for direct mail to constituents (postage and printing)
> $22 million for travel to the home districts

TOTAL annual incumbent office-budget advantage: $504 million for the entire House of Representatives, or, on average, $1,160,000 for each individual member of the House.

All of these funds go to raise the visibility, name-recognition level, and reputation of the incumbent. And the campaign for reelection starts right after the initial election, so for the two-year term the incumbent's office-budget advantage over any challenger comes to $2,320,000.

Now you can start to see why so few incumbents are ousted. But we're just getting started.

The Campaign-Money Advantage for Incumbents

I won't bore you with the intricacies of campaign finance regulations. I'll simply note that pieces of legislation like McCain-Feingold are not "reforms." Such legislation, and all the campaign finance regulations they cause to be created, are, in effect, incumbent-protection laws. They are written by incumbents for incumbents, and their real purpose—to weigh down challengers and protect incumbents—was suggested by formber Congressman Bill Clay (D-Missouri): "If there's one thing we don't need, it's more candidates running for Congress."

To discourage that kind of calamity, Congress restricts the amount of money you can give to a candidate to around $2,100 for each primary or general election. That rule is presented as an effort to keep "big money" out of elections, but in reality it's incumbency insurance. After all, as we've seen, incumbents enjoy tremendous other financial advantages not shared by their challengers, so any limitation on spending works to their advantage; they get a big head start in any race. And since most challengers start off as complete or relative unknowns, they have to raise a lot more money just to become visible themselves.

(Yes, some challengers have their own advantages, as when an incumbent governor runs against a sitting member of Congress. But when I talk about a challenger, I'm usually picturing a true citizen-legislator as envisioned by the Founders, a private citizen who gives up a few years of his life to public service. That sort of person is not likely to have built up a list of people who will give him $2,100. Because of incumbent protection laws, we see professional politicians playing a game of musical chairs, jumping, say, from the House to the Senate to the Governor's mansion. These people have built up donor lists that enable them to challenge an incumbent. But they are still profession-

House incumbents:
Their bottom-line dollar advantage

Thinking of running against an incumbent member of the House? Here's what you're up against:

> \$2,320,000 incumbent's office-budget money advantage
> \$822,000 incumbent's campaign-money advantage
> \$3,142,000 incumbent's total money advantage

In other words, you have to raise \$3,142,000 just to break even with the incumbent. At something like a \$2,100 limit on individual contributions, that means you, the less visible candidate, have to convince almost 1,500 people to give you the maximum contribution, or some 31,420 people to contribute \$100 to your campaign.

And that's just to break even with the incumbent. But the incumbent is raising money, too, so you need a total of almost 1,900 people giving the maximum contribution, or 39,640 people giving you \$100 each, to match the incumbent.

Remember: That's just to stay even with the incumbent in fundraising. To actually *beat* him or her, you need a lot more.

Good luck with that.

al lifetime politicians, divorced from the realities of life as a citizen in private employment.)

Incumbents have other big advantages in raising money: They and their parties know exactly who their most likely sources of funding are – the contributors to their previous campaigns. A typical challenger has to start pretty much from scratch, and that's much more expensive. Also, incumbents have been doing favors for businesses and individuals during the years of their incumbency, and can expect to be paid back at election time with campaign money and votes. Challengers can't.

The result is that it's a lot easier for an incumbent to get \$2,100 contributions at a much lower cost. How much easier? Here are the figures from the Federal Election Commission showing campaign funds raised in contested House and Senate races in 2004:

U.S. House of Representatives
- \$451,731,036 raised by 407 incumbents in contested races
- \$117,105,658 raised by their 798 challengers
- \$334,625,378 more money raised by incumbents than by their challengers

This amounts, on average, to a campaign-money advantage of $822,175 per incumbent facing a challenger.

U.S. Senate
- $171,687,818 raised by 26 incumbent Senators running for reelection in 2004
- $78,701,100 raised by their 123 challengers
- $92,986,718 more money raised by incumbents than their challengers

This amounts, on average, to a campaign-money advantage of $3,576,412 per incumbent over his or her challengers.

You can see how much easier it is for incumbents to raise money than for their challengers. But note that there are a lot more challengers than incumbents, including both primaries and the general election. This means that there are a lot more challengers around to divide up that much-smaller pie.

In the next chapter, let's see what we can do to restore some democracy on Capitol Hill.

RESTORING DEMOCRACY TO THE POLITICAL MARKETPLACE

Few members of Congress have ever had to meet a payroll for a real company. (A law firm doesn't count.) Few members of Congress have any real business experience at all. As a result, few know anything about what it's like to run a business under the laws passed by Congress.

In this regard, George McGovern, who was a Democratic Senator from South Dakota and the Democrats' nominee for president in 1972, was typical of members of Congress. Throughout his political career, he championed efforts to impose more and more obligations and regulations on business. But then, after losing his seat in 1980, he tried to start a business of his own, and when that failed, he admitted: "I wish I had had a better sense of what it took to [meet a payroll] when I was in Washington."

But business experience is not the only sort of experience that's mostly lacking in Congress. What's lacking today is *any* real memory of what it's like to be a private citizen of the United States who doesn't work for the government. We are ruled by career politicians, usually jumping from local politics or state politics to federal politics. They live lives devoted to ruling over people.

It's hard to imagine a greater violation of the vision of this country's Founders. They didn't put term limits into the Constitution, first, because they assumed elections would act as term limits, and second, because they couldn't imagine why anyone would want to spend his or her entire adult life in politics. Just as the role model for the military was the citizen-soldier, who returned to private life after defending his country, the role model in politics was the citizen-legislator, who distinguished himself in a private career, put in a term or two in elected office, then either returned to a private career or retired.

"In free governments," Benjamin Franklin explained in 1787, "the rulers are the servants and the people their superiors and sovereigns. For the former, therefore, to return among the latter is not to degrade but to promote them."

Career politicians have a view of life entirely different from that of citizen-legislators. What we need are fewer career politicians and more citizen-legislators.

A citizen-legislator has many different interests in life, including strong interests in things other than politics. Most of his or her life is spent pursuing those other interests. Success in a nonpolitical career demonstrates the citizen-legislator's competency and leadership ability, and it makes him or her well known. Such a person sees political office as a temporary public service; the citizen-legislator plans to return to a private life surrounded by his or her fellow citizens. Such a person is not likely to risk standing back home by acting like commissars in Washington. Such a person is likely to consider the long-term interest of the people on issues ranging from national defense to public indebtedness.

You can relate to a citizen-legislator. They have real lives. But today it's hard to think of someone in federal office who is a citizen-legislator.

Today, public life is dominated by career politicians. They think about politics almost all day, every day; they eat, drink, and breathe politics. A rare admission of this problem came from Senator Warren Rudman (R-New Hampshire), who explained that he retired voluntarily because "the longer you stay in public office, the more distant the outside world becomes." He said one Democratic senator congratulated him on his retirement, and confessed that "I wish I had the guts to do what you've done, but I'm afraid to leave. I don't know what I'd do with my life."

Why is this distinction between citizen-legislators and career politicians important to conservatives? Because we believe that almost all of the good things that happen in our nation and our society come from the private sector, not the government. A politician who loses that perspective as a private citizen, or worse, never had it in the first place, is truly unbalanced, and in office is a danger to all of us.

Alan Ehrenhalt, editor of *Governing* magazine, explained that career politicians "tend not only to enjoy politics but to believe in government as an institution. The more somebody is required to sacrifice time and money and private life to run for the city council, for the state legislature, or for Congress, the more important it is for that person to believe that government is a respectable enterprise with crucial work to do."

Doug Bandow, a scholar who was then at the Cato Institute, came to a similar conclusion: "Over time, career legislators are more likely to promote the interest of the establishment of which they are part than that of the larger public. And perhaps that is not surprising. If the bulk of one's time is spent meeting with lobbyists, constituents, bureaucrats, and other supplicants—all of them touting the virtues of expanded government power in one form or another—one may actually come to believe in that power."

Thomas Jefferson warned us about this: "Whenever a man has cast a longing eye on [offices], a rottenness begins in his conduct." And what rottenness we see today!

When you read or hear about illegal and immoral conduct in Washington, remember that what you hear and read is just the tip of the iceberg. The great mass of Washington corruption is unseen, hidden beneath the surface.

A study by the Competitive Enterprise Institute found that senior (long-serving) representatives were more likely than junior representatives to vote for pork and special interests. A National Taxpayers Union study confirmed that, on average, members of Congress are more likely to support new spending the longer they stay in Congress. And a study by analyst James Payne found that Capitol Hill has developed a "culture of spending," with the victims of government intervention mostly absent and unseen; Payne found that a congressman's propensity to spend taxpayers' money increases by two-thirds by his eighth term. Career politicians, conservative as well as liberal, tend to "grow" in office – "grow" being Washingtonese for "move to the Left."

Conservative leader Paul Weyrich has said that he's never seen a U.S. Senator have a better second term, from a conservative perspective, than his first term. There are a thousand stories in Washington, D.C. of politicians who eventually learned "to go along in order to get along."

Stop Stacking the Deck Against Challengers and Grassroots Organizations

In the previous chapter, I discussed how incumbents use campaign finance laws to build their fortresses against challengers. It follows that one of our first items of business, as conservatives, should be to repeal these laws, starting with the limitations on individual contributions to political campaigns.

The experience of the past half-century is that allowing large donations, fully disclosed to the public, makes campaigns more honest and more representative of the little guy. The reason is that a principled leader, whether on the Left or the Right, can often find a few big donors—wealthy, civic-minded citizens—who will finance a campaign based on principle. A handful of large contributions can free the candidate to campaign among the people, rather than spending almost all of his or her time raising money.

That is what happened with Senator McGovern, who challenged the Democratic Party establishment in 1972 and won the presidential nomination. Under the current campaign finance law, McGovern's successful candidacy would likely have been impossible.

Of particular interest to conservatives: Former Congressman Jack Kemp campaigned for president in 1988 as a conservative (he was a former Reagan aide) and as the architect of the Reagan tax cuts. Kemp, a pro football great, was articulate and at ease in communicating with voters. But he didn't have a personal fortune to spend on a campaign, and has said it was difficult to run for president because trying to do so with $1,000 contributions (the limit at the time) was like "trying to fill a swimming pool with a teaspoon." So, despite being considered a front-runner for the GOP nomination, he didn't even run when the Republican nomination was up for grabs in 1996.

At the same time, Kemp supporter Steve Forbes *did* have the kind of money needed for a presidential race. He could easily have financed Kemp's presidential campaign, and no one in his right mind would have considered it a sign of corruption. Forbes was a strong supporter, over many years, of the "supply side" ideas for which Kemp was the most prominent spokesman. Unfortunately for Kemp, for Forbes, and for the country, Forbes was forbidden from contributing all but a pittance of his money to Kemp's campaign. However, nothing prohibited him from running himself and spending whatever he wanted of his own money. You can contribute as much as you can afford, as long as you're the candidate. So Forbes ran for president himself.

Now, Steve Forbes is a terrific fellow, a man of great intelligence, a patriot dedicated to conservative principles. But he is not a particularly effective campaigner, and had almost no chance of being elected president. With the same money, Kemp might have been elected, and would have had a chance to continue the Reagan Revolution.

This pattern is being repeated in one campaign after another, at all levels where there are contribution limits. The major political parties now look for "self-financing" candidates – that is, millionaires who can pay for their campaigns themselves. Elective office, to a degree greater than ever before, is filling up with the rich. Typical is Jon Corzine (D-New Jersey), the former Goldman Sachs executive who bought himself a U.S. Senate seat and then his state's governorship.

So-called "reform" laws are increasingly aimed at grassroots organizations that represent the American people in the political process. They are part of an effort to do an end-run around the First Amendment, in order to protect incumbents.

Incumbents are threatened by grassroots lobbyists from a wide variety of organizations that take a stand on issues. From the National Rifle Association to the Sierra Club, ranging from Right to Left, these groups call incumbents on the carpet. So the incumbents pass laws to restrict the activities of these groups.

McCain-Feingold, the most prominent recent addition to campaign regulations, does this by prohibiting these groups from broadcasting any issue ads that refer to specific candidates for federal office in the 30 days before a primary, or 60 days before a general election. Why were those dates chosen? Because "that's when people are most interested in the elections," according to Congressman Martin Meehan (D-Massachusetts), one of the law's most ardent supporters. In other words, McCain-Feingold and similar laws are intended to silence the voices of ordinary citizens who contribute to these organizations. And they are designed to do so at exactly the times when grassroots citizens can have the greatest impact.

The real purpose of McCain-Feingold-type laws is to silence *your* voice in the campaign process, by placing a gag on the organizations that represent you and your views. Such measures are the gravest threat to your free speech that exists today.

Despite all their advantages, incumbents want still more protection from competition. And they are shameless. Now the corrupt politicians who pass corrupt laws like McCain-Feingold are tying to use stories of Washington corruption as an excuse to pass more corrupt laws! The proposed "Honest Leadership and Open Government Act" would impose prior restraints on grassroots organizations, with burdensome quarterly reporting. Such measures are intended to make grassroots lobbying too expensive for various causes, especially those with small followings (and most big causes started out as causes with small followings).

The only true reform needed is *transparency* for candidates and parties. All political contributions should be disclosed to the public, over the Internet, *immediately* as they are accepted by a candidate or party. There's no excuse any more for a 10-day delay, much less a 30-day or even longer delay in disclosing contributions. Simply stipulate that any contribution must be reported on the appropriate Web site before the party or candidate can deposit and use it. Then let the voters decide if they think some contributions are inappropriate, too large, or too anything, and vote accordingly. Passing judgment on the financing of campaigns should be in the hands of *voters*, not self-interested incumbents.

Seeking the Next Jefferson

When it comes to McCain-Feingold-type laws, the relevant part of the First Amendment reads: "Congress shall make no law . . . abridging the freedom of speech, or of the press; or the right of the people peaceably to assemble, and to petition the government for a redress of grievances."

What part of "no law" don't they understand?

To make absolutely clear what the Founders meant when they wrote the First Amendment, it is useful to look at the various wordings they considered. James Madison's original version provided: "The people shall not be deprived or abridged of their right to speak, to write, or to publish their sentiments; and the freedom of the press, as one of the great bulwarks of liberty, shall be inviolable." A special committee of the House of Representatives rewrote it this way: "The freedom of speech and of the press, and the right of the people peaceably to assemble and consult for their common good, and to apply to the Government for redress of grievances, shall not be infringed." Finally, a Senate version read that "Congress shall make no law abridging the freedom of speech, or of the press, or the right of the people peaceably to assemble and consult for their common good, and to petition the government for a redress of grievances."

During the administration of John Adams, Congress passed the Sedition Act, which made it a crime to criticize government officials. Under this law, newspaper editors were jailed. What saved America from totalitarianism was the election, in 1800, of Thomas Jefferson as president, on a promise to dismantle this despicable act. It was a promise he kept. Jefferson referred to his election as the "Revolution of 1800," every bit as important as the Revolution of 1776, and he was right.

President Bush won the Republican nomination in 2000 in part because he promised to veto the anti-First Amendment McCain-Feingold legislation. Once in office, though, he signed it, and the Republican-dominated Supreme Court refused to enforce the Constitution and strike it down.

Who will save us from those who would destroy the First Amendment? Who will be the Thomas Jefferson of the 21st century?

What Needs to be Done

> To reform the federal government, we need to outlaw pork-barrel spending such as earmarks, not only because we can't afford such wasteful outlays but because it constitutes blatant bribery of voters by incumbents. Earmarks serve as payoffs to businesses and special interests for past support or hoped-for future support. Judging by the behavior of our Republican Congresses so far, as with each Democratic Congress before them, there will be lots of talk and promises about this, and no action. In other words: *It won't happen if we practice politics as usual.*

Incumbents have too many built-in advantages over challengers. There's no reason taxpayers should subsidize their use of unsolicited direct mail, including their newsletters to constituents, as well as radio, television, telephone service, and use of the Internet. We should make incumbents pay for these services out of their own campaign treasuries, just as challengers must. *But it won't happen if we practice politics as usual.*

All campaign finance regulations should be repealed, as violations of our First Amendment rights, except for those requiring immediate and total transparency. *But it won't happen if we practice politics as usual.*

George Washington started the tradition of voluntary term limits when he refused to run for a third term. America doesn't need another king, he said. You might say that, a century and a half later, Franklin Delano Roosevelt decided America *did* need a king; he was elected to four terms as president. Toward the end of his life, FDR was so weak that he could only work an hour or two each day—a condition that may have facilitated the Soviet conquest of Eastern and Central Europe and that launched the Cold War.

To guard against such a thing happening again, the 22nd Amendment was passed, limiting a president to two terms.

We need term limits for members of Congress as well.

A vote on congressional term limits was a promise in the Republicans' Contract with America, the party platform that helped lead to the GOP takeover of the House in 1994. But when the new Republican leadership brought the issue to a vote in 1995, it gained a simple majority of "yes" votes, not the two-thirds majority required for a constitutional amendment. Rather than build on that first vote, the Republicans quickly lost interest. By early 1997, it was a dead issue. Potomac Fever, the fabled disease of Washington politicians, was already affecting these self-styled "Republican revolutionaries."

It is clear that we will not get, any time soon, a constitutional amendment imposing term limits passed by a two-thirds vote in Congress. Today it wouldn't get a simple majority vote. So we must bypass Congress, because term limits *won't happen if we practice politics as usual.*

One route to a term limits amendment is to get the legislatures of two-thirds of the states (34 of the 50) to call a constitutional convention to draft a term-limits measure, which then would go to all the states and would require approval by three-fourths (38 of 50) to become law.

Abolish the Two-Party Cartel

Imposing term limits will do much good, but it is not a panacea. By itself, it still leaves the duopoly of the Democratic and Republican parties in control of everything. (Duopoly = a monopoly shared by two.) To make those two Big Government parties truly responsive to the voters, we need another major reform, to make it possible for so-called third parties to flourish.

What are some of the complaints commonly voiced about American elections today? The "good-government" types invariably cite low voter turnout. People who vote on the basis of political philosophy or issues cite the lack of any real choice, because, as Governor George Wallace (D-Alabama) put it, "There isn't a dime's worth of difference between the parties."

I have a solution that will satisfy both those complaints. Give all political parties a level playing field. Remove all the present restrictions on third party and independent candidates that don't apply to Republicans and Democrats. Get rid of restrictions on campaign financing that give Republicans and Democrats a tremendous advantage over third parties and independents. And do as the State of New York does—allow candidates to run on more than one party ticket and add those votes together.

A major reason for the Democrat-Republican duopoly is that people don't want to "throw away" their votes by voting for a third party or independent candidate. Such a candidate must first prove he or she has substantial support, before the media and the voters will pay him or her any attention. But he must get the attention in order to attract substantial support. It's a Catch 22 that keeps most such candidates from having a serious chance.

Jesse Ventura was elected governor of Minnesota only because he was allowed to participate in debates with the major party candidates, something that most independent/third party candidates aren't allowed to do. Most other such candidates who have won in recent years did so only because one of the major parties failed to run a serious candidate.

But if a candidate could run as, say, the candidate of a major party *and* of a Conservative Party or Reform Party or Libertarian Party, or whatever, and add all his or her votes together, alternate parties could become viable. In New York, alternate parties have, in concert with major parties, help to elect many governors, senators, and New York City mayors. Occasionally, alternate parties have even elected candidates on their own, such as U.S. Senator James Buckley, who won in 1970 on the Conservative Party ticket, defeating the Democratic and Republican candidates.

The result of restoring the third party and independent option will be a rebirth of democracy in America. Of course, a rebirth of democracy is the last thing our incumbents from the two major parties want. So how do we push through a reform measure that both parties oppose? I have an idea.

Contrary to what some Americans assume, there is nothing in the Constitution mandating a two-party system. It's true that two major parties are a natural result of a winner-take-all election system such as we have in the United States. But in the past, when Americans enjoyed many freedoms that have now disappeared, third parties played a valuable role in keeping the political process fluid and open to new thinking. Typically a third party would grow until it replaced one of the two dominant parties, and the party that was now No. 3 would gradually disappear, with its former members joining No. 1 or the new No. 2.

Thus the Federalists were replaced in the 1820s by the National Republican Party, they were replaced in turn by the Whigs, and the Whigs gave way to the Republican Party. The GOP began as a minor party in 1856, and its standard bearer in 1860, Abraham Lincoln, became president when the two major parties were still the Whigs and the Democrats. This natural evolution, based on voter preferences, would be all but impossible under today's artificial restrictions.

As I noted, today's campaign finance restrictions shut out third parties. When it takes $100 million for a Republican or Democratic candidate to get his party's presidential nomination, relying on all the proven databases of contributors to his party, how can an independent candidate without those databases find 50,000 people who will give $2,100 each? He might be able to jumpstart his campaign if he can convince 10 like-minded people to contribute $1 million or $2 million each, using that initial $10-$20 million to get the publicity necessary to get traction as a candidate. But existing law doesn't allow that. That's why only billionaires willing to use their own money, people like Ross Perot or Donald Trump, can consider running as an independent for the presidency today. The same goes for independent candidates for Congress or state office; the costs are less, but built-in inequities are the same.

Third parties face state ballot access restrictions that don't exist for the Democrats or Republicans. It's easier for an independent candidate to get on the ballot in the former Soviet republic of Ukraine than in the state of Georgia. And in 35% to 40% of state legislative races, the voters don't even have a choice between a Republican and a Democrat, much less an independent candidate. Why vote? Such an "election" is a farce.

Imagine if this kind of legalized duopoly was allowed in the economic sphere. Coke and Pepsi, not satisfied with being the two most-popular—and profitable—soft drinks, decide they want to be the *only* ones. So they get laws passed to shut out competition.

> No investor is allowed to invest more than $2,100 in another soft drink company.

> Other companies cannot advertise from Thursday to Sunday, when most people do their shopping.

> And, before it can get any shelf space at all, a third-brand company must present petitions signed by 100,000 customers who can prove they have not consumed a Coke or Pepsi that year. Also, those petitions must be approved by people who were appointed to their jobs by the Coke and Pepsi companies.

If we had such a system, would you be surprised when you found *only* Coke and Pepsi on the shelves of your grocery store? And if you preferred mineral water or a Snapple or *anything* else, would you bother "voting" with your grocery money? But this is exactly what we've allowed to happen to our political process, and yet we shamelessly call it "democracy."

One solution is to return to the situation that existed in a much healthier U.S. democracy prior to the 1890s.

According to Census Bureau figures, nearly 80% of eligible voters showed up at the polls between 1876 and 1892, compared to an anemic 50% or less today. We had two healthy major parties with very different platforms, and we didn't have gridlock like today. At the same time, voters who didn't buy into the Democratic or Republican platforms were free to start their own Farmer's Party, Greenback Party, Union Labor Party, or People's Party. The only reasons those parties didn't rise to the top, unlike Lincoln's Republican Party, was either because one of the major parties adopted their most popular programs, or because not enough people believed in their programs in the first place. They didn't fail because the decks were stacked against them.

Political parties should return to being private associations of voters, not arms of the state as they are today. We should repeal all taxpayer financing of campaigns, and require each party to pay for its own primaries and conventions.

Now, I'm not smoking something that makes me hallucinate, so I know that the odds of our Republican and Democratic incumbents returning to our democratic past are nil. They have too much at stake in protecting their legislated duopoly. But I do have a suggestion that might be a bit more feasible.

There are states where the voters are more independent-minded and libertarian (with a small "l") than in most places – Alaska, Washington, Idaho, New Hampshire come to mind, perhaps also Vermont and Maine. Why don't the third parties, from the Libertarian and Constitution parties on the Right to the Green and Socialist parties on the Left, cooperate on this project? Each party can figure out where it might be strongest, then concentrate in that state on a joint Left-Right campaign, based on good-government and democratic concepts rather than one particular ideology, to repeal all of the state's ballot-access laws.

Imagine one state with that kind of freedom, the kind of freedom our forefathers had, up until the twentieth century. I think the results would be dramatic and positive, with a return to real debates on real issues, tough competition and greater turnover between the parties, and a vastly increased voter turnout. And I am confident that the first state's ballot-box democracy would prove so contagious that it would spread rapidly to more and more states across the nation.

Even more significant would be to expand the right of initiative and referendum.

Twenty-three states and many cities provide for the right of the people to enact and repeal legislation through a process of petition and popular vote. Of course, this was the vehicle that Howard Jarvis used to bypass an unresponsive California Legislature and pass Proposition 13, the seminal tax relief measure.

This vital tool of direct democracy should be expanded into every state and at the federal level.

If it existed at the federal level, it could be used to restore prayer in school, to end the raid on the Social Security Trust Fund, to permit public displays of the Ten Commandments, and to require a balanced federal budget, to name just a few issues. Polls have consistently shown extremely high percentages of the people support these concepts, and yet Congress keeps them bottled up.

On the state level, the process of initiative and referendum provides a great escape valve for the actions and inactions of the legislatures. As the saying goes, "The two things you don't ever want to watch being made are sausages and laws."

So, in this second American Revolution, who will take the lead?

"Big Government Conservatism": Corrupt, Not Compassionate

If it hurts people, it ain't compassionate.

"Compassionate conservatism" was a term—a slogan, really—introduced to the public during the 2000 election campaign. But what could "compassionate conservatism" possibly mean? Conservatism (with no qualifier) represents compassion. It seeks to protect the families that nurture children, and to protect the unborn, the sick, the disabled, and the elderly whom some would toss aside.

Conservatism fights for freedom, and the prosperity that goes with it, for anyone and everyone. It works to build a society with a big enough economic surplus that it can afford to train and educate the less fortunate so that they can work and become independent – a society prosperous enough to care for those *incapable* of helping themselves.

Give a man a fish, and you feed him for a day. Teach him to fish, and you feed him for a lifetime. Allow him to sell his fish and use the proceeds to make life better for himself and his family, and you build a civilization.

It isn't fun to demand that people take responsibility for themselves. It doesn't usually make you popular, at least in the short run. But it *is* compassionate.

It's the Left that created the welfare state, making generation after generation dependent on others. It's the Left that made the ghettos permanent. It's the Left that forces people to live behind bars – bars on their windows to protect them from criminals. It's the Left that built the collapsing system of government "schools" that don't teach. It's the Left that taxes away people's earnings, takes a generous cut off the top, and makes people beg to get some of it back. It's the Left that casts its lot with the despots and kleptocrats of the world.

So when the term "compassionate conservative" was first used by George W. Bush, it created confusion. Perhaps, some analysts thought, he wasn't trying to distinguish himself from mainstream conservatism; perhaps he was just trying to emphasize conservatism's compassionate aspects. Or he was just trying to win an election, softening the Republicans' stern image as (in Chris Mathews's phrase) the "Daddy party" by making himself look like a caring nurturer—like the Democrats, the "Mommy party."

Now we know what "compassionate conservatism" is. It is *liberal* conservatism, or, as some put it, "Big Government conservatism." It is an attempt to use liberal means to achieve conservative ends. The Medicare prescription drug benefit, which includes some elements of free choice for seniors. No Child Left Behind, which seeks to create standards for measuring educational success. The Faith-Based Initiative, funneling government money to religious organizations that, in the past, have been denied government funds because they were religious.

Now we also know this about "compassionate conservatism": It doesn't work. It busts the budget, and further federalizes government schools, and tempts religious organizations to subject themselves to Big Government regulation and control. If it was intended to buy votes, it doesn't even do that! Seniors see the drug benefit program as a web of confusion that benefits pharmaceutical companies; the No Child program gives teachers' unions a legitimate reason to attack Republicans for forcing them to "teach to the test"; and the Faith-Based Initiative helps make religious charities dependent on (and loyal to) politicians and bureaucrats.

"Compassionate conservatism" means a runaway federal government that equates compassion with nonstop governmental activity and spending, no matter how feckless the results. It accepts the premise put forth by the Left, that mainstream conservatism is uncompassionate, and it puts Republicans in a bidding war with Democrats and the Left to determine who is more compassionate. (Hint: It's the side that spends the most money and hires the most bureaucrats.)

It weakens state and local governments—levels of government that are closer to the people and more subject to their direct control. That is a violation of one of the key tenets of conservatism, that governmental authority must shift away from Washington and in the direction of states, localities, neighborhoods, families, and individuals.

Decades of social dysfunction should have taught us by now that most government programs labeled "compassionate" aren't compassionate at all. A federal government that infantilizes the people, while accruing more and more power to itself, is practicing a false compassion.

Ending the Culture of Corruption

Perhaps you've heard of the "Culture of Corruption." It's the latest Democratic Party slogan aimed at Republicans, suggesting that Republicans' leadership of Congress has become corrupt and that the Democrats must be voted in to replace them.

Unfortunately, the Democrats have a point. The Republicans on Capitol Hill have begun acting like Democrats used to, when they were in control. They have become too close to the lobbyists that swarm around Capitol Hill like locusts.

As the saying goes: Some people get into politics to do good, and end up doing very well. There's nothing wrong with making a living in politics, as a professional campaign consultant or policy analyst or lobbyist or Capitol Hill aide or in any other legitimate job. Often, though, a person in politics loses sight of the principles that once guided him. He is corrupted by the money and power.

That's why we need to keep politics as moral as possible, to take away the opportunity for corruption. We need to limit access to that money and power, by putting limits on government itself.

Years ago, John Connally, who had been Secretary of the Treasury, was tried (and acquitted) on bribery and corruption charges related to raising the price of milk. Few commentators asked: What in the world is the federal government doing setting the price of milk?

If the government doesn't set the price of milk, no government official will ever be bribed to raise it.

Phony indignation about the latest Washington scandal won't stop corruption. Neither will mountains of new paperwork and "ethics" regulations on people trying to influence officeholders. There are too many ways to get around bureaucratic regulations. (Can't pay off a Senator directly? Hire the spouse.) And such regulations are more likely to trample someone's First Amendment rights, or trip up an honest but disorganized person, than to foil a wrongdoer.

When the U.S. Supreme Court upheld the McCain-Feingold law that limits First Amendment freedoms, it justified the law on the ground that it helps prevent the appearance of corruption. Those of us who don't sit on the Supreme Court are more interested in preventing actual corruption than in preventing the appearance of corruption – that is, in putting a Band-Aid over corruption to hide its existence, which is what McCain-Feingold does.

Only by taking money and power from Big Government – from politicians, bureaucrats, and organized special interests – can we effectively limit corruption.

What Should Republicans Do?

The betrayal of conservatism by Republicans in Washington has reduced or eliminated their advantage on the question of which party will be the better stewards of taxpayers' money. However, there are things that can be done to restore that advantage.

❋ Reverse the Decline in American Education

The federal Department of Education was born out of corruption; it was created in 1979 to pay off the national teachers' union for its 1976 endorsement of Jimmy Carter. In Fiscal 2005, it spent nearly $75 billion; in 2006, its budget is nearly $90 billion. It has more than 5,000 employees, serving as a gigantic jobs program for liberals. And between 2000 and 2005, under Republican rule, discretionary spending by the department increased 60 percent!

Government schools should be run by parents and locally elected school boards, not by the federal government. This department's growth coincides with a dramatic decline in the quality of American education, and eliminating it is a step toward reversing that decline.

Republicans should welcome the growth of charter schools, home schooling, and voucher programs—anything to give parents more choice and children more access to a real education. An excellent example of public service related to this issue is the Children's Scholarship Fund (http://scholarshipfund.org), founded in 1998, which has provided tuition assistance (an average of 50% of tuition) for some 70,000 children to attend non-government schools.

Krista Kafer of the Heritage Foundation reports that the school choice movement is picking up speed:

> School choice is in high demand and growing. Twenty years ago, few states had policies or programs allowing parents the freedom to make choices in their children's education. Today, 11 states and the District of Columbia have state-funded scholarship programs or provide tax relief for education expenses or contributions to scholarship funds. Most states have charter or magnet schools, dual enrollment programs are common, and all 50 states allow parents to home school their children. . . .
>
> From 1994 to 2003, the number of home-schooled students tripled, from 345,000 to 1,100,000. On average, home school students have higher academic achievement than students in public or private schools. Home-schooled elementary school students tend to perform one grade level higher than their peers in traditional schools. By high school, they are four grade levels above the national average. Nearly all home-schooled students participate in at least two extracurricular activities such as dance, sports, music, and volunteerism. In fact, the average home school student participates in five such activities.

The No Child Left Behind program—the creation of President Bush and Senator Teddy Kennedy—rests on the very Democratic Party assumptions that led our schools into the morass which it purports to drain.

Bush did voice certain conservative themes, such as "accountability" and "higher standards," in his advocacy of the bill. But the bill will not achieve any of its ostensible conservative aims. In fact, it has been widely reported that No Child Left Behind is not teaching students how to learn but teaching local schools to cheat; the *Dallas Morning*

News has reported that schools across Bush's home state have been cheating in order to meet NCLB's standards.

✳ Shut Down the Department of Corporate Welfare

Administrations let slip the real purpose of the Commerce Department when they choose its leaders. Secretaries of Commerce are usually operatives from a president's campaign, such as Clinton's Commerce Secretary Ron Brown (who had been Democratic Party chairman and a major fundraiser for Clinton) and Bush's Commerce Secretary Don Evans (who was chairman of Bush/Cheney 2000). The job has become an element of patronage, like the Post Office in the old days, except that Post Office jobs often went to a president's grass-roots supporters, whereas the services of the Commerce Department usually benefit Big Business.

They take their cronies in the corporate world on trade junkets or bring them to Washington to promote Big Government schemes such as disseminating taxpayer money to spur economic growth in communities classified as "distressed." Not surprisingly, most of the beneficiaries, even in programs designed to help the distressed, are well-off to start with.

The Treasury Department or private contractors could execute the Commerce Department's few legitimate activities such as its patent work and the Census enumeration of the U.S. population. The Commerce Department should be paid for by the corporations that use it, or, better yet, it should be shut down entirely.

In fact, all corporate welfare should be eliminated. According to the Cato Institute, it costs the average taxpaying household $860 a year, in Agriculture Department subsidies for mega-farms, Maritime Administration subsidies for ship-buying, and the Overseas Private Investment Corporation, which protects companies that send jobs overseas.

✳ Fold the Energy Department into Defense

Having a federal department of energy makes as much sense as having a federal department of automobiles. The Energy Department is a relic of the 1970s, when political elites ignored science and pursued crackpot boondoggles like ethanol and solar power.

Most of the legitimate functions of the Energy Department involve tasks that the Defense Department could perform more efficiently, such as restricting access to nuclear materials. The Cato Institute's Handbook for Congress in 2003 noted:

> The DOE is demonstrably the most bureaucratically dysfunc-
> tional agency in government. Its inability to provide even the
> most basic security for our nuclear secrets is well-known. Its
> ability to protect workers and communities around its nuclear
> weapons facilities – such as those in Paducah, Kentucky – is
> seriously in doubt. Those problems, however, are simply well-
> publicized manifestations of a deeper problem: the depart-
> ment's inability to competently supervise the activities of the
> contractors who manage and operate its facilities and pro-
> grams.

Cato estimates that taxpayers would save over $10 billion a year if the legitimate activities of the Energy Department were transferred to the Defense Department.

✳ Defund the Left

While the History Channel, C-SPAN, and almost-countless other channels have shown us the potential of television to educate and inform, PBS has shown what happens when the government runs a TV network. The Washington, DC area has three PBS stations, and on one recent weekend the stations showed such programs as "Antiques Roadshow," about expert appraisal of antiques; "The Lawrence Welk Show" reruns; British sitcoms; "Yachting: Ocean Race"; and one cooking show after another. In terms of public service or educational value or, in most cases, quality, the bulk of PBS programming doesn't rise to the level of the lowest-budget cable channel. None of this programming is an essential government service, and the best of these programs might flourish on the many cable channels that did not exist when PBS was created.

Yes, once you look past the pervasive left-wing propaganda in PBS documentaries, there is merit in an occasional episode of "Nova" or "American Experience" or "Frontline," but nothing that justifies spending money from hard-working taxpayers. C-SPAN, with no government funding, does a far better job overall in covering public affairs, politics, history, and science.

Whenever someone in power in Washington suggests a limit on spending on the government's official TV network, the PBS folks launch a massive lobbying campaign that includes commercials on PBS—commercials that taxpayers pay for—and they trot out Big Bird and list "Sesame Street" as an example of the kind of show they'd have to cut. In fact, "Sesame Street" and the like, with countless millions in merchandising revenue, doesn't need to pick the pockets of taxpayers to stay on the air.

Why do Republicans force working people and small business people to pay to make left-wing "documentary" producers rich? Why do they subsidize left-wing shows at all—or, for that matter, right-wing shows? Or *any* TV shows? Why, in the 21st Century, does the U.S. government operate a TV network? Why do we need a government radio network like National Public Radio?

Why, for that matter, does the taxpayer have to pay for politically correct "art" such as a crucifix dipped in urine or a depiction of the Virgin Mary covered with elephant dung? The National Endowment for the Arts has often been deliberately provocative, with (alleged) artists getting grants based on their politics and their connections, not their artistic merit. When Richard Nixon proposed the NEA, First Amendment advocates denounced the idea, because it would inevitably result in the federal government influencing the direction of artistic expression – a kind of backdoor censorship. The late Christopher Reeve, on CNN's "Crossfire," admitted that NEA funding amounts to a seal of approval so that artists can get funding from corporations and other traditional funders of art. Issuing an official seal of approval for art – is that *really* the kind of thing artists want the government to be involved in?

And why does taxpayer money go to the Legal Services Corporation, AARP, Planned Parenthood, and the ACLU? The LSC, which is supposed to represent the poor but, in fact, promotes left-wing causes such as "affirmative action" discrimination and illegal immigration, got $326 million in 2005. (LSC was formerly chaired by a radical named Hillary Rodham Clinton.) AARP gets tens of millions of dollars a year, including $83 million in 2004. From 1987 to 2002, Planned Parenthood received more than $2.4 billion – that's *billion* with a b – in taxpayers' funds.

As for the ACLU, no one knows how much it receives in taxpayers' funds. That's because, when the ACLU sues the government, if it wins it often gets reimbursed for its efforts. But that doesn't work the other way around: The ACLU never reimburses the taxpayer for its often-absurd lawsuits.

Republican politicians wring every last dollar from their conservative supporters...then vote for billions of dollars in funding for left-wing groups. Each dollar they vote to subsidize the Left cancels out a hard-earned dollar contributed by a conservative. How do they justify asking for even more money when they won't stop funding those who are trying to defeat Republicans and conservatives at the ballot box?

When will Republicans stop giving their enemies the rope with which to hang them?

❋ Stop the Government Takeover of Conservative Groups

Conservatives want to defund the Left. But so-called Big Government Conservatives say, "If you can't beat 'em, join 'em!" They just want conservatives to get their share of government largesse.

Make no mistake: If conservative organizations emulate the Left in seeking and receiving taxpayers' money, they will become like the Left in other ways, too. They will orient themselves toward serving the interests and values of the politicians and bureaucrats, not the interests and values of conservatives.

Thomas Edsall of the *Washington Post* reported recently: "For years, conservatives have complained about what they saw as the liberal tilt of federal grant money. Taxpayer funds went to abortion rights groups such as Planned Parenthood to promote birth control, and groups closely aligned with the AFL-CIO got Labor Department grants to run worker-training programs.

In the Bush administration, conservatives are discovering that turnabout is fair play: Millions of dollars in taxpayer funds have flowed to groups that support President Bush's agenda on abortion and other social issues.

"Under the auspices of its religion-based initiatives and other federal programs, the administration has funneled at least $157 million in grants to organizations run by political and ideological allies, according to federal grant documents and interviews. . . 'Quite frankly, part of the reason it went political is because we can't sell it unless we can show Republicans a political advantage to it, because it's not our base,' [Congressman Mark Souder] said, referring to the fact that many of those receiving social services are Democratic voters."

Note what Souder said. The inclusion of conservative groups among the recipients of these funds helps sell programs to conservatives that they would not otherwise accept. It's like when PBS puts on a single conservative show—for years, it was William F. Buckley, Jr.'s "Firing Line"—so that conservatives won't complain as much about PBS, and so that PBS could claim it is balanced.

✳ Dump Environmentalism, Back Conservationism

Former Interior Secretary James Watt was ridiculed when he suggested that human beings are given responsibility for earth's resources by God, but he was right. Republicans must learn to protect the environment while adhering to conservative principles; they must be conservationists, not environmentalists.

Conservation is different from environmentalism in that it recognizes the negative effects of government policies on the environment. Governments are the world's biggest abusers of the environment. The Soviet Union produced the worst pollution the earth had ever seen, long before Chernobyl (which was built to an unsafe design that no democracy would have authorized). In the U.S., there are more trees today than there were in 1920 – but all the increase has come on privately owned land, where at least someone is responsible for the property. Often, when the government is "responsible" for something, *nobody* is really responsible.

A conservative approach to the environment must recognize that the most effective solutions to environmental problems lie in business, rather than government, and in technology, rather than regulatory bureaucracy. In the end, property rights, not property-destroying socialism, provide the strongest incentive to preserve nature.

Conservatives in the conservationist mode have pioneered the use of systems that reduce the total pollutants in the air and water while allowing companies to buy and sell emissions credits—that is, to decide among themselves the most efficient and effective ways to reduce pollution. (An emission credit is a sort of permit to release a given substance into the air or water. A company that needs extra credits can buy them from a company that has a surplus. So, by limiting the total number of credits, and gradually reducing the number, you can cut pollution without forcing massive layoffs or other economic disruption. Through this kind of innovative thinking, conservationist conservatives have discovered ways to help the environment using the free market.)

In contrast to conservation, "environmentalism" makes demands that are often irrational, and conservatives should make no apologies for repudiating and resisting them. A conservationist demands that an oil company drilling in the Alaskan wasteland or offshore take care to prevent any significant damage to the environment; an environmentalist demands that there be no oil drilling at all, even when such a ban puts the country's future at risk.

Around the world, many former Communists (Mikhail Gorbachev included) have embraced the environmentalist movement, hoping to use that movement to take away people's right to private property. They are trying to achieve through the environmentalist movement that which they could never achieve in the heyday of Communism – a complete government takeover of commerce and property.

The Democrats turn conservation on its head by giving environmental preserves to those who have the least stake in caring for them. As Peter Huber argues in *Hard Green: Saving the Environment from the Environmentalists*, "Wealth, not poverty, supplies the means to conserve wildlife, forests, seashore, and ocean. The charge that the rich are the despoilers, the exhausters, the expropriators of the plant's biological wealth is altogether false."

Just as the Democrats' mislabeled "compassionate" welfare policies tend to impoverish the people they are supposed to help, so its much-touted environmentalism ends up endangering the environment. Consider their opposition to nuclear energy, which as even the French have come to learn, is the cleanest and safest source of energy. That opposition has led America toward a greater reliance on coal, which is far less clean than uranium.

In *The Politically Incorrect Guide to Science,* Tom Bethell writes about a grimly ironic turn of events in California under its enthusiasm for "alternative" sources of energy: Over 5,000 wind turbines in Northern California have, according to a legal complaint filed by an environmentalist group, "killed tens of thousands of birds, including between 17,000 and 26,000 raptors."

Conservatives must save the environment from the environmentalists.

✳ Stop Acting Like Democrats

Republicans are so proud of themselves for their Herculean accomplishment in ousting the Democrats from control of Congress in 1994. They are so proud of themselves for supposedly restoring honor to the Oval Office after the Clintons' years. But they are turning into the people they replaced.

Republicans in Washington have become what they beheld.

STANDING UP FOR THE U.S. IN A DANGEROUS WORLD

If anyone personifies Republicans' peculiar impotence on foreign policy, it's Senator George Voinovich of Ohio.

When John Bolton was nominated to be ambassador to the United Nations, Democrats opposed Bolton because of his support for UN reform and his opposition to Fidel Castro, but they didn't dare admit the real reason for their opposition, so they denounced the nominee for his temper. I'm not kidding. To block the nomination of a UN ambassador, they brought forth people who claimed he had yelled at them.

Now, Bolton was one of the most qualified persons ever nominated for the UN post. And it was a measure of the depths to which the once-great Democratic Party had sunk that Democrats' stated reason for opposing him was his alleged rudeness. But even more telling was what Voinovich did.

Voinovich didn't bother to show up for the committee hearings at which the nomination was discussed, until the last day. It was expected that the committee would vote along party lines to send the Bolton nomination to the full Senate, but Voinovich listened to Democrats denounce Bolton and suddenly announced that he was troubled by the nomination. The Senator forced a delay in the committee vote.

When he finally took to the floor to explain himself, Voinovich couldn't control his emotions. He began to break down in such a way that he appeared to be crying. "I'm afraid that when we go to the [Senate] well, that too many of my colleagues" – Voinovich's voice broke – "that too many of my colleagues are not going to understand that this appointment is very, very important to our country. . . . And I just hope my colleagues will take the time"—he struggled to go on—"and before they get to the well, do some serious thinking about whether or not we should send John Bolton to the United Nations."

As noted by James Taranto of the *Wall Street Journal's* OpinionJournal.com: "His crying fit on the Senate floor was a display of weak-mindedness as well as emotional incontinence."

One can imagine Osama bin Laden sitting in a cave, watching C-SPAN, and laughing at George Voinovich.

Voinovich's public breakdown helped Democrats mount a successful filibuster against Bolton, forcing President Bush to give him a temporary "recess appointment" while Congress was out of session.

The Ohio Senator is an example—an extreme example, but nevertheless an example—of Republicans' unwillingness or inability to fight for conservative principle on issues of foreign policy and national security.

The treatment of Bolton shows what often happens to conservatives. When a conservative is up for an important job, the Left launches a preposterous smear campaign, the media repeat charges over and over, and a critical segment of Republicans figures that, where there's smoke, there's fire. *Something* must be wrong with the nominee, or the critics wouldn't be so adamant – right? (See the Clarence Thomas hearings.)

In no area is the anti-conservative Establishment more resistant to progress than in foreign policy. They see it as their domain, into which Neanderthals (people like Ronald Reagan) cannot be allowed. In the 1976 presidential campaign, a Gerald Ford commercial suggested that, although Reagan was a good guy in some ways, he could not be trusted with foreign policy. "*Governor* Reagan couldn't start a war," said the commercial. "*President* Reagan could." A Ford aide, Margaret Tutwiler, declared that the nomination of Ronald Reagan could destroy the Republican Party, but the *election* of Ronald Reagan could destroy the world. In 1980, when Reagan considered offering the Vice Presidential slot to Ford, Ford demanded that he be given charge of foreign policy as a sort of co-president.

Throughout the Cold War and until the present day, members of the Establishment have worked to exclude "right-wingers" from the foreign policy process—"right-wingers" being those, like Ronald Reagan, who have had a reasonable, realistic view of the forces in the world opposing freedom and democracy.

In no area of foreign policy is the Establishment more protective of its prerogatives than with regard to the United Nations. The Establishment hates reformers like John Bolton because it sees the United Nations as one of the highest achievements of mankind, a place where wise men come together to work for peace and brotherhood. The UN, in the view of the Establishment, serves as a check on the right-wing cowboys that Americans sometimes elect as leaders.

The truth, of course, is that the UN is made up mostly of countries where the ruling class came to power by force or fraud. It is an association of dictatorships and kleptocracies (countries ruled by thieves), with a few free democracies in the mix. Indeed, Russia, ruled by the former KGB, and mainland China, ruled by the Communists who butchered pro-democracy activists in Tiananmen Square, both have veto power in the key UN body, the Security Council. So does the corrupt, collapsing government of France.

The UN is the kind of place where Libya is elected to chair the Human Rights Commission and Saddam Hussein's Iraq is elected to chair (with Iran as co-chair) the Conference on Disarmament. It was through the UN that Iraq bribed officials from around the world. It is the UN whose peacekeepers and civilian staffers in the Congo sexually abused young girls. It is the UN that regularly turns a blind eye to genocide.

It is the UN that is currently seeking to impose a worldwide system of taxes (on airplane fuel, the Internet, and other aspects of international travel and communications); it seeks such taxes by means of treaties, which would short-circuit the democratic process and provide an unending source of funding for the UN's corrupt activities. In this effort against democracy, the UN is supported by such organizations as the Clinton Foundation and the Bill and Melinda Gates Foundation, which style themselves as charities.

Heaven forbid that the U.S. send to the UN a man such as John

Bolton, who has criticized UN corruption and fought for American interests and values!

Now that I think about it: Why allow the UN to conduct a "renovation" that will cost billions, a project that no less than Donald Trump has denounced as a boondoggle? Why not take this chance to ask the UN to move somewhere else—somewhere that's not one of the world's most fun, and expensive, places to live? Of course, you might as well ask: Why do we fund the UN in the first place? (The U.S. taxpayer provides 22% of its overall budget and 27% of its peacekeeping costs.)

The UNophilia of the Establishment and the Left is part of their longstanding love affair with dictators. It's virtually impossible to hire a large law firm in Washington to sue the Saudis, funders of Wahhabi terrorist ideology, because all those firms already work for the Saudis. Cuba despot Fidel Castro hosts the president of CBS and assorted Hollywood figures for dinner, and he receives thunderous applause in left-wing U.S. churches, and when the mother of Elian Gonzales dies getting the little boy to freedom in the U.S., Bill Clinton's immigration service snatches the boy from his relatives and hands him over to the mass murderer Castro. (For going along with the kidnapping, Elian's father, a hotel worker, was given a seat in parliament.)

Communist China, which murdered an estimated 60 million people, is the object of billions in U.S. investment. If your investment expert isn't putting your money in China, *USA Today* recently advised, you should fire your expert.

In turn, Red China uses some of that money to buy off U.S. politicians. Remember Johnny Chung, and all those Clintonians who fled the country or took the Fifth Amendment to avoid testifying? Remember the "60 Minutes" report on Bill Clinton selling them missile technology?

The media and the Democrats went ballistic when it was revealed that the United Arab Emirates was to take over management at some U.S. ports—and they were right to do so—but the Chinese Communist Party has controlled such operations at U.S. ports for years, with no discernable reaction.

Google, the search engine company, styles itself as socially responsible. It makes sure plenty of its money goes to left-wing, politically correct causes and to Democratic politicians. The Left doesn't seem to have much of a problem with Google building a special search engine to help Red China oppress its people—blocking access to, for example, information on the pro-democracy demonstrations at Tiananmen Square. If the Left *does* care about this, it doesn't care enough to turn down Google's money.

Another progressive search-engine company, Yahoo, helped the Chinese communists track down and imprison a pro-democracy dissident who had used their system. One is reminded of the U.S. companies that provided information technology to the Nazis, which they used to keep track of Jews and other targets for extermination. The communist Chinese government murders and imprisons people as part of its war on religion, including both Christianity and Fulan Gong; Americans should work to bring peace-loving religion and its moderating influence to mainland China.

And then there's the Kyoto Treaty and its various spinoffs—international agreements to prevent catastrophic, manmade, global warming. A friend of mine has spent years trying in vain to find one "expert" —any expert—who agrees with the premises of Kyotoism: that the world's climate is affected by warming that is *global*, rather than *local* (climate patterns have been shifting since the earth began); that the warming is *catastrophically harmful*, rather than *somewhat harmful* or even, in some locations, *beneficial*; that the warming is *manmade*, rather than *natural* (caused by solar activity or other naturally occurring phenomena); and that the warming can be prevented by means consistent with peace, democracy, and freedom.

The U.S. Senate considered the principles of Kyoto, and voted no 95-0. That doesn't stop the anti-science forces from promoting Kyoto, which, not incidentally, would cripple any economy that adhered to its positions. European nations simply ratify Kyoto and then ignore it, which the U.S. can't do because treaties override the U.S. Constitution, and judges can enforce our treaties with other countries. Meanwhile, the world's largest dictatorship, Red China—which, in the years to come, is expected to pump more (alleged) global warming-related gases into the air than any other country—is exempt from the treaty.

Michael Crichton, the medical doctor and creator of *Jurassic Park* and TV's "ER," exposed the politics of Kyotoism in a recent thriller, *State of Fear*, and in a speech that has been widely circulated on the Internet. Yet, when he met with President Bush, it was hushed up lest the President be seen as sympathetic to Crichton's view. And, at a recent meeting that included almost every person ever to serve as director of the Environmental Protection Agency, not a single attendee took a pro-science position on the global warming issue. I should note that most of the errant EPA directors at the meeting were appointed by Republican presidents.

At the intelligence agencies, the CIA in particular, Republicans tolerate activities that, in any other country, would justly get a person put in prison. Its reputation in shambles—the CIA having failed to detect the huge Soviet biological weapons program, or the impending collapse of the Soviet empire, or Saddam's efforts to inflate Western estimates regarding his WMDs—some of those at the agency went after President Bush.

The CIA is filled with left-wing and "affirmative action" hires from the Clinton Administration and earlier—people hired because of their political views, perceived ethnicity, or gender—and was responsible for perhaps the greatest political blow to President Bush (the Saddam WMD debacle), yet it avoids a thorough housecleaning either before or after the directorship of George Tenet, who was a Clinton appointee, by the way. In one case, the new director, Porter Goss, was denied his choice as executive director because the man, 20 years earlier, had allegedly stolen a $2.13 slab of bacon. Goss, himself, was forced to resign after his effort to reform the agency angered the career bureaucracy.

Apparently, stealing bacon is a career-threatening move, but Republicans have little problem with intelligence officers plotting a coup against them.

On issue after issue, Republicans simply give up without a fight. One reason is that, even when Republicans take a conservative foreign policy position rhetorically, they lack the willingness to do the hard work, year after year, to turn that posturing into policy.

Or they fail to understand what resources are available to them. In any game of strategy, it is critical that you understand your own resources as well as your opponent's. When Ronald Reagan became president, it was hard to find people to staff foreign policy-related jobs. Many if not most of Reagan's best people were those who had gained experience in liberal/Democratic administrations but had converted to conservatism.

Today, there are plenty of foreign policy experts available – people who got experience and credentials during the Reagan years, or who have served with distinction on Congressional staffs or in think tanks or in the media. Some, but only a few, have made it into the State Department, intelligence agencies, and other government bodies dealing with foreign affairs. Today, we can begin to build a State Department and a foreign policy counter-Establishment that represents American interests and values, if only the Republicans will summon the political will to do so.

Putting Big Business Over National Security

Many Americans were upset when they learned that a company owned by an Arab government, the United Arab Emirates, was acquiring contracts to manage port facilities in New York, Newark, Philadelphia, Baltimore, Miami and New Orleans. People were correct to raise serious concerns over the security of those ports, given the UAE's mixed record on issues related to terrorism. Yes, the UAE is one of the U.S.'s strongest supporters in the Arab world, but that's like saying: He's kind of skinny, for a sumo wrestler.

The deal, which was ridiculed and became known as another example (along with Katrina and Harriet Miers) of astonishing incompetence at the White House, was approved by a little-known committee representing various government departments. The Committee on Foreign Investment in the United States (CFIUS, pronounced "siffy-us") is made up of officials from the Treasury, Justice, Commerce, State, and Homeland Security departments, as well as various White House offices. The Secretary of the Treasury is the chairman of the group.

Now, CFIUS is supposed to protect the nation's security. But for the most part it has operated over the years as a rubber-stamp for Big Business and for foreign companies. It's pro-Big Business orientation is apparent from the fact that the Treasury Secretary chairs it, not the Secretary of Defense or Homeland Security, and from the fact that it has approved 451 of 470 deals it examined between 1997 and 2004.

Patrick Mulloy, a member of a commission looking at the U.S.-China relationship and U.S. security, said in June 2005 that the Bush Administration had failed to fulfill a key reporting provision mandated by the legislation creating CFIUS. Even though the White House must report to Congress every four years on "whether foreign governments or companies have a coordinated strategy to acquire U.S. critical technology companies," no such report had been filed since 1993.

Meanwhile, members of Congress were actually putting pressure on CFIUS to become an even tamer watchdog! Congressman Donald Manzullo (R-Illinois) called for the Commerce Department—notorious for its singleminded pursuit of trade deals—to take over CFIUS. And some in Congress demanded that CFIUS give greater weight, not less, to such factors as whether a given deal will help the economy (as opposed to whether it will hurt national security).

With regard to CFIUS, "I am worried that we are letting business trump national security," Senator Richard Shelby (R-Alabama) said in October 2005.

As bad as the Dubai ports deal was, at least in terms of basic politics, what's far more disturbing is that the Chinese Communists manage terminals in the Port of Los Angeles and other West Coast ports. (They also control both ends of the Panama Canal.)

The Chinese Communists methodically milk all their foreign business operations for intelligence that might be useful in a conflict with the United States. And, as in the Internet deals mentioned earlier, they do whatever is necessary to get the technology and strategic resources they need to establish themselves as a world power. They are usually able to find Americans willing to help them. IBM sold its personal computer division, Lenovo, to them – and Lenovo recectly sold $13 million worth of PCs to the U.S. State Department! UNOCAL, the U.S. oil giant, was going to be sold to the Chinese Communists until a massive grassroots outcry killed the deal.

Throughout the Cold War, Big Business was willing to sacrifice the national interest for the sake of profits. IBM sold the Soviet Union advanced computer equipment for the Kama River car and truck plant, and tried to sell the Soviets a computer to be used to track people's movements through the USSR. (Even Jimmy Carter, as a presidential candidate, complained about such sales to the Soviets.)

George Will once remarked that proponents of such deals "love commerce more than they loathe Communism."

It could be worse. No one believes that George W. Bush or any Republican candidate would sell missile technology to the Chinese Communists for campaign contributions, as Bill Clinton is alleged to have done. But in the face of an implacable foe like the butchers of Beijing, sometimes it's enough to simply look the other way.

Another area in which Congress and the Bush Administration put commerce ahead of the best interests of the country—indeed, the best interests of the world—is foreign aid. As Kenyan economist James Shikwati put it, "For God's sake, please stop the aid!"

Shikwati told the German publication *Der Spiegel:* "If the industrial nations really want to help the Africans, they should finally terminate this awful aid. The countries that have collected the most development aid are also the ones that are in the worst shape. Despite the billions that have poured in to Africa, the continent remains poor."

He was asked: Do you have an explanation for this paradox? "Huge bureaucracies are financed [with the aid money], corruption and complacency are promoted, Africans are taught to be beggars and not to be independent. In addition, development aid weakens the local markets everywhere and dampens the spirit of entrepreneurship that we so desperately need. As absurd as it may sound: Development aid is one of the reasons for Africa's problems. If the West were to cancel these payments, normal Africans wouldn't even notice. Only the functionaries would be hard hit. Which is why they maintain that the world would stop turning without this development aid."

Der Spigel: "Even in a country like Kenya, people are starving to death each year. Someone has got to help them."

Shikwati: "But it has to be the Kenyans themselves who help these people. When there's a drought in a region of Kenya, our corrupt politicians reflexively cry out for more help. This call then reaches the United Nations World Food Program—which is a massive agency of apparatchiks who are in the absurd situation of, on the one hand, being dedicated to the fight against hunger while, on the other hand, being faced with unemployment were hunger actually eliminated. It's only natural that they willingly accept the plea for more help. And it's not uncommon that they demand a little more money than the respective African government originally requested. They then forward that request to their headquarters, and before long, several thousand tons of corn are shipped to Africa."

Der Spigel: "Corn that predominantly comes from highly-subsidized European and American farmers."

Shikwati: "And at some point, this corn ends up in the harbor of Mombasa. A portion of the corn often goes directly into the hands of unscrupulous politicians who then pass it on to their own tribe to boost their next election campaign. Another portion of the shipment ends up on the black market where the corn is dumped at extremely low prices. Local farmers may as well put down their hoes right away; no one can compete with the UN's World Food Program. And because the farmers go under in the face of this pressure, Kenya would have no reserves to draw on if there actually were a famine next year. It's a simple but fatal cycle."

Or, as the saying goes: Foreign aid is taking from poor people in rich countries and giving to rich people in poor countries.

And when we lend money to the governments of poor countries (at the expense of U.S. taxpayers), we often put conditions on the loan, such as that the recipient must raise taxes on its people. In other words, we actually encourage the governments to do the worst possible thing they can do if they really want to lift their people out of poverty.

Big Business likes foreign aid, because it supposedly promotes the development of a recipient country's workforce or gives that country the resources to buy U.S. goods. In fact, such aid subsidizes the purchase of goods produced by Big Business, and banks get their ill-advised loans repaid.

In connection with foreign trade, Big Business gets a lot of subsidies—everything from a program that subsidizes U.S. sales abroad to the Overseas Private Investment Corporation, which insures companies that take jobs overseas to countries where the local governments might steal their facilities.

Most conservatives support free trade, that is, open commerce across national boundaries that benefits the people on both sides. But we are as opposed to subsidized trade—taxpayer-funded welfare for corporations—as we are opposed to the kind of trade that helps a foreign country prepare for possible war with the U.S.

Nation-Building in Iraq and Elsewhere

One problem in national security is that we seem unable to set priorities.

Although many conservatives fully supported the invasion of Iraq —and all conservatives prayed for the success of our troops once the war began—many questioned why the U.S. was going after Iraq at a time when, it seemed, larger threats loomed, such as a nuclear Iran and a nuclear North Korea and the general threat of Al Qaeda.

The President's initial military response to the 9/11 attacks was highly praiseworthy. Certainly, he was justified in taking out the Taliban regime in Afghanistan, which provided the principal base for Al Qaeda. Under President Bush's leadership, our armed forces and intelligence agencies made a good start in tracking down terrorists associated or allied with Al Qaeda. The Bush Administration also made progress in tearing down the "Gorelick Wall," the barrier—named after former Clinton Administration official Jamie Gorelick—that prevented law enforcement and intelligence agencies from sharing certain information. That no-cooperation restriction contributed to the success of the 9/11 plot. (In typical Washington fashion, Gorelick was named by Democrats as a member of the 9/11 Commission. In other words, she was in charge of investigating herself!)

(Some conservatives have concerns about the so-called PATRIOT Act, particularly in connection with the open-ended nature of "GWOT," the Global War on Terrorism. Because terrorism, as a tactic,[1] can never

---

[1] Terrorism is the use of violence against civilian targets to cause fear among the general population, in order to achieve a political objective. Sometimes the term is also applied to violence against military targets by groups that *usually* attack civilians.

be eliminated, a Global War on Terrorism promises never to end. And conservatives are reluctant to allow the federal government to expand its powers indefinitely in the name of fighting terrorism. Conservatives remember "Project Megiddo."[2] They also remember that "temporary" expansions of government power tend to become permanent. Most conservatives support the expanded law enforcement powers granted the federal government since 9/11, but also want to make sure that those powers come up for periodic review by Congress. Conservatives believe in a motto from a book published by Benjamin Franklin: "Those who would give up Essential Liberty to purchase a little Temporary Safety, deserve neither Liberty nor Safety.")

After the overthrow of the Taliban and the efforts to tear down the Gorelick Wall, though, the Bush Administration seemed to lose its way. The President turned from finishing the job of eradicating Al Qaeda, to pursuing regime change in Iraq. There is no question that Saddam Hussein, a Stalinist who used chemical weapons against his own people and established "rape rooms," deserved to be overthrown. But was this war justified in the absence of an attack on the United States? Was this "nation building" experiment justified? Was the Iraq War the best use of scarce U.S. resources and of the lives of our service men and women? Did the Bush Administration provide enough troops to get the job done? Given the weakening of the U.S. military under Presidents Bush (the father) and Clinton, *could* the current Bush Administration have provided enough troops to suppress the outbreak of insurgency?

---

[2] "Project Megiddo" was a late-1990s effort by the FBI to warn law enforcement agencies about the threat of domestic terrorism. But, despite Al Qaeda's 1993 attack on the World Trade Center, the report overlooked Islamofascism and suggested that the real terrorist threat sprang from various Christian and pro-life groups, along with Second Amendment supporters, people concerned about the United Nations or the Y2K problem, and other groups that the Clinton Administration considered to be collections of right-wing nuts. In the report, people who are peaceful but out-of-the-mainstream are lumped together with actual threats such as the KKK, in a way that, had it been aimed at the Left, would have been considered McCarthyism. The reference to Christianity is clear from the name of the project: Megiddo is prominently mentioned in the Book of Revelation; "Armageddon" means "Hill of Megiddo."

There is no question that serious errors were made in planning for the period after a successful invasion of Iraq. One error included the failure to seal Iraq's borders from terrorist/Syrian/Iranian infiltration—in, admittedly, one of the most smuggler-friendly regions on earth. Another was the creation of an absurd system of "proportional representation" for the Iraqi parliament. That electoral system had the effect of deepening the divisions among the Iraqi people, discouraging political alliances between members of different religious factions, and helping well-organized extremists by making voting too complicated for most people to understand.

During his 2000 campaign, George W. Bush correctly ridiculed nation-building of the sort Bill Clinton had engaged in, in such places as Haiti and the Balkans. Conservatives oppose nation-building as a matter of principle, even if it's done in a well-organized and efficient way. But doing it badly is even worse.

President Bush has become a nation builder himself, first in the so-called Palestinian Authority, where (beginning under Clinton) the U.S. response to Yasser Arafat's terrorism was to give Arafat his own country to rule and to loot. Since Arafat's death, the Palestinian Authority has fallen into the hands of terrorists even worse than Arafat. This nation that was largely built by the U.S. is a threat to the very existence of Israel, and is in a position to supply diplomatic cover, sanctuary, training, weapons, funding, and murder-suicide bombers to the Islamofascist movement.

Since 2003, of course, President Bush has also been a nation-builder in Iraq, seeking to create a democracy there. That is a difficult task anywhere, but especially in a nation that had been ruled until recently by a horrific dictatorship – a totalitarian regime that did not allow the development of the sort of private institutions that serve as building blocks for democracy.

The result of this nation-building effort is that the U.S. is stuck in a Middle Eastern quagmire that shows no promise of ending. A historical study suggests that counter-insurgency efforts last an average of nine years, and, at this point, there's no reason to think the Iraq effort will be of shorter-than-average duration.

When I am asked what conservatives would have done about Iraq,

I point out that, if George H.W. Bush had listened to conservatives in 1991, there would have been no Saddam to overthrow in 2003. The first President Bush was strongly advised to go straight through to Baghdad and finish off Saddam's regime.

Early in 1992, Steven J. Allen and I wrote that, "as in Vietnam, the victory that was won on the battlefield was fumbled away by the politicians. . . . Bush's order to stop the [first Gulf War]—with allied forces only a few miles from true victory—allowed more than 500 tanks, two Republican Guard divisions, and a fleet of helicopters to escape." We quoted former Reagan aide Mona Charen: "Why didn't we finish the job? Because the president gave all the wrong reasons for fighting – and then found himself boxed into a corner."

And we wrote: "Another harmful effect of the Gulf War may be the acceptance of the necessity of U.N. approval for the United States to take military action." Remember that it was the subsequent desire to get UN approval for the Iraq War that led the Bush Administration to make its strongest claims about Saddam's WMDs—charges that proved politically disastrous later when the U.S. was unable to prove them.

For those trying to analyze the current Iraq War, I would point out some of what I believe are the relevant principles of conservatism. Quoting Steven J. Allen: "A conservative has respect for those who make or have made sacrifices in the cause of freedom, and for those who put their lives in peril to protect others. . . . A conservative believes that military force should be used with care, in a manner consistent with the Constitution, in limited circumstances in which the cause of freedom and the just interests of the United States are at stake. A conservative believes that government officials should not put American servicemen and servicewomen in harm's way without giving them a clearly-defined mission and the resources they need for victory. A conservative believes that the United States should avoid entangling alliances and the trappings of empire. A conservative has compassion for the oppressed and seeks *peacefully* to free them from oppression."

In other words, if President Bush had acted according to conservative principles, he would have been more skeptical regarding the push for war; given the troops more resources and a clearly defined mission; turned the government of Iraq over to Iraqis faster, without waiting for a perfect government to form. His father, had he been a conservative, would have provided support for revolt against Saddam following the first Gulf War (instead of encouraging the revolt and then abandoning the revolutionaries), so that by 2003 there might have been no Saddam to worry about.

Out of personal loyalty to the current President, and out of loyalty to him in his role as Commander in Chief, most conservatives supported the war, though a fair number questioned its wisdom. Conservative journalist Jon Utley, for example, was a leader in opposing the war. Even many conservatives who supported the war have now come to believe that it was a mistake. Unlike the Left, though—many of whose members act as if they want the other side to win—conservatives are united in working and praying for a successful outcome. A defeat in Iraq would be catastrophic. And it would be the foreseeable consequence of not having our priorities in order.

Getting Our Priorities Straight

Iran and North Korea developing nuclear weapons are not the only problems from which the Iraq War has distracted us.

Let me give one example of a part of the world that the Bush Administration is neglecting: Latin America. Over the years, not just in the current Bush administration, we have failed to help build Latin American economies by promoting free markets and encouraging them to reject corrupt, socialist governments. We should have been promoting real freedom in Latin America just as we promoted it behind the Iron Curtain, with Radio Free Europe and our help for Solidarity in Poland and our support of anti-Soviet dissidents. Now, we are paying the price for neglect.

In Latin America, the Left is on the rise. In Venezuela, Hugo Chavez has muscled his way into power, survived a coup attempt and, using the country's oil wealth—Venezuela's a member of OPEC—is steadily eliminating the opposition at every level of government and society and attempting to spread his pernicious ideology to other countries. He sees himself as the next Fidel Castro. At this writing, the leading candidate for president of Mexico is a Chavez ally, and his victory would put Castroites in control of Latin American countries from which the U.S. gets more than 30% of its imported oil.

Meanwhile, the Sandinistas, the Soviet/Castro-backed gang that seized control of Nicaragua in the 1970s, are attempting a comeback. In Peru, Chile, and Bolivia, the Left, aligned with Castro and Chavez, is in position to take absolute power. FARC, a Communist army, controls much of the drug wealth of Colombia. (In Brazil, fortunately, the leftist government is mired in scandal and is teetering.)

The cluelessness of the liberal "mainstream" media on this critical issue was nowhere more apparent than when broadcaster and former presidential candidate Pat Robertson criticized Chavez and suggested that the U.S. might "take him out." Robertson's own TV program, "The 700 Club," had done several reports on the threat of Chavez and his comrades, and Robertson's on-air comments followed one such report. The liberal media, in response, acted as if they had barely heard of Chavez, and treated Robertson as a nut who was randomly calling for the assassination of foreign leaders. Most of the media never even bothered to explain why Robertson might have a problem with the political boss of Venezuela who's using his country's oil wealth to bring about totalitarian revolution in Latin America.

(The same thing happens on issues related to the Middle East. You're more likely to see a sophisticated in-depth report on, say, Israeli politics, on "The 700 Club" rather than "The CBS Evening News.")

This issue is critical for many reasons. Leftist governments in Latin America may provide safe haven for terrorists, and give them access to money, false documentation, places to train, and weapons and weapons technology. Because Venezuela and Mexico control so much of the U.S. oil supply, they will be able to stymie U.S. action against them (while making it more difficult for the U.S. to extricate itself from entangling alliances with oil-producing, terrorist-supporting dictatorships such as Saudi Arabia).

This issue also relates to one of the country's biggest problems, immigration. If Latin America goes communist, the U.S. will be flooded as never before with refugees. This influx of unskilled workers, most of whom speak little or no English, will create crushing burdens as U.S. politicians try in vain to maintain a welfare state that was never intended to handle such an invasion. As our leaders should have realized by now, it is national suicide to offer welfare-state benefits to millions of poor people who are on the other side of an open border.

As I noted, Latin America is just one example of an area we have neglected. Much could also be said about Africa, where we have stood by and allowed the genocide of millions, and where millions of AIDS orphans are recruiting targets for the likes of Al Qaeda.

As European socialism collapses, we must turn away from a foreign policy approach that focuses too much on Europe and too much on commitments that are no longer relevant in the post-Cold War world.

Ask yourself: Why in the world are U.S. troops still in Germany, a decade and a half after the Cold War? Why, for that matter, do we maintain a presence in South Korea that the South Koreans are coming to resent?

And what are we doing to counter the efforts by Russian President Vladimir Putin to reestablish totalitarian rule in his country? It is Putin of whom President Bush said, after meeting him, "I was able to get a sense of his soul, a man deeply committed to his country and to the best interests of his country." It is also Putin who has brought TV news under government control, abolished the election of regional governors, and is most likely responsible for the attempted assassination by poison of Ukrainian leader Viktor Yushchenko. Outside of the praiseworthy decision to pursue a strategic missile defense—a program the Russians strongly objected to, on the ground that the U.S. had signed the ABM Treaty with the defunct USSR—what have we really done to stand up to the reemerging totalitarian Russians?

Why is the State Department continuing to pursue ratification of the Law of the Sea Treaty, which President Reagan rejected in 1982? Secretary of State Condoleezza Rice said "we very much want to see [LOST] go into force." The International Seabed Authority, which the U.S. would join under the treaty, would expand the corrupt power of the United Nations and allow UN taxes to be assessed on U.S. companies operating in international waters – 70% of the earth's surface. And

it would actually overrule rights that are protected by the U.S.
Constitution. In addition, the treaty could end up prohibiting such
measures as the Proliferation Security Initiative, one of the Bush
Administration's best programs for dealing with weapons of mass
destruction.

With regard to efforts against terrorism, why is the Bush administration resisting the use of profiling as a way to ensure that security
resources are allocated reasonably? Yes, if the government searched
only Middle Eastern young men, Al Qaeda and its affiliates might turn
to, for example, Chechen women. But almost any security measure
could be overcome with sufficient resources; forcing Al Qaeda to use
counter-to-the-profile types such as Chechen women would put one
more roadblock in the path of a successful 9/11-type attack. Second, a
responsible profiling system would take all factors into account,
including age, sex, national origin, and apparent ethnicity along with
many other factors such as whether the person is acting nervously.
Every so often, we might still see a situation in which an 80-year-old
Swedish woman is pulled out of line at the airport, but more of our
resources would be directed where they can do the most good. This
has nothing to do with discrimination, any more than when the police
pay special attention to five-feet-tall red-haired men after witnesses
describe a bank robber as a five-foot-tall red-haired man.

The lesson of all of this:

For too long, U.S. foreign policy and national security have been
characterized by inertia—continuing to do the same things, for no particular reason—and by hidebound thinking. Since the Cold War,
Republicans for the most part have been going through the motions,
or "phoning it in," as actors say. It's time for a major effort to apply
conservative principles to the foreign policy and national security
problems of the 21st century.

THE CONSERVATIVE FUTURE

13 NOMINATE, ELECT, GOVERN: TWO OF THREE IS NOT ENOUGH

Morton Blackwell, founder and director of the Leadership Institute, has been one of the key organizers of the conservative movement since the early 1970s. He has a compelling way of looking at the history and progress of conservatism *as a political movement*. He sees the conservative movement as going through three stages.

Phase I of the conservative movement was learning *how to nominate a candidate for president*. We learned how to do that in 1964, when we nominated Barry Goldwater as the Republican candidate for president.

Phase II of the conservative movement was learning how to nominate *and elect* a candidate for president. We learned how to do that in 1980, when we nominated and elected Ronald Reagan as president of the United States.

Phase III of the conservative movement will come when we learn how to nominate and elect someone as president *and then ensure that he or she governs as a conservative.*

Unfortunately, Phase III presents us with a test we have not yet passed.

Let's take a quick look back at phases I and II, to see what lessons we can learn about nominating and electing a president. Then we'll spend a bit more time on phase III, figuring out how to prep for this exam and pass it next time.

Conservatives Learn How to Nominate a Candidate for President

In 1964 we conservatives wrested control of the Republican Party from its entrenched Eastern Establishment led by New York Governor Nelson Rockefeller. Richard Nixon had been defeated by Jack Kennedy in the 1960 presidential election, and the dominant liberal Republican wing of the GOP now saw Rocky as the heir apparent to the presidency by virtue of his unequaled Establishment resume. We thought otherwise.

We nominated Barry Goldwater at the Republican convention in San Francisco, the first Republican candidate to openly wear the new label *conservative*, in the process changing the future course of both the Republican Party and American politics in general. Yes, as everyone knows, Goldwater—and conservatism—suffered a disastrous defeat at the polls in November. But conservatives also learned many important lessons in 1964, lessons we used to become the dominant political movement in the coming decades. Among those lessons:

> *The mainstream media are incurably liberal. They will never give conservatives a fair chance, so you have to do an end-run around them.*

Boy, did we learn this lesson the hard way! We were called fascists, Nazis, bigots, racists, and reckless crazies who might destroy the world in a nuclear holocaust.

Barry Goldwater was declared psychologically unfit to be president by more than a thousand psychiatrists, in an article in *Fact* magazine. Columbia professor Richard Hofstadter published, in the November 1964 issue of *Harper's*, the essay "The Paranoid Style in American Politics," an attack on conservatives, whom Hofstadter preposterously lumped together with the Klan and other bigots.

When President Kennedy was assassinated by a Communist sympathizer, somehow that was turned into a conservative deed. But we didn't let that stop us. We created our own channels of communication—publications such as *National Review* and *Human Events*, Goldwater's own book *The Conscience of a Conservative*, and below-the-radar bestsellers such as Phyllis Schlafly's *A Choice Not an Echo*, John Stormer's *None Dare Call It Treason*, and J. Evetts Haley's *A*

Texan Looks at Lyndon. All of those books sold millions of copies without the benefit of a New York publisher or a favorable review in the *New York Times.*

Our network was openly underground, that is, we operated openly but the Establishment ignored us. It represented a new phenomenon in modern American politics and helped us get the nomination in 1964 but it wasn't sufficient to convince a majority of the American people —not yet. But we would continue to work at that.

Properly mobilized by a shared ideology, the grass roots can take on the combined forces of Wall Street, the entrenched political machines, and the mainstream media.

Logistically, an estimated four million men and women took an *active* part in the Goldwater campaign, contacting many millions more. This was unprecedented in modern American politics. LBJ had only half as many workers, even though the Democratic voter pool was 50 percent larger.

This populist reach was even more apparent in fundraising. The Goldwater campaign was the first popularly financed campaign in modern American history. The 1960 campaign, with between 40,000 and 50,000 individual contributors to Nixon and some 22,000 to Kennedy, was typical of the approach from previous years. Estimates of the number of contributors to Goldwater in 1964—combining federal, state, and local campaign groups—range from 650,000 to over a million. As you'd surmise from such an explosion in the number of contributors, individual and smaller contributors became hugely important. Only 28% of the Goldwater federal campaign contributions were for $500 or more, compared to 69% of the Democratic contributions.

In short, we were learning how to mobilize the grass roots for door-to-door campaigning as well as raising the money. We'd continue to develop our expertise in the years to come, while the Democrats were stuck with labor unions as their chief source of financial support and manpower, and Establishment Republicans remained dependent on fat cats for financing and paid party workers for logistical support.

The value of a defeat can be highly underestimated.

Yes, you read that right. None of us goes into political battle *hoping* to be defeated, but good can come out of defeat if you learn your lessons well and apply those lessons to open up new opportunities.

In 1964, we were learning our lessons even as a lot of deadwood was cleared out of the Republican Party. This made it easier for us to continue our takeover of the GOP, utilizing new technology, more effective techniques, and fresh ideas. At the same time, the Democrats were saddled with the same old leadership, the same old sources of manpower and money, and the same old approaches to issues. The Watergate scandal in 1974 eliminated more of the Republican office-holders who had stood in the way of creating a more broadbased party.

Defeat stings, but conservatives should keep this in mind: In 1976, had Ford been elected, it is highly unlikely that Reagan would have been elected in 1980, or ever. The conservatives-can't-win stigma, which largely disappeared with Reagan's 1980 and 1984 landslides, would have continued indefinitely. Without Reagan's policies, we would probably not have experienced the technological revolution of the past 20 years. But it's possible that none of that would have mattered, because without Reagan's policies, the Soviet Union and the Soviet Empire probably would have remained in place, even as internal pressures pushed the USSR toward war using its full arsenal of nuclear and biological weapons.

Defeat stings, but in 1992, had the hapless President George H.W. Bush been reelected, it is a near certainty that the Democrats would have retained control of Congress in 1994. In fact, they would probably have gained congressional seats in 1994, then picked up the White House as well in 1996. Someone like Al Gore might have been in the White House on 9/11.

Sometimes a *loss* for the Republican Party can be a *gain* for conservatives, Americans, and the world.

Conservatives Learn How to Nominate *and Elect* a Candidate for President

Between 1964 and 1980 we conservatives refined and expanded the techniques we learned in the Goldwater campaign, creating what was called "the New Right." The payoff was the key to the White House, an accomplishment that seemed like an impossible dream in the early years of the movement. Here are some of the lessons learned that contributed to that victory:

A successful movement needs a leader, not just a spokesman.

Barry Goldwater will always hold a special place in our hearts because of his courage in speaking the truth, no matter what the consequences might be to his career. "In your heart you know he's right" was not just our 1964 campaign slogan, it was our motivation to keep working when things were the darkest. But Goldwater always made it clear he didn't really want the nomination, much less to assume the leadership of an ongoing movement. We pretty much forced the nomination on him, but after 1964 he just wanted to be a senator from Arizona and to work on particular issues such as improving the organization of the military. You could hardly blame him, considering the calumnies that had been visited upon him.

But, as my wife Elaine reminds me periodically, when God closes a door, he also usually opens a window. In this instance it was movie and TV star Ronald Reagan, who made his political debut with a 30-minute narrative, "A Time for Choosing," broadcast when things were their bleakest, toward the end of the Goldwater campaign. That stirring endorsement of Goldwater created a new political star and a new spokesman for conservatism—a far more effective spokesman than Goldwater.

More importantly, in the years following 1964 Reagan proved he wanted to be more than our spokesman—he wanted to be our leader. In 1966 he became governor of California, by then the largest state in the union, and used that as a bully pulpit for his national ambitions. And he was in the trenches with us every step of the way, speaking to any political or civic group that would listen, raising money for our candidates and causes, and listening to our concerns.

Capturing the White House in a nation as large as ours is no job for a dilettante. It requires someone who really *wants* the job enough to put in years of grueling work. For a movement, it is equally important that this is an *ideological* ambition, not just a desire for personal power. As we'll see, this is one of the missing ingredients for a successful conservative movement today, but in the 1970s we had that kind of a leader with Ronald Reagan and it gained us the White House.

A successful movement must constantly enlarge its constituency.

Conservatives started doing this in the 1950s and 1960s, when we used the anti-communist issue to begin to wean northern ethnic Catholics—Irish, Italian, Polish and other Eastern Europeans—away from the Democratic Party, which had become a party of appeasement. Of course it didn't hurt that the Democrats were also driving these people *away* with their increasingly secularist orientation and their stand on the social issues of that day, such as school busing and the destruction of neighborhoods through "urban development." The important point for our success was that we didn't follow the "me too" approach of Republican liberals. We offered a real alternative and invited—begged—this new constituency to join us.

In the 1970s, this process continued as we expanded our outreach to Southerners and Evangelical Protestants. As late as 1976, these groups were mostly Democratic, but the Democrats took them for granted and began to look down on them. Indeed some liberals and Democrats came to hate them with a passion that burns today, calling Southerners rednecks and calling conservative Evangelicals "the Religious Right." (Conversely, they began to refer to Islamic extremists as "fundamentalists," which is a name for a group of mainstream Christians.) Unlike liberals and Democrats, we treated Southerners and Evangelicals with respect, courted them, and actively addressed the issues that were important to them.

Ronald Reagan would never have become President without the support of "Reagan Democrats," who were mainly Catholic in the North and Evangelical in the South. Eventually, by the 1990s, most of them would be fed up with the Democrats and would become Republicans.

We learned how to use "social issues" to get the extra 5% of the vote that made the difference between defeat and victory on Election Day.

After the Great Depression of the 1930s and the disastrous policies of Big Government Republican Herbert Hoover, Republicans got used to being the minority party. A war hero like Dwight Eisenhower could win the Oval Office as a nominal Republican, but as a general rule the White House was conceded to the Democrats. The same pattern held for the Congress. At the state and local levels, in the races for the Senate and the House, most Republicans outside the South would get 40%, 45%, sometimes even 47% or 48% of the vote—close, but usually not enough to win. (In the South, except for east Tennessee, Republicans had hardly any presence at all.)

That pattern held until the second half of the 1970s. That's when a group of conservative leaders known as the "New Right" developed a plan under the leadership of Paul Weyrich to reach out to conservative religious leaders and their followers. Traditionally most conservative Protestant ministers had preached that a good Christian was *in* the world but not *of* the world—in other words, leave the business of running the country to the non-Christians. Alarmed by the increasingly immoral tone of American life in the 70s, some of these ministers changed their tune. And with the mobilization of this Christian Right, Republican candidates for state and federal offices started getting 51%, 53%, 55% of the vote in the 1978 and 1980 elections. And that formula has served Republican candidates well to this day.

Consider: During the period when the Democrats became the party associated with the so-called pro-choice position on abortion, the Democratic Party picked up three House seats for "pro-choice" Democrats ... and lost 100 seats that had been held by pro-life Democrats!

Let me be clear about this: The positions that brought Southerners and Evangelicals into the Republican Party were mainstream positions. The overwhelming majority of the American people agree with conservatives on social issues such as prayer in school, abortion on demand, and opposition to "homosexual marriage." Decades of polling prove that. But for something like 5%-8% of the population, it was these social issues—and these issues alone—that got them to the polls. When they got there they voted for the Republican candidates who shared their values, and their votes made the difference between defeat and victory.

The Republicans had been trying to win at politics by sitting on a stool with two legs, economic issues and foreign policy issues. It didn't work. We added a third leg to the stool—social issues—which gave us a stable platform for victory.

Occasionally I run into business types who don't want social conservatives to have an equal seat at the table. Social conservatives are not usually the kind of people with whom a corporate executive hangs out at the country club. But business Republicans and others, such as libertarians, have to decide whether they want to be in a 52% majority, or in a 45% minority that sits on the sidelines complaining while the likes of Teddy Kennedy, Hillary Clinton, Al Gore, and John Kerry run the government.

This "big tent" approach is exactly what kept the Democrats in power for so long. FDR's coalition brought together people who felt very uncomfortable being in the same room with each other—white Dixiecrats, Jews and blacks, farmers and university intellectuals. That coalition fell apart for the Democrats as conservative Republicans stole some of their key voting blocs and created a new coalition.

A successful aspiring movement needs to be in the forefront of utilizing the new technology of the day. It cannot afford to rest on the old ways of doing politics.

We conservatives knew, from our experiences in 1964, that the old ways would not work for us. The liberal "mainstream" media wouldn't give us a fair break; they saw themselves as "gatekeepers" protecting people from views they considered radical, such as those of conservatives. Wall Street had an agenda quite different from ours. The entrenched political machines didn't want newcomers who would threaten their control of the political process. If we wanted to advance, we had to create end runs around those forces of the status quo—which is what we did.

The critical technological advance we developed took the form of alternative media—media that gave us a way to get our message across directly to the American people, without the distorting filter of the liberal media "gatekeepers." From the aftermath of the Goldwater campaign to the mid-1980s, direct mail was *the* alternative medium that gave us our edge.

Democrats, liberal Republicans, and independent liberals weren't interested in direct mail. The old ways – relying on labor unions or fat cats—were working fine for them, or so they thought. With those avenues shut off to us, we were hungry for new ways to reach the American people, and hungry enough that we did the necessary work to create the new medium of political direct mail.

Direct mail—reaching Americans through their mailboxes—was already a proven successful technique in the commercial realm. (Think of Sears, Roebuck with its catalogue, and *Reader's Digest*, the world's largest-circulation magazine.) But direct mail had not been used in the political realm except in isolated, temporary situations. I applied the techniques used successfully in the commercial world to the political realm, learning as I went along. For some 15 years I had little competition from the Democrats and the liberals, and in that period of time we used direct mail to help build the conservative movement that, in turn, elected Ronald Reagan as president.

We kept growing, step-by-step, under the radar of the Liberal Establishment. We used direct mail to explain our positions to the American public, and we used direct mail to greatly expand our lists of contributors and activists.

Some people wrongly think of political direct mail as just a form of fundraising, and it's true that we used it for that purpose – fundraising in small amounts from large numbers of people, rather than large amounts from a few wealthy people. But political direct mail is primarily a form of advertising and organizing. It is a way of getting one's message to the world, like television, except that we could campaign relatively cheaply by sending our messages only to the people most interested in them. (How much TV advertising money is wasted on telling 10-year-olds about the new Cadillac or trying to sell dog food to cat people?) And it is a way of creating a community of supporters for a particular candidate or cause.

Thanks to this secret weapon of direct mail—actually, we did it openly but our adversaries ignored us—conservatives were able to become an independent, vibrant force, free of the fetters imposed by the Republican political hierarchy and the liberal media. Direct mail also freed conservatives from the influence of the big corporations and millionaires which had traditionally financed GOP and Democratic politics (and which expected to be paid back with favors).

Eventually, our adversaries started adapting our techniques, and we didn't really mind. With our victories, it was inevitable that they would catch on to what we were doing. Second, our causes were more populist, thus more suited to grassroots organizing through direct mail. Third, we were confident that if Americans were exposed to messages from both sides, they would line up with us. Liberals didn't *need* alternative media, because they already controlled the "mainstream" media.

In the years after Reagan's election, new alternative media would be added, such as talk radio, cable television, and the Internet. But up to the point of Reagan's election, direct mail was the key. (For the full story, see my 2004 book, *America's Right Turn: How Conservatives Used New and Alternative Media to Take Power.*)

With real leadership, an active outreach to potential new constituencies, and an openness to new technology and new ways of "doing" politics, we conservatives proved in 1980 and 1984 that we could nominate *and* elect a president of the United States.

The Unfinished Business:
How to Nominate and Elect a President
Who Will Then Govern as a Conservative

As it turned out, nominating and electing a president was the easy part. With a quarter-century and almost four presidencies behind us, we can see now that *governing* as conservatives is the hard part. This is where we have to go back to school and cram real hard, now and for the next couple of years, to pass the exam.

It was M. Stanton Evans, the conservative journalist and author, who first framed the problem in a witticism that conservatives instantly recognized as the truth. "The trouble with our people," Evans says to this day, "is that once they come to Washington, they no longer act like our people."

This apostasy of our national politicians from conservative principles didn't begin yesterday, nor with the Republican takeover of 2000. Back in 1976, a high percentage of the officeholders and GOP officials backing liberal President Gerald Ford against conservative Ronald Reagan were veterans of the Goldwater campaign! They had taken, as a lesson from the Goldwater effort, the idea that no conservative could be elected president. In fact, by the early 1970s, they had pretty much given up on conservative policies entirely, backing Nixon's wage-and-price controls, the Nixon-Kissinger-Ford "detente" foreign policy, and the selection of liberal Nelson Rockefeller as vice president. They traded their rebel status for a seat at the table of power, but in the process forgot the reasons they got into politics in the first place.

It happens over and over again. Washington power and money is enticing and corrupting both for elected officials, and for their staffs, and for lots of others who leave Iowa or Alabama or Montana behind. How many elected politicians, political staffers, think tankers, movement organizers, and political reporters ever leave Washington once they get there? My guess is that for every one who returns home while still active in his career, at least nine will stay in Washington. If one Washington job ends, another one beckons. For people who are interested in politics, Washington is an addiction. There's even a well-established name for this addiction: it's called "Potomac Fever".

Elected officials are merely the most visible among the corrupted. This happens across the ideological and party spectrum, of course. On the Right, which is what concerns us, these politicians campaign as conservative Republicans and are elected as conservative Republicans. Once in office, though, they too often develop a severe case of dual personalities struggling for control.

One personality—Mr. Conservative—is very good at verbal skills, and so he concentrates on mouthing conservative platitudes to the voters back home. It doesn't matter if this becomes utterly divorced from reality. Mr. Conservative is so good at this that he convinces *himself* he's still a conservative as he votes for a bankrupting new entitlement.

The other personality—Mr. Republican—is very sociable and has a deep need to be admired and *accepted* in Washington, where it's a lot harder to get into the country club than back home.

If Mr. Republican is the president, he wants to be accepted by—well, everyone. And especially those misguided people who said nasty things about him or didn't vote for him in the last election. Suddenly *their* acceptance is more important than acceptance by the conservatives who voted for him, and so he starts to modulate his positions and "reach out."

If Mr. Republican is a new Senator or Representative, he wants first and foremost to get along with his party leaders. They control his committee assignments, and thus affect the headlines he can get as well as the favors he can dole out. And in a few short years they will have bundles of cash to hand to him when he's up for reelection—if he plays the game right. He learns to "get along by going along."

In almost all instances, this is an irreversible disease process. Whether the politician's term in office lasts two, four, or six years, *the longer he remains in Washington* the stronger Mr. Republican becomes, at the expense of Mr. Conservative, who atrophies everywhere except in those speech muscles.

As I say, this disease process—Potomac Fever—is most apparent in our elected officials because they are so visible. But it also affects non-elected conservatives in Washington.

The staffs of these elected officials aren't in civil service. They serve at the pleasure of their boss, who wants to "get along by going along," so they help him do it. If the boss retires, dies, resigns, or fails to be reelected, or if jobs are lost when the party loses the White House or a majority in Congress, staffers have a relatively small pool of prospective new employers, so they know to stay closely connected to special interest group lobbyists.

More and more, the main career path for ambitious Capitol Hill staffers is to switch to one of Washington's K Street lobbyist firms. This is even encouraged by politicians like Tom DeLay, who are eager to use such "family" connections on K Street to bring in campaign contributions from the lobbyists.

Washington is a small town dominated by a major employer (the government) and by organizations that depend on and deal with that employer. It's what they used to call a "company town," and the cost of living is very high. Good luck finding a high-paying job if you are seen as opposed to the company.

Think tankers live in an even smaller, more inbred world, though they remedy this situation sometimes by switching from jobs in think tanks to jobs as political staffers. Still, many think-tankers are too much in the academic mold to enjoy the constant chaos of life as a Capitol Hill staffer, so their options are limited. It's either "get along by going along" in Washington or return to that dreadful state college you escaped from.

"Going along" at some think tanks can also mean going along with the big business desires of wealthy contributors whose agendas may be more self-serving than true-blue conservative. Consider the case of Bruce Bartlett. He was fired by the National Center for Policy Analysis even though they admitted he was doing an excellent job as a senior fellow. His transgression: being too critical of the liberal policies of President Bush. The final straw came when the Center's president read the manuscript of Bartlett's new book *Imposter: How George W. Bush Bankrupted America and Betrayed the Reagan Legacy.*

Organizational leaders presumptively are in Washington to press the agenda of their conservative constituents with the political powers that be. Too often what happens is the opposite. They are courted by those politicians (who, after all, got where they are by being super persuasive), and they end up representing the politicians' agenda to their constituency. This is one reason I am so adamantly against Bush's Faith-Based Initiative. It is hard enough to maintain your independence without going on the federal dole. When it comes to taxpayer monies, we need to defund the Left, not fund the Right.

Conservative media are just as susceptible to Potomac Fever as all of the above. When we talk about conservative media, of course, we're talking mostly about the new and alternative media—primarily direct mail, talk radio, cable TV, and the Internet, including bloggers. Their track record as consistent conservatives was a lot better *before* the Bush GOP takeover of Washington than since.

Access to high administration officials and their allies can be very important to people in the political media, and the Bush administration doesn't hesitate to cut off access if a reporter or commentator is even mildly critical of the president. (Interestingly, this is not true for the liberal media. The Bush people have a record of leaking stories to their media opponents, presumably in an effort to curry favor. It's only *conservatives* who get cut off for their criticism.)

Because of the Bush people's record of cutting off conservative critics, conservative media are forced to choose—they can have "access," or they can do honest reporting on Bush Administration activities, including the administration's mistakes. The Bible warns, in another context, "no man can serve two masters," and unfortunately some of the conservative media choose loyalty to the president rather than to conservative principles. This is why many of them are excusing, justifying, or even praising actions by the Bush GOP that would have horrified them during the Clinton era. In effect, they have become the Fourth Branch of the Big Government Republicans. This does the conservative cause no good.

From 1965 to 1978, I pretty much had the field to myself in efforts to grow the conservative movement through direct mail. Then in 1977 the Republican Party decided it wanted to tap the new medium and hired one of my executives to show them how. He offered me the opportunity to raise money for them, but I turned down the offer because I wasn't happy with the drift of the Republican Party and didn't want to be co-opted by the GOP establishment. Another of my executives did leave to join the Republican effort, though, and it paid off handsomely for the GOP.

I relay this not as criticism—the Republican Party has every bit as much right to use direct mail as do conservatives, and indeed GOP direct mail (as well as conservative direct mail) played a significant and valuable role in Reagan's landslide election and the GOP's capture of the Senate in 1980. Rather, I mention this to emphasize that the conservative movement and the Republican Party are *two distinctly different entities*, each with its own interests and its own agenda. Sometimes those agendas are in agreement, other times not so. Every conservative has to make the conscious decision as to which agenda he's going to serve when the conservative agenda differs from the Republican agenda.

The Rise of Blind Partisanship

I've said above that our unfinished business, as conservatives, is to learn "how to nominate and elect a president who will then *govern* as

---

*That part was mostly a joke, because of the notorious fractiousness of the YRs.

a conservative." Actually the mission is broader than that. We must also nominate and elect Senators and Representatives who will legislate as conservatives. And those of us in the private sector must similarly learn to put our conservatism first and foremost.

With the benefit of hindsight, it's easy to see how we confused our mission as conservatives with our mission as Republicans. In 1957 Stan Evans stated our goals so succinctly to his very first *Human Events* journalism class: "First we take over the Young Republicans.[*] Then we take over the Republican Party. Then we take over the nation. Then we defeat world communism."

It was such a utopian agenda for the handful of 1950s conservatives as to sound almost like lunacy, which is why it was usually stated that baldly after work hours and a few rounds of beer. And remember, everyone around the table was young and full of youthful bravado as well as beer. But it was wonderfully logical in the progression of its vision. And, unbelievably, we actually made it happen.

Well, sort of. We have learned from experience that the Republican Party—as one of our two historic national parties—represents far too many interests to be "taken over" Soviet-style. At best an ideological movement can assume the *leadership* of the party, and then only temporarily. Arguably the only time we conservatives "took over" the Republican Party was in the few months between the nomination of Barry Goldwater and his defeat in November 1964. But did we really take it over even then? The liberals in the party simply sabotaged our efforts and then stayed home (or voted Democratic) on Election Day, thus assuring our crushing defeat at the polls. Some "takeover"!

But we returned to the task, and again we *thought* we had taken over the GOP in 1980. The results this time proved far more measurable and permanent (such as the defeat of the Soviet Empire) than in 1964, but we never had anywhere near a complete takeover of the Republican Party. "Personnel is policy," as they say in Washington, and Reagan's conservative advisers were far outnumbered by moderates and even liberals. Then any semblance of conservative "control" of the GOP collapsed with the tax-raising, left-of-center presidency of

---

[*]Soon after the 2000 election, the closely divided Senate fell under Democratic control for 18 months.

George H. W. Bush.

The Bush people loved pointing out how they had cleaned house of the right-wing crazies, the Reaganites, right up 'til the moment the Clintons' moving van pulled into the driveway.

Again we returned to the task, and in 1994 Republicans, led by conservatives, took over the Senate for the first time in eight years and the House of Representatives for the first time in 40 years. In 2000, when we elected George W. Bush as president, with Republicans in control of Congress, many thought it was the beginning of a golden age of conservative government. What could hold us back? The Democrats were no longer in power *anywhere* to stop us.*

Boy, were we wrong! The results of the Bush Era, from a conservative perspective, have ranged from good (for example, judges) to disastrous, as detailed in this book. We have learned from experience that the ascent of Republicanism is not the same as the ascent of conservatism.

I am not saying we were *wrong* to seek control of the Republican Party and to work for GOP victories in 1964, 1980, 1994, or 2000. Far from it. The problem is that decades of partisan battle against a solidly liberal Democratic Party have unintentionally led us to subjugate the cause of conservatism to the cause of the Republican Party, threatening the loss of our soul as a movement of ideas and principles.

We've got to get our mojo back as conservatives. I'll discuss how to do that in the next chapter.

14

BRINGING BACK THE CONSERVATIVE MOVEMENT: A CONSERVATIVE DECLARATION OF INDEPENDENCE

"A little rebellion now and then is a good thing."
– Thomas Jefferson

Political movements think in terms of issues and philosophy. Thus conservatives judge partisan allies by how faithful they have been to conservative ideas such as limited, constitutional government.

Political parties, on the other hand, think in terms of partisan loyalty. Republicans are no different from the Democrats in this regard. Republicans judge their political allies by whether they vote for "us" or "them" (the Democrats).

The difference between conservatives and partisan Republicans in priorities and goals must inevitably lead to conflict. It's like a marriage in which a man and woman disagree about fundamental values and about critical questions such as whether to have children. The differences go to the heart of the concept of marriage.

In the union between the conservative movement and the Republican Party, the movement has fulfilled its obligations faithfully. The Republican Party has been caught stumbling home after midnight, smelling of booze and cheap perfume.

As long as we serve as its enabler, the Republican Party will never change. They'll keep promising not to do it again, and we'll keep forgiving them. It's time to say:

No more!

Republicans are running scared in 2006. That's appropriate, given their sorry record. Conservatives will make personal decisions about whether to vote for Republican candidates for the House or Senate. But conservatives don't have to feel an *obligation* to vote for Republicans just because they are Republicans.

Nor should we feel that a Republican victory is essential for the future of conservatism. The opposite may be the case.

Conservatives must rid themselves of the notion that a Republican victory in a given election is essential to the future of conservatism. We need to make clear the differences between conservatism and Republicanism, so that a repudiation of the Republican Party is not, and is not seen as, a repudiation of conservatism. In fact, a defeat of the GOP in the House or Senate might be just the wake-up call the Republicans need, and it could work to rejuvenate the conservative movement.

In modern times, the federal government has never shrunk, but its expansion was the slowest during two periods of divided government, the Reagan years and the Clinton years. Divided government may be our best bet until we can re-build the conservative movement into a force sufficient to turn back the size of government.

Conservatism as a Third Force, Not a Third Party

Third parties (other than the Democrats and Republicans) have a valid role in American politics, but they stand almost no chance of winning a national election. The system is rigged against them. Democrats and Republicans have successfully conspired to shut out competition, through onerous ballot access restrictions, limits on campaign contributions, and other legal ploys. Only under unusual cir-cumstances can a third party even get into the double digits in a pres-idential election, and, because of the way the Electoral College works, a third party would probably have to get at least 38 percent of the vote to win the White House. Ross Perot's candidacy in 1992 assured the defeat of the first President Bush, but how many billionaires are public minded enough to sacrifice a hundred million dollars in such a cause?

Rather than follow a third party route to defeat, conservatives should concentrate on becoming a Third Force in American politics that determines the nation's political agenda. Who cares what party controls the White House or Congress if *we* control the nation's political agenda on all the issues of importance to us? *This is not a pipe dream. It has happened before.*

It happened in the years 1977 to 1980. Jimmy Carter was in the White House, and the Democrats enjoyed lopsided majorities in both the House and the Senate. You'd think it would have been a golden age for liberal Democrats. Think again. Carter couldn't get most of his key proposals passed. Very little went through.

In 1979 the dean of Washington correspondents, the *Washington Post's* David Broder, paid a visit to my office. He was full of questions and very perplexed. Why weren't the Democrats able to implement their agenda? Broder had just talked to people in Vice President Walter Mondale's office, and to numerous liberal Democratic strategists, and they had not been able to provide a plausible explanation. Broder wondered if I had any idea why the Democrats were so strong, yet so weak.

I did. I explained to Broder that direct mail was the second largest form of advertising in America, and for the previous decade conservatives had been spending tens of millions of dollars to apply direct mail to politics. Those expenditures were paying off. My own direct mail operation was sending perhaps 70 million letters a year at that time for conservative organizations opposing Jimmy Carter's initiatives. I gave Broder the obligatory tour of my computer room—the machines were giants in those days and had to be maintained in temperature-controlled rooms—containing thousands of magnetic tapes with the names and addresses of millions of conservatives on the mailing lists.

These conservative organizations and their agendas were a new Third Force in American politics. It wasn't the Republicans who stopped Jimmy Carter and his peanut brigade in the Congress; it was conservatives, acting independently of the GOP and the Wall Street establishment. Not only were we able to stop Carter's agenda, we organized and then turned out the troops to elect Ronald Reagan as president, to defeat five powerful Democratic Senators and replace them with conservatives in 1980, and to elect around 35 of the "Newt

Gingrich class" of Republicans in the House of Representatives. So, good things can happen in elections, but they come *after* the ground-work has been laid with independent conservative Third Force politi-cal action.

Let me give you two more examples of successful conservative Third Force political action. As I've noted, a major achievement for conservatives is to take a key liberal issue *off the table* – to make it so toxic for the liberals and Democrats that they retreat in a rout and don't dare bring up the issue again. Conservatives did that with at least two of the liberals' top-priority issues.

The Equal Rights Amendment: By early 1972 this misnamed proposal seemed unstoppable. It had passed the House 354 to 23, and the Senate by 84 to 8. Even prominent conservative politicians like Strom Thurmond and Spiro Agnew had supported it; they didn't want to be seen as "anti-women" when half their constituents were women. Now it needed the approval of three-fourths of the states, and the states were rushing to see which could ratify the fastest. Fourteen states ratified the ERA in the first month after Congress's approval, and by the end of the first year 30 states had done so. Only eight more states were needed, and the ERA would be part of the United States Constitution.

How do you like them odds? Well, that didn't stop conservative activist Phyllis Schlafly. She had actually read the proposed amend-ment and was alarmed by its hidden and massive dangers. She turned grassroots conservatives into a Third Force that stopped ERA in its tracks at that critical final stretch of the ratification process. It *can* be done, and if it can be done with an issue deemed as "unstoppable" as this one, it can be done with the far less popular proposals the Republicans and the Democrats will put into the hopper in the next Congress.

The gun issue: There was a time, not so long ago, when Democrats competed with each other to craft the most restrictive gun-control bill in Congress. They saw that as a surefire way to achieve victory, and to heck with the Bill of Rights. But they failed to reckon with the growing clout of the National Rifle Association under its aggressive executive director, Wayne LaPierre. Nearly half of

American voters were gun owners, and LaPierre organized millions of them into an effective new Third Force in American politics.

Al Gore learned, too late, just how powerfully this issue resonated with ordinary Americans. He had spent almost all of his life in Washington, D.C., and other gated liberal enclaves, not enough in his purported home state of Tennessee. In the 2000 presidential election, he lost West Virginia, which had been one of the most reliably Democratic states, and he lost Bill Clinton's Arkansas, and he lost Tennessee, where both he and his father had been elected Senator. Simply carrying his "home" state would have been enough to make him president. And he probably lost all three because of the gun issue.

After that you didn't hear much at all about gun control from Democrats who actually had a chance to become president. In the 2004 Democratic primary debates, only the Reverend Al Sharpton supported Al Gore's position on handgun licensing. The others waffled or ran from it. Senator John Kerry went pheasant hunting a few days before the election, but that wasn't enough to undo the damage done by his support for gun-control measures—legislation against a person's right to protect himself, his family, and his business.

Six Steps to Bring Conservatives Together Again

During the time of its greatest successes, the conservative movement was a network that brought together people from a wide variety of backgrounds with widely varying priorities. From movement activities, pro-lifers learned why it was important to cut taxes, taxpayer activists learned why the Second Amendment must be protected, NRA members learned how Big Business subsidies often hurt national security, and so on. All these groups, and many, many more, learned how to work together to promote policies and candidates. In the 1970s, '80s, and '90s, a conservative gathering would feature 100 different causes, all coming together in a single, unified effort.

Big Government Republicans have learned how to divide these groups. It's time to re-establish and re-invigorate the conservative movement. Here's how:

Step 1: Create a New Mindset

We used to talk about "knee-jerk liberals" whose reflexes were on auto-pilot to back whatever nonsense the Democratic Party proposed. Now we have to worry about knee-jerk conservatives who automatically back anything proposed by the Republican Party. Decades of partisan combat to take over the GOP and defeat the Democrats have dulled their memory of why we got into politics in the first place: to turn back the growth of Big Government and to restore political, economic, and religious freedom to the American people.

Conservatives must put principles first, not parties and politicians. As long as those parties and politicians pursue conservative principles, we should support them. When they violate those principles, we must defeat them. Whether a leader or potential leader has a "D" or an "R" after his or her name is not as important as what he or she believes and what actions he or she takes in pursuance of those beliefs.

In the future, we must use every opportunity to let our fellow conservatives understand just how bad the Republican record has been since 2000, so that nothing like this disaster ever happens again.

Step 2: From This Moment Forward, Put 100% of Our Money and Our Organizational Efforts into <u>Conservative</u> Causes

You may be getting dozens of appeals from Republican campaign organizations asking for your financial support. The proper place to file these is in your wastebasket.

Don't worry – the Republican Party isn't going to starve without your money. Wall Street and the lobbyists on K Street will keep the party well fed. It's appropriate that they do so; the GOP has been doing their bidding for years. The GOP has *not* been doing *our* bidding, though, so why should we give them our hard-earned money? When the Republicans come up with conservative results, not just promises, we can reconsider supporting their party.

Although the Republican Party doesn't need your money, grass-roots conservative organizations and principled conservative candidates *do* desperately need your support. Keep in mind that every dollar you give to the GOP is a dollar that does *not* go to support conservative causes. Unless you have almost unlimited resources, it is time to choose. Choose to support conservatism, not Republicanism that will be controlled by Big Government special interests.

What I say about money applies to your human energy as well. Devote your organizational energy to *conservative* causes. Do your part to make them as effective as they can be.

Step 3: Let a Thousand Conservative Organizations Bloom

Some people think there are too many conservative organizations now. They assume that the size of the conservative "pie" is fixed, so if more groups are formed, there's less money and energy to go around for each of the groups.

I heard this argument 30 years ago, and it was as untrue then as it is now. I guess I was a supply-sider before that economic term was coined, applying the concept to politics, because I realized that more organizations would "grow" the conservative movement. I realized the conservative "pie" would get larger and larger. And that's exactly what happened.

There are good reasons why more groups and efforts result in a bigger conservative movement.

For one thing, you don't put all your eggs in one basket. A single all-purpose conservative group certainly would be a tempting target for liberals. It would allow them to focus their energies in one direction.

For example, the liberals could hire private detectives or just unleash a bunch of "journalists" to look into the backgrounds and private lives of everyone associated with the group. As would be true with any large group, they might find some moral flaw or act of corruption on the part of a former staffer or other associate. Once armed with incriminating information or mere allegation, they could make the organization seem guilty by association. This is the kind of thing we see in politics all the time, but having a single conservative organization would make it much easier.

Moreover, an all-purpose group may seem like a good idea in the abstract, but trying to be all things to all people often means you lose focus; no one issue is deemed important enough to go all-out for it at the expense of the others. Members who don't share the priorities of the leadership would begin to get frustrated, and if they had no place else to turn, they would lose interest entirely.

With a specialized group, on the other hand—groups such as Stop ERA and the National Rifle Association—a grassroots supporter can put all his or her energy into the issue that he or she cares about most. Activists can connect with people who believe just as strongly about the issue as they do. Since they're ardent about that issue, they'll put their money and energy into the group. They bond with it in a personal way that's not usually possible with an all-purpose group. Over time, they may get interested in the conservative issues put forth by other, allied groups—or not, as they please.

Remember that today nearly everyone is bombarded with hundreds, even thousands, of advertising images and appeals every day. You can reach through that clutter more effectively when you use a rifle approach rather than a shotgun. It may sound counter-intuitive, but the more narrow your focus, the larger the base you can create for your organization. I learned in the 1970s how to talk to people about one single issue—whether it was a balanced budget, abortion, or the Panama Canal—and get their initial approval on the issue that was most important to *them*. Once I succeeded in that, I could send them further mailings to see what other conservative issues appealed to them.

Today's technology makes single-issue groups even more feasible. Because of the Internet, it's easier than ever to identify the people across the nation who share your passion for *your* issue. Before you had to spend large sums of money advertising via direct mail, hoping to find two or three people out of every 100 pieces of mail who shared your passion. Now you can set up a Web site for your organization and your issue, use viral marketing and guerilla marketing to let people know of its existence (much cheaper than direct mail), and like-minded citizens come to *you*. From every hamlet in the nation, people who share a single passion can come together with the click of a mouse.

Initially, each single-issue group will attract people interested in that one issue, but eventually many of them will become all-around conservatives as they learn how their issue fits into the conservative agenda and philosophy of government. That's what happened with Stop ERA and the NRA. People who joined solely because of the ERA or gun control started talking to others who shared their passion on that issue, and often found that they shared a value system on a host of issues. In effect, they discovered that they had been conservatives, but just didn't know it before.

That's why I say: Let 1,000 conservative single-issue groups form! I mean that literally. After all, the Left easily has more than 300 civil rights organizations alone, as well as more than 300 environmentalist groups ranging from a major player like the Sierra Club to specialized groups promising to save the Amazon Rainforest.

So let's start dozens of groups for every important issue before Congress, as well as all the issues that should be before Congress but aren't. Let's bring together the Americans who share a strong interest in each of those causes, and – equally important – let's train people from each of these organizations on the ways to present their case effectively. If the conservative point of view prevails on those hundreds of issues, who cares which party is in control?

Step 4: Make Sure Conservative Voters Challenge the Candidates Who Want to Represent Them

Republican politicians too often assume that the conservative vote can be taken for granted in November—that we have "no place else to go." Not so! We can stay at home and rake the leaves in our yard, or go fishing, or whatever. The possibilities are endless. When you come across a Republican who assumes that you have no place else to go, remind him that conservatives have sometimes stayed home resulting in the defeat of a Republican who betrayed conservative principles.

Don't just accept their word that they have voted, or will vote, conservative.

If they are incumbents, check their voting record in detail and corner them one-on-one, with a conservative delegation, or at a public campaign appearance about their liberal, big-spending votes. Don't accept excuses.

Politely but firmly let them know that whether you vote in November will depend on their voting record, no matter which party they belong to or how conservative they claim to be. And if you're not going to vote for them because of their compromises with Big

Government, let them know why. Cite their wrong votes and their failure to oppose publicly the Big Government drift of their party.

If the candidates you are interviewing are not incumbents, but are seeking office, your job may be harder because of their lack of a record. In that case, question them about their political principles. Get them to explain their views in detail. Don't let them simply agree on general principles or use weasel words. Ask them about specific legislative proposals and demand specific answers.

Even "safe" liberal incumbents seeking reelection—those who received 55% or more of the vote last time—should be questioned firmly. This lets them know there *is* concern in their district, it encourages others to speak out too, and it may even cause these liberal incumbents to moderate their votes in the future. It is especially important to let big-spending Republicans know they cannot take conservative votes for granted.

Also, don't hesitate to ask personal questions that can give you clues as to their inner convictions. "When a man assumes a public trust, he should consider himself as public property," Thomas Jefferson wrote to Baron von Humboldt. The same holds true with *candidates* for a public trust.

Put them on the spot with such questions as "Will you disavow pork-barrel earmark projects for *our* district?" and "What is something you have done because it was right, even though you knew it would hurt you politically?"

Conservatives shouldn't confine themselves to questioning incumbents or aspirants for office. Big Government Republican incumbents need to be challenged in their primaries, which is the kind of thing that *really* gets their attention.

Step 5: Improve and Refine Your Own Political Skills

In order to get our movement back on the correct path, conservatives must do more than complain. It's time for armchair conservatives to get out of their chairs and take an active role in politics.

We certainly need more good candidates for office, at the local, state, and federal levels. But that's just the most visible need. In order to get more and better candidates, we need more and better skilled precinct captains, candidate and campaign advisers, and local conservative organizational leaders. Alternatively, a person's communications skills may suggest that he or she move into television, radio, or print media, or perhaps start a political blog. Maybe he or she should join a politician's staff, or go to work for a government agency. Students can stand up and challenge the leftists on their campus, or organize fellow students and get them involved in local political campaigns.

Conservatives have a valuable resource available to help you hone political skills. In 1979 Morton Blackwell opened the Leadership Institute, and in the years since then more than 48,000 conservatives have taken the institute's intensive classes and become more effective. Leadership Institute programs include: Grassroots Campaign School, Grassroots Activist School, Campaign Leadership School, Candidate Development School, Public Speaking Workshops, Public Relations School, Broadcast Journalism School, Effective TV Techniques Workshops, Direct Mail School, Political Voter Mail School, Internet Leadership School, Student Publications School and Workshops, Freshman Legislator Training School, Capitol Hill Staff Training School, Legislative Project Management School, and Foreign Service Opportunity School. (For more information, go to the Leadership Institute's Web site at http://www.leadershipinstitute.org.)

Step 6: Continually Enlarge Our Constituency

Much of the growth of the conservative movement in past decades could be attributed to appeals to broad constituencies that had previously voted Democratic.

Early in the history of the conservative movement, we appealed to northern Catholics first on the issue of anti-Communism; later we also focused on domestic issues such as urban renewal and forced busing, policies that were wrecking neighborhoods. Beginning in the late 1970s, we persuaded Southern Baptists and Evangelicals from various denominations to get involved in politics, not to treat politics as something dirty that should be avoided.

These efforts paid huge dividends in growing the conservative movement. Now we must be concerned about future growth. In particular, I see two constituencies worthy of intensive attention by conservatives in the years ahead.

Hispanics/Latinos are the largest ethnic constituency in American politics, and the Latino portion of the electorate will continue to grow for a long time. Conservatives need an active outreach effort to make certain that Latinos don't fall to the liberal Democrats by default, due to our neglect or indifference or because we state poorly our position on immigration. Most members of the Latino community have strong, conservative beliefs on issues related to family, faith, hard work, and small business entrepreneurship. If we reach out, I believe we can incorporate much of the community into the conservative movement.

Does our stand for secure borders and against illegal immigration doom us in our quest to add Hispanics/Latinos to the conservative coalition? Not if we are taking those positions for the right reasons. If we support policies that are tough but fair, and that encourage legal immigration even as they discourage illegal immigration, we will find broad support among immigrants who played by the rules and among Latinos whose families have been part of America for generations. As I have noted, Arizona's Proposition 200, which required proof of eligibility in order to receive welfare or to vote, was supported by 59 percent of the state's Hispanic Republicans and 47 percent of all Hispanic voters.

The critical point is that we have to take our conservative case *directly to the community*. You can't just publish a conservative position paper and assume that people will come to us. That's not the way Tammany Hall and other northern big-city machines made Democrats out of the European immigrant groups in the 19th century! Those "bosses" got the new immigrants on the local government gravy train, of course, but they also did valuable work helping them integrate into American life and get established economically. In the 21st century, we have an opportunity to help and assist the new wave of immigrants and help them build businesses that will make them independent of the government. If we don't do this outreach, we can be sure the liberal Democrats will seek to recruit them using their usual strategy of legal bribery, hoping to use the growing Hispanic/Latino vote to offset their losses elsewhere.

To his credit, George W. Bush has sought, as governor of Texas and then as president of the United States, to integrate Hispanics into the Republican Party, rather than ignore them or alienate them. To his discredit, he has distorted the message and the goal by pursuing open borders and amnesty. That's a mistake on politics as well as principle: Republicans will never be able to outbid Democrats on providing services and political power at the public's expense. Conservatives have the opportunity and the duty to get the message right.

Independents are another voter constituency that need to be courted vigorously by conservatives. After all, more U.S. voters now identify themselves as independents than as Republicans or Democrats.

Polls repeatedly show that many, if not most, independents are conservative not only in their economic beliefs but also in their positions on religious, cultural, and family issues. What they object to is the often vitriolic partisanship between the two major parties, along with the hypocrisy common to both parties. Their desire for what is called "good government" makes them fearful of deficit spending, no matter which party is doing it, and repulsed by negative TV ads.

Consider the last gubernatorial race in conservative Virginia, in which the Republican candidate unleashed a barrage of vitriolic and emotional TV ads on the death penalty issue. It is clear that this approach backfired, especially among independents.

Economic conservatism, cultural conservatism, and disgust with deficits, corruption, and vitriolic partisanship: Independents' views present a great opportunity for conservatives. With their record of deficit spending and political chicanery since 2000, Republicans now face an uphill battle trying to appeal to them. But that same matrix spells opportunity for conservatives who are willing to separate their *conservative* message from a partisan *Republican* message. But again, conservatives have to actively reach out to this constituency in a voter-to-voter way, not just by issuing position papers.

Making the GOP Come to Us!

Senator John F. Kennedy understood the occasional necessity for creative destruction. Kennedy knew his corrupt Massachusetts party had to be purged. As Arthur M. Schlesinger, Jr. relates in *A Thousand Days*, Kennedy had detested Democratic Governor Foster Furcolo for many years. With Furcolo planning a challenge to popular GOP Senator Leverett Saltonstall in 1960, Kennedy mused: "Sometimes party loyalty asks too much." He added, gloomily, that "Nothing can be done [about the state Democratic Party] until it is beaten—badly beaten. Then there will be a chance of rebuilding."

Republican defeats in the 1970s cleared out deadwood GOP leadership and allowed conservatives to advance the cause.

I've spoken about the attractions of power and how it leads to Potomac Fever. The only antidote for Potomac Fever is the threat of *losing* that power. By reinventing the conservative movement as an independent Third Force in American politics, we will be able to accomplish what we can't accomplish as loyal house servants. We will get the Republican Party to come to *us*, begging for our support—which we will deliver, of course, only after they have first earned it with a record of solid accomplishments rather than mere promises.

15

A CALL TO ARMS FOR
CONSERVATIVES

We conservatives are responsible for bringing the Republican Party to majority status. For many years, polls have conclusively and repeatedly shown that many more Americans consider themselves conservative than liberal—or Republican. Our hard work in taking over the GOP from its Eastern Establishment wing, and presenting the new Republican Party as a conservative party, has been responsible for its ability to win the White House, Senate, and House of Representatives.

Now it has become apparent, however, that the Republican leadership in the White House and Congress is conservative in name only. They have used the popularity of the word "conservative" to cloak their Big Government, Big Business agenda. And the growth of the federal government and the intrusiveness of the federal government have exploded under all-Republican control. It is far worse today than during the divided government of the 1990s.

We conservatives have every right to be disappointed, frustrated—even angry. But we should not be despondent. As a movement we have had long, dark nights before, and each time we have persevered and come back stronger than before.

- We had been marginalized in the Republican Party, and were castigated by the liberal mass media, but through hard work we secured the nomination of Barry Goldwater as the GOP presidential candidate in 1964.

- We were written off as an historical aberration after Goldwater's defeat, presumed dead as a movement. But again we refused to play dead. Utilizing the new alternative media of direct mail, we learned not only how to nominate a conservative, but how to elect one in the person of Ronald Reagan. While there were inevitable disappointments during the Reagan years, we won the Grand Prize: the dismantlement of the Soviet Union and its evil empire.

- And in the early years of the Clinton presidency, the GOP leadership in Congress was advising us to face political "reality" and capitulate on Hillarycare, gun control, and other Clintonite socialist measures. We refused, and created our own political reality, utilizing direct mail and the new alternative media of talk radio. The result was the defeat of Hillarycare, and the Republican takeover of the House of Representatives in 1994 for the first time in 40 years.

Each time we followed our heart and our conscience, and refused to let the *New York Times* and vacillating Republican leaders dictate our future or our agenda. And each time we prevailed.

Today we have far, far more resources available to us than we had in 1964, or 1980, or 1994. If we were able to accomplish what we did back then, we can accomplish much more today. We now have a panoply of alternative media at our disposal—not only direct mail and talk radio, but also cable television and the Internet and its blogosphere. We have dozens of conservative magazines, hundreds of Web sites, thousands of organizations, millions of grass roots activists and donors, as well as tens of millions of voters.

But we are seriously short of good leaders. Most who want to lead conservatives are not conservative themselves, or their first loyalty is to the Republican Party rather than conservatism.

Where is the political leader who will publicly challenge the big-spending GOP president of the United States, as Senator Barry Goldwater did in 1960 when he labeled Eisenhower's "me too" policies as "a dime store New Deal"?

Where is the political leader who will publicly challenge George Bush as courageously as Ronald Reagan did in 1975 and 1976 when he said GOP President Jerry Ford was wrong on detente, the Panama Canal, and other national defense issues?

None of those being mentioned today as possibilities for the next GOP presidential nomination have earned conservative support, the way Barry Goldwater and Ronald Reagan did in their day.

What we did before, we can do again. Heeding Barry Goldwater's advice to conservatives at the 1960 GOP National Convention, we *can* once again take over the Republican Party. And this time with *real* conservatives at the helm.

Toward that end, I call on all conservatives to rededicate ourselves to a rebirth of conservatism in these ways:

Our first loyalty will be to the conservative movement and conservative principles, not the Republican Party. We can identify ourselves as *Reaganite conservatives*, to distinguish ourselves from the "compassionate" and "neo" conservatives who have led us down so many disastrous paths.

We will think of conservativism as a Third Force rather than a third party. Our goal will be to take over the Republican Party and move the Democratic Party to the right as well.

We will hold each party responsible and accountable for its actual conduct, not just its promises. We will not be intimidated by the "lesser of two evils" rationalization of transgressions against our liberties, but will demand positive accomplishments in restoring our liberties. And we will support only those political candidates and groups that advance liberty in a substantial and consistent manner.

Since money for most of us is a finite resource, we will not give our financial support to the Republican National Committee or the Senate and House GOP fundraising committees. Instead we pledge to give our political dollars only to conservative organizations and principled conservative candidates. And the foremost way to determine whether candidates are principled conservatives is whether they will publicly oppose the big government policies of the Bush GOP.

We call for the wholesale replacement of the Republican leadership in the House and the Senate. Like the Biblical Jews, we need new leaders, a clean slate, and a new start in order to get to the promised land.

We will withhold our support from any of the candidates for president in 2008—until someone truly earns our support. And again, the best way to determine who earns our support is whether they will publicly oppose the big government policies of the Bush GOP.

And we will renew and expand our efforts to make the voices of the American people heard through a wide variety of new conservative organizations, media outlets, political strategies and techniques, and most importantly *new leaders*.

Conservatives, we are in a battle for the survival of freedom under God's laws. None should stay on the sidelines. Working together, we must save America for our children, grandchildren, and future generations.

Let the real conservative revolution begin!

APPENDICES

In The
Court of Public Opinion
Conservative Articles of Indictment Against President George W. Bush

1. Federal spending has increased by 33% since George W. Bush became President, including a 48% surge in discretionary spending.

2. The *increases* in spending during the Bush administration have exceeded the *entire* federal budget under President Jimmy Carter.

3. President Bush has given his tacit approval to this out-of-control spending, by choosing never to veto a single bill. In contrast to the zero vetoes cast by the current president, President Bill Clinton had 38 vetoes, the first President Bush 44, President Ronald Reagan 68, and President Gerald Ford 66.

4. In 2005, President Bush signed a $286.4 billion transportation bill with 6,371 pork barrel spending projects, including the $224 million Bridge to Nowhere in Alaska. (In 1986, President Reagan vetoed a transportation bill because it contained 150 pork barrel projects.)

5. In 2002, President Bush signed a $180 billion farm bill, an 80% increase in agriculture spending, including the largest "corporate welfare" payment ever made to Agribusiness.

6. In 2003, President Bush pushed through Congress a prescription drug plan that will cost more than $1.2 trillion in its first 10 years and $2 trillion in the decade after that. It was the biggest expansion of the federal government since President Johnson.

7. Since Bush became President, spending for the Department of Education has nearly doubled, from $35.7 billion to $70.9 billion—for a federal department that serves no legitimate purpose. (Under the Constitution, government schools are a concern of state and local governments only.)

8. The Bush Administration's deficit in FY 2006 is an estimated $390 billion, and that does not include the $174 billion borrowed from the Social Security Trust Fund. The real deficit for 2006 is about $564 billion.

9. During the first five years of the Bush presidency, $809.3 billion was raided from the Social Security Trust Fund to pay for the general operations of government. As of the end of April 2006, the IOUs in the Trust Fund amounted to $1.914 trillion. This amount increases every month and no one has any idea how this money can be paid back.

10. Under President Bush, the national debt has gone from $5.7 trillion to $8.35 trillion—an increase of $2.65 trillion in just five years. Much of this debt is owed to foreigners, including enemies such as the government of Communist China.

11. President Bush has done nothing to oppose corporations that provide aid and comfort to the Communist dictatorship in China – corporations such as Yahoo, which helps the Communists track down and imprison dissidents, and Google, which helped the Communists censor the Internet.

12. There are at least 11 million illegal aliens in the U.S. with 4,000 more streaming across the border every day. Yet the President has refused to enforce the immigration laws. In fact, work-site arrests for immigration violations fell by 95% from 1999 to 2005. Instead of enforcing the law, the President has proposed what amounts to an amnesty for illegal aliens.

13. The Bush administration wants the Senate to ratify the Law of the Sea Treaty (LOST), which would effectively give taxing authority to the United Nations, would interfere with efforts to protect U.S. national security, and was strongly opposed by President Reagan. Former Attorney General Ed Meese said ratification of LOST would be a "surrender of sovereignty."

14. The Bush administration has opposed the United Nations Reform Act, which passed the House 221-184. The measure would require that U.S. funding for most UN operations be cut in half by 2008 if basic reforms have not taken place.

15. Despite his promise to nominate highly qualified conservative judges in the mold of Antonin Scalia and Clarence Thomas, President Bush nominated the unqualified, near-unknown Harriet Miers for the Supreme Court. Only in the face of solid conserva-

tive opposition did he back off from apparent plans to nominate "moderate"-to-liberal Alberto Gonzales to the Supreme Court.

16. President Bush has appointed very few conservatives—persons who are active members of the conservative movement, or who supported Ronald Reagan's 1976 campaign—to policy positions in the federal government. Almost all appointments have come from the anti-conservative/anti-Reagan/Big Business wing of the Republican Party.

17. He has refused to pursue the many alleged crimes committed by the Clintons, including the possible sale of presidential pardons and the sale of missile technology to Communist China.

18. He has weakened the national security by holding over officials from the Clinton administration, particularly in the State Department and the CIA.

19. After being elected in part due to his opposition to McCain-Feingold, President Bush signed the anti-First Amendment legislation. McCain-Feingold restricts citizens' right to criticize politicians.

20. President Bush has taken no action in support of a constitutional amendment to overturn *Roe v. Wade*. For six consecutive years, he has been "out of town" and supposedly unable to attend the March for Life (the major pro-life event in Washington) held on each January 22nd. He has refused to take advantage of a president's greatest asset—"the world's biggest microphone," also called "the bully pulpit"—to bring people to the pro-life cause in the U.S. and around the world.

21. He has done nothing to de-fund the Left—that is, to cut off the flow of billions of dollars of taxpayers' money to leftwing organizations that lobby and campaign for more taxpayers' money—even though neither conservative nor liberal groups should get government money.

22. In partnership with Teddy Kennedy, President Bush pushed the "No Child Left Behind" legislation through Congress—legislation that furthers the federal takeover of local schools, expands the power and money of the Washington bureaucracy, puts students into categories based on skin color and perceived ethnicity, and interferes with education by forcing teachers to "teach to the test" (and encourages cheating and statistical manipulation of test results).

23. In an attempt to get support from Big Business and Big Unions, he imposed tariffs (taxes) on imported steel, helping domestic steel companies while hurting other businesses and the American people in general.

24. He has done nothing to abolish atrocities like the National Endowment for the Arts. To the contrary, he actually hosted a White House tribute to the NEA.

25. In fact, he has not abolished, nor sought to abolish, *any* significant government program.

26. He has pursed an "energy" policy that will benefit special interests while doing almost nothing to increase U.S. oil-producing capacity (other than a weak effort to allow drilling in a tiny part of Alaska).

27. He has given only lip service—perfunctory support—to promote a constitutional amendment to establish marriage as between one man and one woman.

ADDENDUM: On the plus side, President Bush pushed through an income tax cut that was half the size of Reagan's. It was better than no tax cut at all but hardly sufficient. And even that achievement is now threatened because the cuts are set to expire automatically unless extended.

Regarding the courts, the President has made some good appointments, although not as many as people think. But when you look at lower courts as well as the Supreme Court, you find that, for every thoughtful jurist like a John Roberts type or a Sam Alito type, there's a Harriet Myers type. (Remember that it was a George W. Bush-appointed federal judge who, in the Ohio "intelligent design" case, trashed religion and ignored science.)

There are very few cases of Bush appointments similar to Antonin Scalia and Clarence Thomas—legal scholars who combine great intellect with the courage to stand up for the Rule of Law, who are willing and able to articulate their reasoning and "create a paper trail." Again, one could criticize Ronald Reagan for many of his court appointments, but he was starting almost from scratch. Today, there are scores of highly qualified Scalia/Thomas types in the judiciary and in the legal profession as a whole. Unfortunately, the lesson that young conservatives have taken from the Bush appointments is: Keep your mouth shut, and do not express your opinions in writing, or you will never have the chance for a seat on the Supreme Court. Not even a Republican president, backed by a Republican Senate, will pick you if you are seen as controversial in any way.

In general, President Bush has done very little to move the country in a conservative direction, the way Ronald Reagan did. It is perfectly reasonable to say (as candidate Bush did, regarding an abortion ban) that the country is not ready for a given policy shift, and that it may take years of debate and hard work to move the country in the conservative direction on a given issue. But at least Ronald Reagan took the lead. At least he *started* the process. He took positions and made proposals that, at the time, were considered radical, but that are now part of the accepted wisdom. In contrast to Reagan, Bush has rarely pushed the envelope.

Ronald Reagan faced the fact that there were not enough experienced conservatives to fill all the top jobs in his administration, so in some cases he appointed competent people who disagreed with him but would (mostly) follow his orders. But he kept his eye on the ultimate goal, that one day conservatives would govern the country. He appointed conservatives to lower-level positions so that they would have the credentials for future conservative administrations.

Alas, many of those credentialed conservatives are still waiting for appointments in a Bush administration. As I note above, President Bush has appointed very few conservatives—persons who are active members of the conservative movement, or who supported Ronald Reagan's 1976 campaign—to policy positions in the federal government. Almost all appointments have come from the anti-conservative/anti-Reagan/Big Business wing of the Republican Party. And, unlike Reagan, he has not created a new generation of credentialed young conservatives who can help a future conservative president govern.

In fact, President Bush drags conservatives down precisely because he is *seen* as a conservative. So, when he massively expands government, or fails in preparing the Iraqi occupation, or nominates Harriet Miers, or seems to stand idly by during Katrina, or okays United Arab Emirates management of U.S. ports, conservatives are blamed for policies and actions that we had nothing to do with.

In politics, the most advantageous position is power without responsibility. (Like Washington special interests, you can get things done in your favor, but never have to answer for the consequences.) The worst position in politics is responsibility without power. In the Bush Administration, conservatives are not empowered, but they are blamed when policies fail.

When Republicans, running as conservatives, captured the White House and both houses of Congress, I told a reporter: "Now comes the revolution."

Who would have thought that it would come to *this*?

WHERE DO *YOU* STAND?

What do you think about the state of the union? About the direction of the conservative movement today? About the record of the Republican Party since 2000? I've had my say. Now I'd like to hear from *you*.

Each month I will send a report to the national media on the state of conservative opinion, so this is your chance to make your voice heard.

Just go to *ConservativesBetrayed.com* and sound off!

Here are the kind of questions we'll be asking:

> What grade would you give President Bush for his performance in each of these areas:

    Foreign policy
    Reducing the size and scope of government
    Government spending
    Illegal immigration
    Governing as a conservative

> If you could, would you vote for President Bush again?

> What grade would you give Congress for its performance in each of these areas:

    Foreign policy
    Reducing the size and scope of government

Government spending
Illegal immigration
Honesty and morality

Given the following choices, which would you prefer?

- Republican Party control of *both* the White House *and* Congress?
- Democratic Party control of *both* the White House *and* Congress?
- Government divided between the two parties?
- A third party option

In the next Congressional election, do you plan to?

- Vote for the Republican candidate
- Vote for the Democratic candidate
- Vote for an independent or third party candidate
- Stay at home (not vote)
- Undecided

If you get requests for contributions in the next year from national Republican groups, you will:

- Contribute at the same level as before
- Increase my contributions to the GOP
- Decrease my contributions to the GOP
- Refuse to contribute to the GOP until it becomes conservative

Make your voice heard on these and other questions! Let the national media know where you stand! Cast your vote today at ConservativesBetrayed.com.

THE SHARON STATEMENT

The Sharon Statement was the founding declaration of principles for Young Americans for Freedom (YAF), the conservative youth group. It was adopted in conference at Sharon, Connecticut, on September 11, 1960. Written largely by conservative journalist M. Stanton Evans, it remains to this day the best concise summary of conservative principles that guided the new movement.

> In this time of moral and political crises, it is the responsibility of the youth of America to affirm certain eternal truths.
>
> We, as young conservatives, believe:
>
> That foremost among the transcendent values is the individual's use of his God-given free will, whence derives his right to be free from the restrictions of arbitrary force;
>
> That liberty is indivisible, and that political freedom cannot long exist without economic freedom;
>
> That the purpose of government is to protect those freedoms through the preservation of internal order, the provision of national defense, and the administration of justice;
>
> That when government ventures beyond these rightful functions, it accumulates power, which tends to dimin-

ish order and liberty;

That the Constitution of the United States is the best arrangement yet devised for empowering government to fulfill its proper role, while restraining it from the concentration and abuse of power;

That the genius of the Constitution—the division of powers—is summed up in the clause that reserves primacy to the several states, or to the people, in those spheres not specifically delegated to the federal government;

That the market economy, allocating resources by the free play of supply and demand, is the single economic system compatible with the requirements of personal freedom and constitutional government, and that it is at the same time the most productive supplier of human needs;

That when government interferes with the work of the market economy, it tends to reduce the moral and physical strength of the nation; that when it takes from one man to bestow on another, it diminishes the incentive of the first, the integrity of the second, and the moral autonomy of both;

That we will be free only so long as the national sovereignty of the United States is secure; that history shows periods of freedom are rare, and can exist only when free citizens concertedly defend their rights against all enemies;

That the forces of international Communism are, at present, the greatest single threat to these liberties;

That the United States should stress victory over, rather than coexistence with, this menace; and

That American foreign policy must be judged by this criterion: does it serve the just interests of the United States?

IV

A CONSERVATIVE BIBLIOGRAPHY

Here are some books that might be considered "the conservative basics"—books that helped define modern conservatism, that recorded the movement's successes and failures, or that inspired people to become conservatives, plus a book I wrote on the rise of the "New Right."

- *The Law*, Frederic Bastiat
- *The Closing of the American Mind*, Allan Bloom
- *Slouching Towards Gomorrah*, Robert Bork
- *Up from Liberalism*, William F. Buckley Jr.
- *Witness*, Whittaker Chambers
- *The Conservative Revolution: The Movement That Remade America*, Lee Edwards
- *The Theme is Freedom: Religion, Politics, and the American Tradition*, M. Stanton Evans
- *Free to Choose: A Personal Statement*, Milton and Rose Friedman
- *The Conscience of a Conservative*, Barry Goldwater
- *The Road to Serfdom*, F.A. Hayek
- *Economics in One Lesson*, Henry Hazlitt
- *The Conservative Mind: From Burke to Eliot*, Russell Kirk
- *When Character Was King: A Story of Ronald Reagan*, Peggy Noonan

- *Atlas Shrugged* [fiction], Ayn Rand
- *The Rise of the Right*, William A. Rusher
- *A Choice, Not an Echo*, Phyllis Schlafly
- *A Time For Truth*, William E. Simon
- *The New Right: We're Ready to Lead*, Richard A. Viguerie
- *The Mainspring of Human Progress*, Henry Grady Weaver
- *Ideas Have Consequences*, Richard M. Weaver
- *Abortion: Questions & Answers*, Dr. and Mrs. J. C. Willke
- *America's Right Turn: How Conservatives Used New and Alternative Media to Take Power*, Richard A. Viguerie and David Franke

V

QUOTATIONS FROM RONALD REAGAN

Do you hear any public officials or candidates making these kind of statements today?

Individual liberty depends upon keeping government under control.
> —*Interview with Radio News West, Los Angeles,*
> *December 30, 1974*

Government always finds a need for whatever money it gets.
> —*Remarks at a White House luncheon for out-of-town*
> *editors and broadcasters, July 22, 1981*

Government's view of the economy could be summed up in a few short phrases: If it moves, tax it. If it keeps moving, regulate it. And if it stops moving, subsidize it.
> —*Remarks to state chairpersons of the National White*
> *House Conference on Small Business, August 15, 1986*

No government ever voluntarily reduces itself in size. Government programs, once launched, never disappear. Actually, a government bureau is the nearest thing to eternal life we'll ever see on this earth!
> —*"A Time for Choosing" Television Address,*
> *October 27, 1964*

Our government is too big, and it spends too much.
> —*Address to Congress, April 28, 1981*

One thing our Founding Fathers could not foresee...was a nation governed by professional politicians who had a vested interest in getting reelected. They probably envisioned a fellow serving a couple of hitches and then looking...forward to getting back to the farm.
    —*Meet the Students, taping for television, Sacramento, September 17, 1973*

We don't have a trillion-dollar debt because we haven't taxed enough; we have a trillion-dollar debt because we spend too much.
    —*Remarks to the National Association of Realtors, March 28, 1982*

Balance the budget by bringing to heel a federal establishment, which has taken too much power from the states, too much liberty with the Constitution, and too much money from the people.
    —*Remarks at a rally for a proposed Constitutional amendment
    for a balanced federal budget, July 19, 1982*

Our loyalty lies with little taxpayers, not big spenders. What our critics really believe is that those in Washington know better how to spend your money than you, the people, do. But we're not going to let them do it, period.
    —*President's news conference,
    The White House, June 30, 1982*

Simple morality dictates that unless and until someone can prove the unborn human is not alive, we must give it the benefit of the doubt and assume it is. And, thus, it should be entitled to life, liberty, and the pursuit of happiness.
    —*Alfred M. Landon Lecture Series on Public Issues, September 9, 1982*

Eight Steps <u>You</u> Can Take to Help Free Conservatism from Big Government Republicanism

1. Cut off your support of the Republican National Committee and other party fundraising committees. Tell them you are not willing to have your money and political energy used mostly to support Big Government Republicans who don't share your conservative views. Give 100% of your political donations to principled conservative causes and candidates.

2. Withhold support for now of all 2008 GOP presidential candidates. Support only a candidate who "walks with us" like Ronald Reagan and who will publicly criticize and oppose Big Government Republicans.

3. Demand sweeping changes in the Republican congressional leadership. Only with new, principled conservative leaders will the Republican Party be worthy of support from the conservative majority in America.

4. No longer think of yourself as a Republican, but rather as a Reagan conservative committed to building the conservative movement into an independent Third Force (not a third party) pushing both major political parties to the Right.

5. Express your outrage over the country's direction wherever an opportunity presents itself—at political town hall meetings, on call-in talk shows, with personal visits and in letters and telephone calls to your political representatives, and in letters to the editor and participation in online chat rooms/discussion groups.

6. Leadership begins with each of us. Set up a Web site to express your views, become a blogger, and e-mail good conservative articles to family and friends. Get involved in political campaigns, either as a candidate or to support others who will challenge Big Government Republicans.

7. Launch your new leadership role by going to ConservativesBetrayed.com. Sign our petitions, vote online, and participate in our political soap boxes to express your disappointment and frustration, as well as to present your ideas for constructive action.

8. If you generally agree with the message of ***Conservatives Betrayed***, give your copy to someone else and buy bulk discounted copies at ConservativesBetrayed.com to spread the message. Also, go to ConservativesBetrayed.com to e-mail this page to others who want to send the Washington politicians a message they will hear loud and clear.

Conservatives, if we unite and work, we can save America from the Big Government politicians who have betrayed us!

ACKNOWLEDGEMENTS

This book has been over a year in the making. Unfortunately for the conservative cause, as the weeks and months went by, I was presented with more and bigger examples of how conservatives and the conservative cause are being betrayed.

No doubt whatsoever, the Big Government Republicans will continue to produce more and bigger disappointments that I would include in my book, but as one of my associates says, "A work of art is never completed; it is merely abandoned."

Most of the help with this book came from my friend of over 47 years, David Franke. In fact, without David, I might never have had the opportunity to come to Washington, D.C. and become involved with the national conservative movement.

So, David, once again, I'm in your debt. However, I feel I owe it to David to say that, while he helped research and organize my thoughts, they are my thoughts and not his. Because, while my disappointments and anger at the GOP come and go, David long ago gave up on the Republican Party and considers himself a libertarian.

Also, John J. Miller, Mike Long, and George Neumayr provided significant advice and writing assistance. Bill Schulz, one of the early leaders of the young conservative movement, graciously provided wise counsel, as he has to me and many others for over 45 years.

And completely indispensable to the final project was my friend and fellow Houstonian, Art Kelly, who helped with research, critiqued my thoughts, and ran interference between me and all of the others involved.

Also, from my company, I thank Nancy Bakersmith, Cat Tiernan, Carl Hieronymous (artwork/design), and Mark Fitzgibbons for their unique and special help.

In addition, Michael Marshner helped with research and Chris Broomall worked on development of the website associated with this book.

A special thanks to my longtime friend, Connie Marshner, who volunteered to weigh in on some of the social issue sections.

And, this book may not have seen the light of day without the encouragement and almost limitless patience of my publisher, Jeff Stern, president of Bonus Books, as well as his team in Los Angeles.

Lastly, I am so grateful for the many patriotic conservative activists who, over the decades, have been faithful to principles above politics.

ABOUT THE AUTHOR

RICHARD A. VIGUERIE transformed American politics in the 1960s and '70s by pioneering the use of direct mail fundraising in the political and ideological spheres. He used computerized direct mail fundraising to build the conservative movement, which then elected Ronald Reagan as the first conservative president of the modern era.

As the "Funding Father of the conservative movement," Viguerie motivated millions of Americans to participate in politics for the first time, greatly expanding the base of active citizenship. He is our era's equivalent of Tom Paine, using a direct mail letter rather than a pamphlet to deliver his call to arms. *George* magazine credited this as one of the defining political moments of the 20th century.

Viguerie's advertising firm has mailed more than two billion letters over the past 41 years. Ronald Reagan's 1968 campaign manager Cliff White and journalist William Gill wrote in their book *Why Reagan Won:* "In every election from 1966 onward, the Viguerie Company and its score of imitators…brought information to millions of Americans; information that quite often the people could not obtain from newspapers or television or mass-circulation magazines."

The *AFL-CIO News* has said that Viguerie "made it all possible" for conservatives, and the *Washington Post* has called him "the conservatives' Voice of America." In 1979 *Time* magazine listed him as one of 50 future leaders of America, and in 1981 *People* magazine named him one of the 25 most intriguing people of the year. In December 1999 he was cited in the *Washington Times* as one of 13 "Conservatives of the Century."

Viguerie's most recent book is *America's Right Turn: How Conservatives Used New and Alternative Media to Take Power* (Bonus Books, 2004). Written with David Franke, it is the first in-depth look at how direct mail, talk radio, cable TV, and the Internet have changed American politics. *America's Right Turn* was widely praised by Left and Right alike.

Mr. Viguerie and his wife, Elaine, are natives of Houston, Texas, and have been married for 44 years. They have three children and five grandchildren and live in the Virginia countryside on 230 acres of conservative-friendly environment.

Mr. Viguerie may be contacted at P.O. Box 4450, Manassas, VA 20108, or at RAV@ConservativesBetrayed.com.

INDEX